Quincy's Market

Quincy's Market

A BOSTON LANDMARK

John Quincy, Jr.

Northeastern University Press
Boston

Northeastern University Press
Copyright 2003 by John Quincy, Jr.

Library of Congress Cataloguing-in-Publication Data
Quincy, John, 1951–
Quincy's Market / John Quincy, Jr.
p. cm.
Includes bibliographical references (p.) and index.
ISBN 1-55553-552-6 (acid-free paper)
1. Quincy's Market (Boston, Mass.). 2. Boston (Mass.)—History. 3. Boston (Mass.)—Buildings, structures, etc. 4. Architecture—Massachusetts—Boston. 5. Markets—Conservation and restoration—Massachusetts—Boston. 6. Boston (Mass.)—Economic conditions. I. Title.
F73.8.Q56 Q56 2003
711'.552'0974461—dc21   2002015422

Designed by Joyce Weston
Composed in Bembo. Printed and bound by Butler and Tanner, Somerset, England. The paper is Daytona Silk, an acid-free stock.

Manufactured in Great Britain
07 06 05 04 03   5 4 3 2 1

Frontispiece: Mayor Josiah Quincy (1772–1864) with Faneuil Hall Market behind him. Portrait in oil by Gilbert Stuart, 1824. Quincy sat for this portrait (his second by Stuart) in November 1824, while the market's foundation walls were still being laid. He appears seated inside the Faneuil Hall mayor's office, holding plans from the architect Alexander Parris. This is the first representation of the market house, and it is at odds with the completed building—most notably in the front elevation's windows, the main entry, the linear detail etched into the granite work, and the extent of the tapered granite columns, as well as the fact that the actual market building looms larger in reality than the view of it from Faneuil Hall depicted in the portrait. The portrait was donated by Josiah's daughter, Eliza Susan Quincy, in 1876 to the Museum of Fine Arts, where it remains today. COURTESY OF THE MUSEUM OF FINE ARTS, BOSTON.

To the memory of my father,

John Quincy, Sr.

(1917–1983),
who introduced me to Boston when I was a boy

and

To my Puritan ancestor,

Edmund Quincy

(1602–1637),
who introduced the family name to America,
where it still endures twelve generations later

Sine macula macla
(A shield without a stain)

Contents

Acknowledgments   VII

Introduction   XIII

1. Divisions over a Marketplace: From Open Fields to Faneuil Hall   I

2. Faneuil Hall and the Marketplace Witness a Revolution   21

3. A Need for Renewal: Josiah Quincy Proposes a New Marketplace   40

4. Negotiating for a Grand Market   60

5. Building the New Market   81

6. Faneuil Hall Market Is Born   108

7. Quincy's Market: Decline and Survival   144

8. Rebuilding the Markets   181

9. Faneuil Hall Marketplace: Sustaining the Results   207

Conclusion   229

Author's Note   235

Notes   239

Bibliography   268

Index   275

Acknowledgments

I am greatly indebted to many people who believed in my effort to complete this book and to those who provided invaluable services. I am especially indebted to all who took time out of their hectic schedules and enlightened me with tales of their experiences and treasured memories. I am honored to recognize everyone whose love for Faneuil Hall Market and its unique history led them to tirelessly breathe new life into the new Faneuil Hall Marketplace. These include the following:

Architects Frank Adams, the late Bruno V. D'Agostino, Richard Detwiller, Christopher Dean, John E. Dobie, Fred Groff, William L. McQueen, and Thomas D. Quirk; I owe a special debt of gratitude to Frederick "Tad" A. Stahl, who gave generously of his time and provided recollections of the physical condition of the markets before, during, and after renovation (his anecdotes, drawn from his extensive experience with Faneuil Hall Markets, could form their own book); architect Jane Thompson, whose brilliance and enlightenment still shine as radiantly as when she and her husband, architect Ben Thompson, first opened the eyes of the world to the "Festival Market" in 1976 that pumped new life into the old buildings; of the late Ben Thompson, who spoke to me through his wife, Jane, I remain in awe, forever appreciative.

Boston Redevelopment Authority (BRA) staff: former directors Robert Walsh and the late Edward J. Logue, attorney Edward J. Lonergan, executive assistant to the director Paul L. McCann, Patricia Twohig, David B. Weiner; and other BRA staff members, especially, former director Robert T. Kenney, whose knowledge proved to be invaluable—I sincerely thank you for continually making yourself accessible and patiently clarifying many significant details with your remarkable recollection and insight.

Archivists Dave Nathan, Larry Gillis, and especially Kristin Swett of the City of Boston Archives, who worked tirelessly on my behalf searching for materials that I would have otherwise overlooked; senior civil engineer John M. Fleming Jr. of the City of Boston Engineering Division, Public Works Department; records manager Jim Cyphers of the Boston Neighborhood Development; the administration and staff of the Boston Landmarks Commission; and Charles J. Speleotis, former general counsel to the Boston Redevelopment Authority.

Former general managers and vice presidents of Faneuil Hall Marketplace Joseph "Skip" Coppola and James "Jim" B. McLean Jr., both of whom went far beyond my expectations in providing insight, recollections, and points of view that would never have been brought to the text otherwise; also, to general manager and vice president Michael Kelleher, Donna M. Crotty, Deborah Fernandes, Erin L. Roberts, Erica Lohr, and Vicki Stonestreet from Faneuil Hall Marketplace and the Rouse Company, my gratitude for your time and extensive support of the project.

Boston Athenaeum curator of prints and photographs Sally Pierce, whose critical skills and scholarly example proved crucial in conveying a factual history; head of reference Stephen Z. Nonack for his knowledge and appreciation of many generations of the Quincy family; former Bostonian Society chief librarian Doug Southard; current chief librarian Nancy Richard; librarian Robyn L. Christensen; former director Anne Emerson; and the distinguished staff of the Bostonian Society, Old State House; Richard Lahue and Judy Fichtenbaum of the Chelmsford Historical Society; Massachusetts Historical Society director William M. Fowler Jr., to whom I owe a great debt of gratitude, and assistant reference librarian Carrie Foley for her extensive knowledge of the Quincy family papers; Museum of Fine Arts acting co-chair, Art of the Americas, Erica E. Hirshler; David Sturtevant; Christopher Atkins; Elizabeth Dione; and Leah Ross; research director Patrick M. Leehey of the Paul Revere House; the late H. Hobart Holly, president of the Quincy Historical Society, Quincy family historian, and lifelong personal friend of the Quincy family, and his loving wife, Virginia Holly; Quincy Historical Society president Joyce I. Baker; director Edward Fitzgerald; and Research Library volunteers Beverly M. Erikson, Bernice A. Murphy, Andrew J. Dooley, William B. Gallagher, and especially Barbara R. Stamos; Society for the Preservation of New England Antiquities director Richard Nylander; chief librarian Lorna Condon and the distinguished staff of SPNEA, curators of the Colonel Josiah Quincy Homestead; museum director Marilyn Day and Barbara E. Ricker of the Westford

Historical Society; Aaron Schmidt of the Boston Public Library photo collection and print department, and other staff members; Harvard University Graduate School of Design's Francis Loeb Library librarian of special collections Mary F. Daniels, and reference assistant Desirée Goodwin, both of whom located critical historical data; Harvard University archivist Harley P. Holden and senior reference archivist Brian A. Sullivan, who gave generously of their time while sharing amusing anecdotes about legendary Harvard president Josiah Quincy; and supervisory park ranger John B. Manson and park ranger Matthew P. Greif of the Boston National Historical Park.

Of the numerous facilities that were necessary for research I would like to acknowledge the staff members of the following Massachusetts repositories: Adams Library, Chelmsford; Crane Library, Quincy; Westfield Public Library, Westfield; American Antiquarian Society, Worcester; New England Historic Genealogical Society, Boston; Chelmsford Historical Society, Chelmsford; Lowell Historical Society, Lowell; and the Massachusetts Historical Commission, Dorchester.

I am also indebted to the following individuals: Robert L. Beal, president of the Beal Companies (formerly vice president of the Beacon Companies); Paul G. Boudreau, Paul Boudreau Associates; Kevin Cain and the Washington Street office staff of Copy Cop, for providing exceptional professional services preparing reductions and enlargements of researched materials, some of which were irreplaceable; Jack Connors of the advertising firm Hill, Holliday, Connors, Cosmopulos; Herbert E. Fletcher II and his son Herbert "Hobie" Ellery Fletcher III, former owners of the Fletcher Granite Company in Chelmsford, for giving generously of their time and sharing their family papers; Sandra Heaphy, business manager of Maritime Heritage Prints; the Kelley family, owners of Durgin Park restaurant, especially Seana and Suzanne Kelley; Lee M. Kaplan, M.D., Ph.D., and Gerald J. Doyle, M.D.; Claudio Krause, president of the Faneuil Hall Merchants Association; Norman B. Leventhal, former chairman of the Beacon Companies; Peter "Pete" C. Leyden, construction manager and project supervisor, Walsh Brothers Construction Company, who gave me many opportunities to physically inspect secured areas around the marketplace that were under reconstruction and allowed me the opportunity to examine the complexities of the original market house construction; attorneys Peter Lyons and Ronald Wysocki; the late Walter Muir Whitehill; the late Edmund Quincy and his insightful correspondence; and the late William F. Morrissey, MAI, friend and business associate of my father and grandfather whose vivid memory of the markets during the early twentieth century proved invaluable; William J. Pastuszek, MAI, MRA, SRA; Ed Pignone, chief of staff and vice president of communications, Greater Boston Chamber of Commerce; Lawrence Rosenblum, for his archival film footage of the old markets; Ellen Smith, Ph.D.; James A. Visbeck, Isaiah Thomas Books and Prints; Roger S. Webb, Architectural Heritage Foundation, for providing me with abundant materials, factual data, and other crucial information; artist and illustrator Gary Irish, whose enthusiasm for redrawing the market buildings was undeniable; my good friend Bill "LBG" Griffin, who contributed his extensive computer skills to my research, for which I remain indebted; former mayor Kevin White, who graciously extended his time and knowledge to my research; Boston College historian Thomas H. O'Connor, a longtime friend of the Quincy family, who provided me with extensive historical reviews—for his participation and tutorial advice I remain humbled and honored; William F. Looney Jr., my friend, mentor, attorney, and Latin interpreter who never let me relinquish my goal, together with the law office of Looney and Grossman in Boston and especially Rob Barber; William A. Frohlich, director and editor-in-chief of Northeastern University Press, who encouraged me to be patient and persistent, as well as former senior editor John Weingartner, both of whom showed a personal interest from the beginning and professionally guided me through the project, current senior editor Robert J. Gormley, production director Ann Twombly, associate director Jill Bahcall, and copy editor Diana M. Donovan; my sister Carolyn J. Quincy, who since I was young encouraged me never to give up the quest of writing this book; my mother, Madeline J. "M.O." Quincy, who has never let any of her children or her grandchildren forget about our Quincy family ancestry.

Lastly, I would like to recognize the twelfth generation of American Quincy family members, who continue to give me great pride and inspiration: Richard Peter Quincy Jr., Laura Dorothy Quincy, Caroline Elizabeth Quincy, Christopher John Quincy, and Elizabeth Condry Quincy. I have now shown you what some of your Quincy family ancestors have accomplished. Do honor to your distinguished name and let the world remember you as a blessing to your generation.

Introduction

Since the founding of the Massachusetts Bay Colony, the market area near Faneuil Hall has been at the heart of the Boston's long history. Its story begins with the arrival of the Massachusetts Bay colonists in 1630, and the settlements and open-air trading that followed. The marketplace became more permanent in 1742, when Peter Faneuil donated the much needed market house that still bears his name. Faneuil Hall housed merchants for many years and hosted a succession of Revolutionary War events. In the early 1800s Josiah Quincy responded to the growing crowds at the market. The story of how Mayor Quincy enlarged the markets in such a grand way and of how they were rescued in the late twentieth century is an inspiring one, for it is in keeping with the grand ideals of our nation, many of which were first emphasized in old downtown Boston, the city's birthplace.

The story of this marketplace parallels the shifting fortunes of its city, from its days as a primitive colony to its present existence as a modern urban center. The marketplace was so prosperous that Bostonians built wharves upon wharves and filled in the water to make more room for trade. It served the everyday needs of citizens for years on end. And when it fell into need of renewal, an extraordinary person always stepped forward to pull it out of chaos.

By the time Boston was incorporated into a city in 1822, the almost two-hundred-year-old market district, then centered around Faneuil Hall, had become overwhelmed by the volume of its trade by ship. In addition, multitudes of regional farmers converged upon its narrow streets on market days, bringing produce and livestock to sell to city dwellers. Conditions continued to worsen until the market area became so congested and unhealthy that it was characterized as "a labyrinth of crooked and narrow alleys, frequently choked with farmers' wagons and trucks" that "mingled the offensive odor of the salt ooze with that of garbage and filth peculiar to such a locality."[1] These conditions were the result of the city's recent population boom, the inability of the city to respond immediately, and a severe depression that followed a long period of economic expansion.

In 1823, in order to remedy the markets' situation, the new City of Boston, under its second mayor, Josiah Quincy, demolished most of the market district's buildings and wharves, and created new land between Faneuil Hall and the water. Upon this filled land three new colossal buildings were constructed: two long, four-and-a-half-story warehouselike buildings that would hold individual multifloor units for stores and a central market house just as long as its flanking warehouse/store buildings. This central building looked not unlike an oversized ancient temple, but instead of European marble, it was built of New England granite. The three new buildings, called by their collective and formal name Faneuil Hall Markets—or simply "the markets"—served Boston as its chief wholesale and retail food distribution center for the next 125 years.

By the early 1950s, however, the market district was again in desperate need. The victim of urban flight to suburbia, its meat, produce, and fish vendors had experienced such a drop in business that many of them had relocated to more profitable centers. Blight set in to such an extent that the very existence of the markets seemed threatened. Fortunately, the marketplace was not demolished.

In 1969, the City of Boston secured a $2.1 million federal grant to restore a portion of its market district. It took several more years of studying the situation and clearing red tape before the city was ready to begin work on the restoration. This was one of the first major waterfront renewal projects in the country, and it soon became a model for other cities. As the project developed, city, state, and federal agencies began working with private industry. Renovations of all three buildings and some of the nearby streets were completed, and the newly named Faneuil Hall Marketplace reopened in phases, between 1976 and 1978. The costs were truly astounding, but so was the result.

The restoration of this important part of Boston's heritage added to downtown Boston's overall sense of prosperity. Along with its neighboring renewal projects of the new Government Center and the waterfront, it greatly contributed to the long-term economic health of the city as well.

Today throngs of visitors stream through its buildings and patronize its specialty shops, restaurants, food stalls, and pushcarts. Little do most of these visitors realize, as they stroll through the buildings and along the outside brick and cobblestone concourses, that they are walking on land that covers the remnants of Boston's old wharves, which still lie buried beneath.

My own fascination with the markets began when I was twelve years old. On a snowy afternoon in December 1963, before the renewal, my father took me to Durgin Park, a restaurant in the old North Market building, not far from Faneuil Hall. At that time, the traditional markets had become a meager collection of meat and fish vendors who sold their wares from partially abandoned buildings and timeworn stalls. Over a steaming lunch of grilled franks, Boston baked beans, and Indian pudding with ice cream, my father told me a story. It was a story that had been told to many Quincy sons at this same restaurant, possibly at the same table, by many Quincy fathers. Quincy Market, he said, using the popular name given to the market house and its warehouse/stores, was named after Josiah Quincy, a Quincy family ancestor.

On that snowy day I learned that Josiah Quincy was of the sixth generation of Quincys in America and that he was renowned for his fortitude, impartiality, and perseverance. A restless man, he never walked when he could mount his horse. He was often seen galloping through the streets of Boston with the long cape of his greatcoat flowing in his trail.

He was Boston's second mayor and, from the spring of 1823 until the end of 1828, he unselfishly led Boston through its infancy as a city. I was told that he was a highly disciplined, tenacious, resourceful, and sometimes obdurate public officer. His natural powers of persuasion and manipulation were enhanced by his talent for stirring oratory and challenging debate.

One of his greatest achievements, my father told me, came from his resolve to overcome his detractors and to execute a project Herculean for that time—or any time. Initially ridiculed by Bostonians as the "mammoth"[2] project of the mayor, the marketplace he built quietly earned respect, and then affection and awe. Mayor Quincy's foresight and determination helped him complete the project—on time, despite an unthinkable schedule, and on his own terms, which meant no new taxes to subsidize the endeavor, I was informed. The project had done more than give the city a sense of pride; it had probably saved the new city from bankruptcy, for there had been a major depression at the time, and the marketplace he built served as a center for new business. Had a less able administrator been in office at that time, my father told me, the project would probably have succumbed to its initially strong public opposition or to budget problems.

After lunch on that snowy December afternoon in 1963, filled with pride in

Mayor Quincy's accomplishment, I followed my father as he led me along slushy North and South Market Streets. He showed me the remains of the granite and brick structures and told me of the first time he had seen the marketplace as a boy. I could see in my father's eyes how saddened he was by the sight of the deteriorating warehouse/stores and the soot-darkened granite market house. When we stopped at its west portico, across the street from Faneuil Hall, my father remarked, "Look at the massive weight of these solid granite columns and the proportions of the granite block walls. Imagine what it must have taken to transport this stone to Boston during the early 1800s. What a colossal job it must have been to lift these pieces and put them into place so precisely by hand, not to mention the exhaustive hand-hammered details of the granite everywhere you look."

I gazed in awe at the magnificent structure, dreaming of what it must have been like in the past. Then my father brought me back to earth. "Appreciate what you see here today, son, because there's been talk around the city that the markets may soon face the wrecking ball." Stunned with disbelief, I reached out my hand and touched a soot- and age-blackened granite column. Its past spoke to me as the present could not. At that very moment, I'm sure, the ghost of Josiah Quincy crawled under my skin, where he has remained to this very day.

Whether this conviction is based on reality doesn't matter. The experience was real to me, and later I took solace in the discovery that Josiah Quincy, too, believed that spirits guided him during his own life. When he was twenty-two years old, in December 1794, he made an entry in his journal which said, "I have always encouraged myself to believe that all men are at times, if not always, subject to invisible influences, suggesting thoughts and communicating impulses which give direction to the whole course of their lives. True or false, this belief is consolatory and useful."[3]

In the years since, I studied the history of Quincy Market and was amazed at what I found. Many of the circumstances that led to the market's inception have been mistakenly reported by storytellers. Numerous legends have grown up around this landmark, most of which have little truth to them. And for good reason.

Apparently, after Mayor Quincy left office, all the architectural records for the markets' development—from the initial drafts to the conceptualized drawings and scale models—were lost. The small amount of information that survives is fragmented and provides only cursory, often contradictory data.

In addition, Josiah Quincy publicly refused all recognition for his efforts. Instead of telling stories about the project's development, he attributed the success of the marketplace to his colleagues and fellow citizens by stating in his book *A Municipal History of Boston,* "It is due to the men who constituted the city councils at that day, whose intelligence devised, and whose energy effected these great results, and also to the spirit of the citizens, whose votes sustained and encouraged them, through good report and evil report." And he went on to conclude, "[T] he difficulties with which they had to struggle, and the course of measures by which they were surmounted and success ultimately obtained, should be permanently recorded, as an honor to the past and an example to the future."[4]

The most accurate of the surviving evidence, however, suggests that the present configurations of the buildings, their physical components, and the street layouts—despite Mayor Quincy's denials—were indeed the result of his actions while he was in office. This corroborates Quincy family tradition, and it is indeed a story that should be told.

Josiah Quincy's accomplishment is best described, I think, by Edmund Quincy, who wrote, "The circumstances of the greatest local interest in Mr. Quincy's municipal administration was the building of Faneuil Hall market-house. The conveniences for the provisioning of the city were at that time of a very limited description, and one of the first considerations which occurred to him after entering on his office was, how these could be enlarged and improved without great expense to the city. From the first to the last he encountered opposition in every shape—of the selfish interests of the property-holders whom it was necessary to buy out, of the parties whose vested interests in the old state of things were endangered, of demagogues who were ready to lay hold of any occasion of persuading the people that they were in danger of ruin, and of cautious citizens who dreaded the creation of an unmanageable city debt. The land made by filling up the dock on a part of which the market-house stands sold for enough to pay for the whole expense of the operation, while the taxable property was increased by the value of the warehouses built upon it."[5]

I believe that Josiah Quincy's contribution to Boston is not only unique but inspirational. In terms of its political birth, the marketplace came about through innovative planning. In terms of scale and aesthetics, the buildings are a masterpiece of civic design, both technically and in terms of ornamentation. In terms of business needs, the marketplace gave Boston an elegant center in which new business could transpire. And in terms of history, a vital relationship to the American Revolution's "Cradle of Liberty" (Faneuil Hall) and Boston's ever-evolving waterfront was maintained.

Boston's signature institution is indeed—literally and in the memory of its people—Quincy's Market.

"Old men dream dreams. Young men see visions."

—Josiah Quincy to Samuel Hurd Walley

May 24, 1854

Divisions over a Marketplace:
From Open Fields to Faneuil Hall

T he peninsula that holds today's downtown Boston was first named Shawmut, meaning "living fountains or waters," by the Native Americans. This desolate peninsula wilderness was less than four miles in circumference and surrounded by Massachusetts Bay. Barely linked to the mainland by a narrow ribbon of land called the Neck, at flood tides Shawmut became a virtual island because the waves of the bay washed across this bridge of an isthmus. Mauled by the sea for centuries, the coastline had been shaped with shallow coves and small hallows. Yet, up from its barren shoreline, through the middle of the peninsula swept lofty hills. The highest hill was named Tramountain (or Trimountain)[1] by early white explorers because of its three bold peaks. And from that hilly landmark the peninsula received its second name, Tramountaine.

The native inhabitants of the area used the barren peninsula and its nearby harbor islands only for access to good fishing, especially during the warm summer months. Shawmut remained an otherwise uninhabited windswept tract until 1625. It was then that Reverend William Blackstone, or Blaxton, a bachelor Anglican minister, abandoned a Rhode Island expedition led by Robert Gorges and was mysteriously lured northward to the uninhabited Tramountaine. Blackstone, an admitted eccentric and bookish recluse, claimed settlement rights to the peninsula and built a solitary dwelling on the west side of the three hills.[2] There he planted a sizable orchard, tapped a freshwater spring, and lived in solitude for five years until the arrival of the Puritans, who came to settle somewhere along the coast of Massachusetts.

In the summer of 1630, a convoy of eleven ships arrived from England in search of a site for a new colony. Led by the *Arbella* and carrying mostly English Puritans known as the Massachusetts Bay Company, the group was enticed by Tramountaine's deep and protected harbor waters. Governor John Winthrop, the steering force and righteous minister of this company, was in charge. The new settlers first disembarked across the harbor, on a nearby spit of beach on what is now called Charlestown, and during that summer they hurriedly erected a primitive settlement with crude and drafty shelters. Over the long weeks crossing the Atlantic, the lack of food and fresh water had caused rampant illness. Such diseases as scurvy and hectic fever had lowered their number from the original group of about a thousand. Recovery was hampered by the settlers' discovery that there was a lack of fresh drinking water where they chose to disembark. Running springs were scarce and those that were there were tainted with brine. The use of wells was not an option for them, since it was a Puritan custom at the time to shun well water unless absolutely necessary.

A scouting party discovered Reverend Blackstone's solitary habitation at Tramountaine and conveyed to him the misfortunes plaguing their settlement. Blackstone led the party to a freshwater spring not far from his home and pointed out that it would amply accommodate the group.[3] Although Blackstone was sympathetic to the plight of his fellow Englishmen, he insisted that if the Puritans were to relocate to Tramountaine, they would have to respect the sanctity of his seclusion and not encroach upon his cottage, gardens, or apple orchard.

That September, the Puritans moved across the harbor and founded a permanent colony not far from that spring, alongside Mill Creek, which flowed down Tramountain to the harbor. The creek connected a pond (later called Mill Pond or Mill Cove) to an inlet of Massachusetts Bay. There, nestled on a small plain at the base of Tramountaine's hills, Governor Winthrop proclaimed, "We shall be as a City upon a Hill."[4] The settlers renamed the peninsula Boston, in honor of the city in northeast England whence many of them had emigrated.[5] This area, at what is now known as Adams Square, was the birthplace of Boston.

Unlike Blackstone, who had settled on the sunny western declivity of the three hills, the Puritans built rudimentary huts and thatched-roof houses at the base of the eastern side, directly facing the harbor and the weather it brought to the land. Enclosed by the headlands of two hills (later called Copps Hill and Fort Hill), the Great Eastern Cove or Great Cove, as they called the inlet, divided the north and

Shawmut Peninsula and the Town Cove, 1630.
ILLUSTRATION BY GARY M. IRISH, ASAI, 2002.

south ends of the marshy coastline. It also afforded a most convenient access to the sea. The Puritans soon built a common dock there, extending into Great Cove, to make access even more convenient. They removed timber, stones, and other obstructions, then piled rocks to build a common dock where vessels could be loaded and unloaded. It was decreed that the land near this "orderly and convenient Town Dock"[6] was their "chief landing place."[7] Soon Great Cove became known as Town Cove, and the chief landing place used for trading and storing goods was called Town Dock.[8]

Once settled, the Puritans began to set up a government; to do so, they executed the terms of their Massachusetts Bay Company charter: "By that charter a governor, deputy-governor, and eighteen assistants were annually to be chosen out of their own number by all who, as 'freemen,' had the franchise in the Company." A

Great and General Court was convened four times a year to create the first laws of the colony and "to elect and commission the officers and to vote upon the admission of new members, or 'freemen.' The Assistants soon assumed the name of 'Magistrates,' with all the requisite and implied functions."[9] A year later, membership in the First Church of Boston was made a requirement to being elected.

The Bay Colony charter, signed by King Charles I, was intended to set up not a government but a business venture by which private English investors would profit from an overseas plantation. But the Crown became preoccupied with other affairs, and the colonists were left to set up their own form of government. Inevitably, without close monitoring from the mother country, these idealistic Puritans converted many of their religious and political ideals into law. In doing this, they developed a habit of resistance to arbitrary political and religious authority. This sometimes worked for them and sometimes against them, but they based their civil government on the needs of the people.

These independently written laws were tolerated back in England because of more immediate turmoil occupying the Crown's attention around the world. From almost the very beginning, Boston became accustomed to functioning on its own, thus laying the foundation for an eventual free and independent republic. As one source aptly described the situation, "[T]hrough temporary experiment of the Puritan Commonwealth, the corporation of the Massachusetts Bay Company became, by anticipation, the Commonwealth of Massachusetts."[10]

These early settlers were faced with hostilities and hardships totally alien to life back in England. Yet, they were somehow able to survive the ordeals of the wilderness and maintain their seaport colony, and in late 1633 other settlers arrived from England. Among them were two people who would make their names in the New World for different reasons. The Reverend John Cotton later became known for his controversial stands against dissenters. Edmund Quincy, who lived for only four years after his arrival, served the colony wherever he could and left a line of heirs who would do the same.

Trade was intrinsic to the colony's existence. In an effort to aid the ships now approaching Boston on a regular basis, the Court of Assistants ordered that a signal light be placed atop the highest peak of Tramountain. On March 4, 1634, a lantern was positioned there, and the hill became known as Sentry Hill. (It was later renamed

Beacon Hill.) Ships could now bring supplies and take goods for trade more safely. But during the winter, the precarious icy conditions of Massachusetts Bay forced many merchant ships laden with supplies to bypass Massachusetts for the southern colonies. This left Boston to fend for itself during the harsh winters, when much of the livestock succumbed to exposure or to natural predators.

The most crucial element of winter survival became the availability of food. A bounty of one penny was awarded to any man who killed a wolf while protecting the cows, horses, goats, and swine. There were widespread shortages of grains, fruits, vegetables, and meat (which depended on grains to survive). Although some fish, along with mussels and clams, could still be easily gathered along the seashore in winter, many colonists died from starvation. "Muscles [*sic*], groundnuts and acorns, the chief dependence now of many, the snow and frozen state of the earth rendered hard to be procured. Under these distressing circumstances, the perils of the ocean, danger from pirates, and the hostility of known belligerent powers, were taken into view."[11]

Despite all this, the colony grew. When the weather permitted, native men and women, led by Chief Chickatabot, visited Boston and exchanged goods like pumpkins and baskets of corn for cutlery and clothing. And ships from Holland, Ireland, and the southern colonies brought provisions like salted beef and pork, porridge, and coffee beans.[12]

Since most of Boston's commerce was conducted around the Town Dock, all merchandising, town meetings, and public gatherings also took place there. It was therefore natural that the Town Dock should host the colony's marketplace. This makeshift marketplace was, at first, devoid of any suitable structure, so a nearby field was used. It was called, at various times, the Corn Market or the Dock Market. (There was also an open-air market called the Fish Market, which was situated a little north of the Town Dock.) In order to clear the Town Dock area for the market, in 1634 the Court of Assistants ordered "that all of the timber [trees] be taken away from the market, and gotten clear, and . . . pitts gotten filled up."[13]

During the ensuing years the open marketplaces at the Town Dock and elsewhere were used for the buying and selling of goods. But the old English custom of hucksters and peddlers selling foodstuffs house-to-house continued in the New World as well. This method had the added benefit of being unregulated by government, which appealed to the colonists' independent way of thinking.

Still later, according to a 1635 entry in John Winthrop's diary, "By order of Court a mercate [market] was erected in Boston to be kept upon Thursday the 5 day of the week, being the Lecture Day. Samuel Cole set up the first house for common entertainment, and John Cogan, merchant, the first shop."[14] This new market was situated on the spot where the Old State House stands today, just southwest of the Town Dock.

Held once a week as the decree states, the gathering of buyers and sellers was mostly convened, as it had been before at the Town Dock area, at an open-air market, not within a structure. "It [the field where the open-air market was held] was a convenient place, and a safe shelter [haven] for the fishermen who supplied the inhabitants with cod and mackerel, and for farmers who came down the Charles River in their boats with vegetables. It was equally convenient for farmers of Roxbury and Dorchester, coming over the 'Neck' with their teams. The topography made it a natural market-place and commercial center of the town."[15] Boston's market district changed into one with structures only gradually during the seventeenth century.

As more colonists immigrated, the need for regulating trade grew. "The market was an important institution in the mother country, and its need was early recognized by the founders of Boston, who brought with them the ancient 'common law of the market.'"[16] Boston's early seventeenth-century laws attempted to provide reliable, fairly priced food and to protect both buyers and sellers. But the Puritans, who saw themselves as escaping the power of the Crown, objected to regulated trade, which had been strictly enforced in England, following them to Boston.

Nevertheless, the laws provided for officials to inspect the market for cleanliness, to regulate weights and measures, and to settle any disputes through a court proceeding. The court used to settle such contentions was conducted at the market with few formalities; it was called the Pie Powder Court, named after the appearance of its members, who often ended up with baking flour covering their feet.

By 1649 the position of "Clerks of the Market" was created. There would be two of them and their duties were similar to those of the Market Clerks of England.[17] The first clerks were Jeremy Houchin and James Penn; they served two years and were compensated "one third part of all forfeit for his pains [with] the remainder going to the poor."[18]

In 1658 the Town House was built of wood on the first open-air marketplace site, adjacent to the Town Dock (just southwest of Faneuil Hall today), by an order of the General Court. This two-story structure was intended for public gatherings of all sorts. It was begun with capital donated by Captain Robert Keayne in his voluminous 1656 last will and testament. One of the founders of the oldest military company of citizen-soldiers in the Western Hemisphere, the Ancient and Honorable Artillery Company,[19] he left the "sum of £300, current money,"[20] for the building of the Town House. Two years later an equal amount of money was contributed by the citizens to effect its completion. "The town, in accepting this legacy, was under obligation to make provision for the Artillery Company [to store their supplies there]. . . . It is the reason that no rent is charged to the Company—a fact which . . . at times caused considerable controversy."[21]

The Town House provided rooms for a court, a library, and the artillery company; it also had an open ground floor to shelter a merchants' exchange. At first, this merchants' exchange was open only on Thursday, and most merchandise was sold in bulk at wholesale prices. Those who purchased smaller amounts of goods were charged excessively. Then, in 1695, "An Act was passed forbidding the sale of imported provisions at wholesale, until after three days' notice had been given by a public crier; this was considered to be in favor of the poor, who were thus to have an opportunity to buy in small quantities at wholesale prices."[22]

The second floor of the Town House was constantly in use as a court or as a gathering place for town meetings, which had evolved into a cornerstone of colonial practice. Here, voters annually chose a host of officials that included selectmen and constables; shire reeves; water bailiffs and wardens of the waterworks; hog reeves; the measurer of salt; town scavengers; town criers; and a keeper of the town clock. Ironically, there were, at times, more office holders at a town meeting than voters, since every adult male was compelled to serve the town at least once during his lifetime.

Just outside the Town House, the Puritan magistrates enforced their strict moral corrections at the stocks, pillory, and hanging posts there, or led the accused away to the more publicly oriented Boston Common to be shamed. "Boston had a Town Court as early as 1651, and its Municipal Court, with wide jurisdiction but summary proceedings, is modeled after the pattern of the old Pie Powder Court which used to sit on market days to dispose of cases arising among those who congregated in the market places."[23]

In the spring of 1696, it was ordered that the market be held open in Boston every Tuesday, Thursday, and Saturday. It was further ordered that a bell should be rung at the opening of the market, at 7:00 A.M. from March to May, at 6:00 A.M. from May to September, and at 9:00 A.M. for all the remaining months. Like other customs adopted by the colonists, the ringing of the market bell had originated in early England, "but public sentiment was greatly against this measure, one reason for which was the fear that 'the Market Cross' often set up in England and on the Continent might be introduced here, and the citizens were willing to submit to almost any inconvenience rather than to have the semblance of that power of which they had striven hard to rid themselves."[24]

Clerks were ordered to be appointed by the selectmen for the enforcement of rules whereby "retailers, hucksters, and traders could not buy until the afternoon, in order that the house keepers have the benefit of the early chance."[25] Presumably, these clerks also enforced payment of licenses, fees, rent, and fines. The seeds of independent American enterprise had already taken root, however. Many country farmers and local butchers still found it more profitable to peddle directly from their wagons than to abide by English customs that ultimately taxed their profits into nearly nothing. So, by 1700 Boston remained one of the few towns in the civilized world without an adequate common market.

There were, by this time, three factions of governance affecting market trade. First, there were the townspeople as lawmakers, who passed laws through their selectmen at town meetings. Second, there was the Crown—in the form of its appointed governor and his councilmen, who enforced the laws. And last, there were the merchants themselves, who benefited from the effect of the laws that ensured open competition. But despite the intent to provide fresh food, honest measure, and fair prices, government attempts to more fully regulate trade failed for some time. Citizens seemed to prefer not only the convenience of country farmers peddling from their wagons but the opportunity to barter or bargain on price without the interference of regulations.

There may have been other reasons for the delay in having a regulated marketplace. English Captain Nathaniel Uring, during a stay in Boston in 1700, wrote of the reasons he saw for the townspeople's opposition: "The reason is, if the market days were appointed all the country people coming in at the same time would glut it, the townspeople would buy their provisions for what they pleased. So they rather choose to send them in as they see fit, and sometimes a tall fellow brings a turkey or goose to sell, and will travel through the whole town to see who will give the most for it, and it is last sold of 3s. 6d. or 4s., and if he had stayed at home he could have earned a crown for it."[26]

While Bostonians of the early 1700s were left without a permanent public marketplace, the population multiplied to six thousand. People moved out of the central town and began to fill the peninsula. In those years, too, the owners of property along the coast continually filled it in, to extend the land and build wharves out into the harbor.[27] This alteration of Boston's land mass both accommodated the expanding population within the confined wilderness and led to unprecedented economic growth. A parochial seaport became a center of commerce that looked to foreign lands as trading partners.

As the town expanded, no thought was given to overall planning. Boston was shaped by the needs of its inhabitants. From its birthplace at the head of the Great Cove, starting from the Town Dock, the settlement gradually moved north and south, following the shoreline. For many years not a single building appeared on the eastern slope of Tramountaine. Boston's earliest streets followed the curves of the hills, crossing their slopes at the easiest angles. Cows were driven to pasture on Boston Common, along paths that circumvented the blueberry bushes on Beacon Hill. Horses laden with grain or corn were led across the low banks of Copps Hill to the gristmill. Thus, the narrow and winding streets, with their curious twists and turns of this rugged promontory, came about by means of shortcuts and convenience; they remain substantially unchanged in the downtown Boston of nearly four centuries later.

By about 1710 Boston's population had grown to 12,000, making it the largest town in British North America. It was also considered to be the continent's chief commercial port, now having forty wharves and twelve shipyards. King Street (earlier called Great Street, and, after the Revolution, State Street) went past the Town Dock to High Street (known as Washington Street today), which connected Boston to the mainland, across the Neck. Portions of King Street, Elm Street, and Market Square were officially designated Dock Square.

Although prosperity led to the construction of additional piers, by 1710 the largest development in Boston took place not far from Dock Square. Named Long Wharf, it was built by Oliver Noyes and Associates, and it extended about two thousand feet into Boston Harbor's deeper waters from the foot of King Street. The north side of the wharf was occupied by an unbroken line of shops and warehouses, while the south side of the pier provided berths. The seaward end was reserved for the town battery and for docking the deep-draft oceangoing vessels.

Until 1710, Philadelphia and New York surpassed Boston in size and power, but once Boston's great fleet of tall ships opened trade with the Far East (importing its silk, tea, opium, and spices), it began to dominate foreign commerce in the colonies. It continued to do so for the next 150 years. Along with New York, Boston became a major port of trade with Europe, the West Indies, and Australia (which provided gold and wool). Boston also became one corner of the highly lucrative and infamous triangle of slave trade, which stretched from Africa's Gold Coast to the West Indies back to the northeast colonies. This shameful trade was responsible for the enslavement, even deaths, of millions of Africans. Trading, smuggling, slaving, and pirating made the fortunes of the city's principal merchants during those days of Boston's square-rigged sailing vessels.

In 1711 a fire along King Street destroyed the second story of the Town House. Although the market bell was saved by sailors who ascended to the cupola and hoisted it down, the men perished in the falling ruins. The Town House was rebuilt with brick in 1712 but was again damaged by a fire that destroyed most of the early library books, records, and valuable papers.[28]

With the loss of the Town House, farmers from the outlying countryside again traversed the peninsula, fervidly hawking produce, meat, eggs, and other goods from their carts and wagons. Loyal, affluent, and conveniently located customers were favored with grocery deliveries. But those situated less conveniently to the Neck, specifically at the west and north ends of the peninsula, found themselves at a disadvantage, because the farther a farmer traveled through town, the less he had to sell, in terms of both quantity and quality.

A controversy therefore arose that created complex alliances. Not only were the central townspeople pitted against the residents of the west and north ends, but recent English immigrants, who were familiar with the benefits of public markets and who insisted on rebuilding the Town House as a central market, found themselves at odds with these now "native" Bostonians, who remained determined to trade without any regulations. In February 1717 the selectmen reconsidered creating a permanent public market, and the town subsequently voted to erect a market building. Action on the measure, however, was delayed for two years; it was then debated again, and disallowed.

For the next seventeen years the issue was not raised. The closest thing to a law restricting trade was a ban instituted in 1725 that prohibited dogs over ten inches in height from entering Boston. This was in response to numerous complaints that ravenous dogs were following peddlers who sold meat door-to-door and were attacking buyers who approached their wagons.[29]

A century after the first order was given for a public market, proponents emerged victorious on March 12, 1734, when the town, in a vote of 517 to 399, established three markets. The sum of £700 in tax money was appropriated and three freestanding buildings were erected. "That the Vacant place at or near the Town Dock be one of the Places. That the Open place near the old North meeting House be another place for a market. That the Third place be at or near the Great Tree at the South end, near mr. Eliots House."[30] North Market was located in North Square, near the Old North Meeting House, Centre Market at Dock Square (close to where Faneuil Hall is presently located), and South Market on Boylston Street near the "Great Tree" or Liberty Tree (currently near the intersection of Boylston and Washington Streets).

On Tuesday, June 2, 1734, all three markets were opened with the ringing of the bells. From that day forward every day except Sunday was a market day, and a bell was rung to give notice of opening at sunrise and of closing at 1:00 P.M. Farmers were allowed to sell their own produce, and the fishermen their own catch, without the interference of meddling middlemen. "The newspapers of that day said, 'it was a day of history for the Town of Boston.' There was a large concourse of people, buyers, sellers, and spectators, and an abundance of provisions were brought in for sale; those that excelled in goodness and cheapness sold quickly."[31] The first clerks of these three markets were Captain John Steele, who was stationed at the North Market, Francis Willoughby at the South Market, and Captain James Watson at the Centre Market at Dock Square. From the start, the Centre Market was the most frequented because of its harborfront location.

There remained many dissenters to the organized and regulated market system, however. They contended that people would be better served by peddlers than by a market system of fixed localities. Many of the town's butchers also loudly protested, claiming a threat to their livelihood if they were allowed to sell beef only at a permanent marketplace. Soon the regulations became so confusing that they were not effectively enforced, and a boycott resulted. Within three years of this grand experiment, the clerks at two of the markets were dismissed and their buildings were abandoned. The South Market was converted into a storehouse and rented; the North Market was disassembled and its components were used to erect a workhouse.

In 1737 motions to resurrect the issue for debate incited a riotous band of market opponents into action. Under the cover of darkness a furious mob "disguised as clergymen,"[32] in defiance of two ministers who had been vocal proponents of a public market system, ransacked and destroyed the Centre Market. The incident was considered a symbolic gesture intended to terminate the debate for good.

Market proponents circulated a number of petitions to create another public market but it was impossible to gather enough support to persuade the selectmen to underwrite the cost of another building with tax dollars. Opponents continued to cite the Crown's rigid economic restrictions, royal authority, and strict market controls imposed upon any publicly funded markets.

By 1740 the controversy had turned passionate and violent. And then something unexpected happened: Peter Faneuil, Esq., a flamboyant and wealthy Boston merchant, offered to personally pay for the creation of a market house, provided it be fairly regulated. Such a gesture by a living person was highly unusual by the standards of Boston's colonial society. Yet, Peter Faneuil's gift not only furnished Boston with a permanent market house and meeting hall, but also provided a historic memorial that kept the Faneuil name alive long after the death of its benefactor.

Peter Faneuil, the market hall's munificent donor, often complained that his fellow townsfolk never said his family's name correctly.[33] He insisted that his last name was pronounced "Fan-nel," but most Bostonians found it easier to say "Fan-u-ell" instead. The first Faneuils emigrated to Boston in 1691 and the names of Benjamin, John (Jean), and Andrew Faneuil appear on the list of the French nationals admitted to the Bay Colony as French Huguenot refugees. Although some Huguenots came to the New World destitute, others had extensive wealth, which they succeeded in bringing with them to this country. Apparently, the Faneuils were among those more fortunate, as they had liquidated extensive holdings in France.

Benjamin Faneuil, Peter Faneuil's father, immediately left Boston to seek enterprise in New York, where he married Anne Bureau. While in New York, Benjamin and Anne took up residence at the nearby settlement of New Rochelle, where they produced a family of eleven children.[34]

Little is known about Benjamin's brother John (Jean).[35] But the third brother,

Andrew Faneuil, found Boston a more favorable place. He flourished there in both the social and business aspects of the town. By 1709 Andrew Faneuil owned a wharf just to the north of the end of King Street (not far from Long Wharf), a warehouse, some merchant ships, and extensive interests in real estate. He even purchased the stately Bellingham mansion that stood on the slope of Beacon Hill. Situated on seven acres of abounding gardens, this estate had long enjoyed a colorful history; it was believed that the original cellar had walls made of false foundation stones that could conceal smuggled goods.

When Benjamin and Anne Faneuil died in 1719, their six surviving children—Peter, his younger brother, Benjamin, and the four girls—were sent from New Rochelle to Boston to live with Uncle Andrew in the Bellingham mansion. Uncle Andrew's strict upbringing included compelling them each to adhere to celibacy. Andrew became bitter after the tragic death of his wife, Mary Catherine Faneuil, on July 16, 1724. She left him with no direct heirs.

Although Peter had begun working for his uncle when he was nineteen (about 1719), Andrew chose Benjamin to become the master of his fortunes. His sole condition was that Benjamin never wed.

At first, Benjamin agreed to his uncle's terms, but a highly cultivated young maiden named Mary Cutler captured the young man's heart. For a time Benjamin tried to conceal his affections for Miss Cutler, but when Uncle Andrew learned of his nephew's "indiscretions" he chased him from the family mansion and dismissed him from the business.[36] Since Peter was thoroughly enjoying bachelorhood, Uncle Andrew transferred the same proposal to Peter, and the two entered into a celibacy pact before Andrew Faneuil died in 1738. Peter Faneuil inherited the bulk of his uncle's estate, including holdings in Boston and throughout New England, Great Britain, France, Holland, and many other countries, becoming the wealthiest man in Boston. He would remain so, as long as he never married.

Peter was known to throw a party or two, however. One night, while sipping port with friends around the Bellingham mansion hearth, perhaps after running short of some foodstuff or other, Peter Faneuil expressed annoyance over there being no local market to readily supply his household needs. He went on to express the opinion that a permanent public market was vital not only for his personal use, but for the growing population of the town. And he implied that he would be willing to make sure the town soon had one. Without his knowledge, his overture was made public. It was received with such great favor by market proponents that a petition bearing the names of 347 prominent citizens was quickly circulated and sent to the selectmen.

In 1740 Peter Faneuil formally stepped forward and proposed to the selectmen to "[o]ffer at his Own proper cost and Charge, to Erect and Build a nobel and complete Structure or Edifice, to be Improved for a Market, for the sole Use, Benefit, and Advantage of the Town."[37] In order to avoid any personal liability, he specified that the building be constructed with masonry materials, to withstand the elements and the potential destruction by fire. He hoped, too, that such sturdy construction would discourage future dissenters from tearing the building down!

Keenly aware of the anger of market opponents, his offer also came with stipulations that the town legally authorize the market's creation by a vote, that it enact proper but fair regulations, and that it maintain the premises permanently by never altering the building's use from that of a market.

Many Bostonians immediately became suspicious. Market opponents responded by saying that Faneuil's offer was merely a means to bring the vitriolic debate over regulated markets back to the surface. But on July 14, 1740, Peter Faneuil's gesture was accepted by a narrow margin of seven votes (367 yeas to 360 nays), whereby the selectmen were instructed to "Wait upon Peter Faneuil Esquire, and to Present the Thanks of this Town to Him, As Voted in the Forenoon: And also to Acquaint Him, that the Town have, by their Vote, come to a Resolution to Accept of his Generous Offer of Erecting a Market House of Dock Square, According to his Proposal."[38]

Opposition to a public market house remained strong, so a petition was circulated among the citizens requesting the following: "[W]e the said subscribers would humbly propose that, notwithstanding the said building should be encouraged and come to effect, yet the market people should be at liberty to carry their marketing wheresoever they please about the town to dispose of it."[39] The petition was subsequently passed by vote of the selectmen.

The building was positioned at Dock Square near the site chosen for the Centre Market erected in 1734. On September 2, 1740, "the Selectmen accordingly met . . . Mrk'd and Stak'd out a Piece of Ground for that use, measuring in length from the lower or Easterly end fronting the Ware houses in Merchants Row, One Hundred feet, and in Breadth Forty feet, which leaves a Passage Way of Thirty feet Wide Between the Town's Shops and the Market House to be built."[40] The Scottish artist

John Smibert, an intimate friend of the Faneuil family, was engaged as the architect. Smibert was among a new wave of British immigrants who had entered Boston during the early eighteenth century, bringing masons, carpenters, and artisans familiar with the English Renaissance styles. The new market hall was Smibert's only architectural commission. He devoted the remainder of his life to painting portraits and landscapes.

In his design for the building, Smibert recreated an open arcade with a large hall based upon the two-story English market plan. Collaborating with Smibert were master mason Joshua Blanchard and carpenter Samuel Ruggles. They based the style of the building upon the civic form of the post-Reformation era in England. It was the first building in Boston that utilized all four sides, instead of having only one or two prominent sides. Because Smibert included a second floor in his design, the selectmen "induced Faneuil to make an addition of a large hall over the market

Faneuil Hall as seen by the Town Dock at its waterfront location, looking northwesterly, in 1742.
DRAWING BY GARY M. IRISH, ASAI, 2002.

house for public meetings, and for transacting the business of the Town."[41] The town had, they pointed out, outgrown the public meeting room in the Representative's Chamber of the now rebuilt Town House. The new building gained its second story because of an extended act of generosity by its benefactor.

The two-story building (with additional attic space) was 40 feet wide by 100 feet long. There were three ground-floor arched bays on the structure's ends, and nine bays along each side. The second floor had arched windows and a central domed cupola perched on the gable roof. The cupola contained the bell that would toll to signal the start and the end of market day.

Faneuil personally involved himself in many of the decisions on materials. He imported from England all the glass for the building, using his own merchant ships. And he had mounted atop the cupola a gargantuan grasshopper weathervane weighing thirty-eight pounds. He specifically had it modeled after the grasshopper vane at London's Royal Exchange, which had been built by Sir Thomas Gresham in the 1500s.[42]

The signature grasshopper was designed and assembled by Deacon Shem Drowne, the first known professional weathervane manufacturer in New England and the creator of what is undoubtedly the most famous weathervane in the country.[43] A master craftsman and coppersmith, he fashioned the weathervane out of hammered copper and gold leaf, then inserted green glass doorknobs for its eyes and long metal antennae to seek the wind.

Various legends have given reasons for the selection of this peculiar grasshopper weathervane. Many thought it represented Peter Faneuil's motive for donating the market: to accommodate his own personal need for provisions. Some thought the grasshopper design was part of the Faneuils' crest. But two legends regarding the grasshopper have endured. The British version has it that once, during a picnic, a baby belonging to the Gresham family became lost in a nearby field of high grass. The infant was recovered thanks to the attention drawn by a swarm of grasshoppers fleeing the toddler's grasp. Subsequently, the insect was adopted as a good-luck symbol for British banks. The other is an American tale. Shem Drowne claimed that as a young man he "became discouraged with his repeated failures in the New World, and going out into the country, he lay down to sleep in an open field, and was awakened by a boy chasing a grasshopper. Shem became interested in the sport and acquainted with the boy, who was the son of a wealthy man, and accompanied him

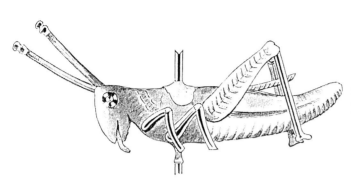

The Faneuil Hall signature grasshopper weathervane. Designed and assembled by Deacon Shem Drowne, this is undoubtedly the most famous weather-vane in the United States. DRAWING REPRINTED FROM ABRAM ENGLISH BROWN, *Faneuil Hall and Faneuil Hall Market* (BOSTON: LEE AND SHEPARD, 1900), 137.

to his home, where he had supper, and was later adopted by the boy's parents. When he became a successful coppersmith, he made the weathervane in commemoration of the part a grasshopper had in the turning incident of his life."[44]

As the brick walls rose from their stone foundations between 1740 and 1742, many citizens considered the architecture imposing and ornate. Rumors of villainous speculation, evil motives, and corrupt profiteering upon the town's public land became widespread. But as the building neared completion, there was more unanimity from its opponents. "When his proposal met with the approval of many towns-people, and Faneuil, when passing down King Street to his office, frequently heard them remark, 'Good thing; hurrah for neighbor Peter!' There was nevertheless a great deal of opposition on the part of the voters."[45]

Opposition aside, the building was finished. At the meeting of the selectmen held on September 10, 1742, "Mr. Samuel Ruggles who was Employed in Building the Market House this Day Waited on the Select men by order of Peter Faneuil Esq. & delivered them the Key of said House, which they accordingly received."[46]

On October 13, 1742, the selectmen conducted their first formal meeting in the new building and announced that three new offices had been located along the eastern end of the ground floor for "use of the naval officer, notary republic, and Surveyor of the Markets. The Selectmen's chamber was located in the second-story and the garret space above was divided between the Assessor's Office and the town's armory."[47]

The ground floor of the public market had stalls where citizens could purchase meats, fish, fruits, and vegetables. Besides the rooms for town officials, the second floor contained a sizable hall for town meetings and civic gatherings, which could accommodate a thousand persons. It was in this hall that the selectmen expressed the gratitude of the whole town by voting to "Wait upon Peter Faneuil, Esq., in the name of the Town, to render him Their most hearty Thanks for so Bountiful a Gift, with their Prayers that this and other Expressions of his Bounty and Charity may be Abundantly Recompensed with the Divine Blessing."[48]

The selectmen approached naming the building with caution, however. Before then, buildings weren't named to honor citizens still living. Thomas Hutchinson, later the Royal Governor of Massachusetts, motioned "that in Testimony of the Town's Gratitude to the said Peter Faneuil Esq., and to perpetuate his Memory, the Town now pass a Vote that the Hall over the Market place be named Faneuil Hall, and at all times hereafter be called and known by that Name."[49] When Peter Faneuil learned of this overture he responded, "I hope what I have done will be for the service of the whole country."[50]

The selectmen allowed Peter Faneuil the privilege of nominating his friend Thomas Jackson as the first clerk of Faneuil Hall market. Jackson was entrusted with the duties of judge and jury of the Pie Powder Court. He was also granted an assistant, Joseph Grey, who swept out the market and disposed of the rubbish in the nearby harborfront.

The Ancient and Honorable Artillery Company of Massachusetts moved their storage from the Town House to the third-floor attic area of Faneuil Hall. On March 3, 1743, six months after Faneuil Hall opened its doors, the bachelor benefactor died at the relatively young age of forty-three from "dropsical complyca(tion),"[51] or "dropsy."[52] His body was interred in the family tomb at the Granary Burial Ground alongside his uncle Andrew, whom he had outlived by only five years.

The first public oration delivered in Faneuil Hall, the first of many memorials to the honored dead, was Peter Faneuil's eulogy. It was delivered by John Lovell, headmaster of Boston Latin School. Headmaster Lovell concluded his sermon by stating, "And may there always remain in this town, the same grateful sentiments, the same virtuous dispositions to remember their benefactors with honor."[53] The selectmen ordered that the bell in Faneuil Hall be tolled from one o'clock until the ceremonies were concluded.

Peter Faneuil died without a last will and testament, and his younger brother, Benjamin, inherited the bulk of the family fortune along with his four sisters.[54] Benjamin Faneuil, who was banished from his uncle's home and business while still a

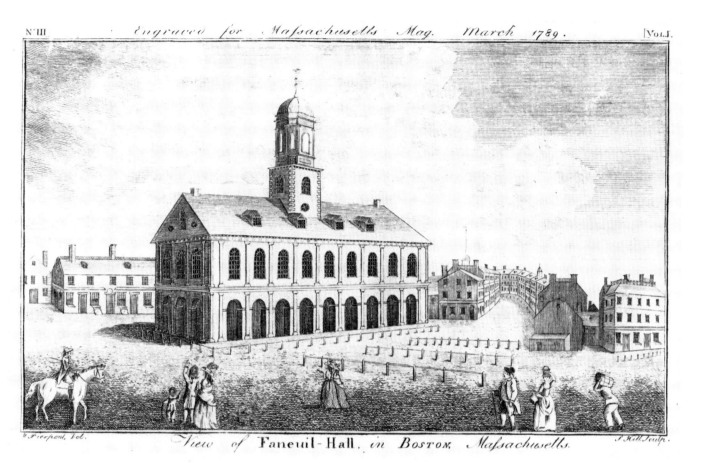

Nº III   Engraved for Massachusetts Mag. March 1789.   [Vol. J.

View of Faneuil-Hall, in Boston, Massachusetts.

*View of the original Faneuil Hall, after completion in 1742. Engraving by Samuel Hill,
from a drawing by W. Pierpont. Reprinted from* Massachusetts Magazine, *March 1789.*
Courtesy of the Boston Athenaeum.

single man, returned as master of Bellingham mansion with his wife, Mary (Cutler),
and their three children, Benjamin Jr., Peter, and Mary.

At first, Faneuil Hall was dedicated to "Liberty and Loyalty," meaning loyalty to
the Crown. On March 14, 1743, the first recorded town meeting in America was
held at the upstairs meeting hall. Later, "[o]ne of the earliest gatherings was on Oct.
10, 1744, to celebrate the King's Coronation-day 'with concert and music.' In May
1747, a series of concerts were given there, thus inaugurating the long series of banquets for which the Hall has been famous."[55]

Despite the initial enthusiasm over the building of Faneuil Hall, the downstairs market had difficulty being accepted. Competition from peddlers, hucksters, and the roving country farmers remained strong. Although the market was opened on September 25, 1742, the first single stall was not leased until three months later, to Anthony Hodgson, who "was granted liberty to occupy No. 8 for one month, to sell butter, cheese and flour, three days in each week, on the condition that he would sell to the inhabitants as cheap as they could buy at wholesale. This pioneer of Faneuil Hall stall-keepers made a specialty of Irish butter, which he imported from the Emerald Isle, and also of Cheshire cheese, which was claimed to be far better than the domestic manufacture, brought in by the countrymen and sold from their saddle-bags at the houses of their customers."[56] (It is interesting to note that specialty foods are much of what is still sold in Quincy Market today.)

Almost a year passed before a second stall was rented. Bostonians remained divided between "pro-market" and "anti-market" in every area of public affairs. The market was closed from 1747 to 1748, from 1752 to 1753, and for several months during 1759 for lack of interest from vendors and customers alike. At times the weathervane caused the "anti-market" faction to ridicule the building as the "Grasshopper Market."[57]

For the first eighteen years of Faneuil Hall's existence, the first-floor market was closed, then reopened several times. And then disaster struck.

Faneuil Hall and the Marketplace Witness a Revolution

O n the night of January 13, 1761, a destructive fire broke out in one of the shops along King Street and swept through the nearby waterfront. Dwellings, wharves, warehouses, and ships' cargoes were destroyed. Faneuil Hall became completely engulfed by the flames and only two elements of the original building survived: the charred brick walls and the fire-damaged grasshopper weathervane. One of the town's most popular periodicals, the *Boston News-Letter,* reported on January 15 that the "stately edifice, Faneuil Hall Market . . . was consumed, except the brick walls." The newspaper went on to say, "[F]ortunately the records, papers, etc., with such other things as could be removed, were mostly saved."[1] Clerk of the Market Abijah Adams had heroically saved many historic documents until he was driven back by the flames.[2]

In order to safeguard against future fires, the town voted to rebuild Faneuil Hall by using the standing brick walls and by using as little wood as possible in the remainder of construction. They would cover the roof with slate and install stone frames around the windows and doors. On April 18, 1761, the General Court approved funding through a public lottery. John Hancock, who was then new to politics and just beginning to acquire influence, was asked to sponsor the lottery, so some of the tickets bore his famous bold signature. Two years later the necessary sum of £2,000 had been raised.

Shem Drowne's son, Thomas, having apprenticed to his father, was enlisted to repair the weathervane. He had already fixed it after an earthquake in 1753, when it fell after some ground tremors occurred.[3] He tucked the following note into the cavity of the sculpture: "Shem Drowne Made Itt, May 25, 1742: To my brethren and fellow grasshoppers, Fell in ye year 1753, November 13, early in ye morning by a great earthquake by my old Master above. Again Like to have met with my Utter Ruin by Fire but hopping Timely from my Publik Scituation Came off with Broken bones & much Bruised. Cured and fixed (by) Old Master's son, Thomas Drowne June 28th 1768, and Though I promise to Discharge my Office, yet shall vary as ye wind."[4]

Past animosities resulting from fear of overregulation of trade were hardly apparent after the fire. Bostonians had become aware of the importance of not losing a structure they now saw as a landmark. When Faneuil Hall market was reopened, the sales of meats, fish, and produce flourished. During this era the market achieved great success, as it was recounted years later: There was "a morning ritual observed by all leading townsmen whether they set forth from Bowdoin Square, Beacon Hill, or the South End. Determined mercantile figures, followed by a servant, turned down every respectable street to converge on Faneuil Hall. There they wandered, among mountains of meat, fish, fowl, vegetable, fruits and dairy products displayed in a confusion never entirely rectified by . . . market regulations. When all the makings of an early afternoon dinner were stowed away in a servant's basket, the merchants marched off to counting houses along the wharves or offices in State Street."[5]

The ceremonial reopening of Faneuil Hall was held on March 14, 1763, at a time when tensions between England and the colonies were mounting. The British were insisting on searching goods for customs violations. The outspoken patriot James Otis, a staunch critic of British rule in Boston, dedicated Faneuil Hall to the "Cause of Liberty." Otis was known, among other things, for his leadership of the Sons of Liberty, a fraternal band of patriots that included John Adams, Adams's cousins Sam Adams and Josiah Quincy Jr., and Dr. Joseph Warren. (Dr. Warren later served on the committee that sent Paul Revere and William Dawes on their famous rides to alert Lexington and Concord that the British were coming.)

Not all of the opening ceremonies were rabble-rousing, however. During the following week, "the *Boston Gazette* related that 'a profusion of wine and other liquors was prepared in Faneuil Hall, to collect the genuine sons of Liberty, to celebrate this happy festival.' Besides what wine and liquors the Selectmen provided, John Hancock and other merchants kept open house, and it seems probable that during the late hours of the night many of the citizens found that the streets were unusually crooked on that joyful occasion!"[6]

Time and again over the following years, Bostonians came to Faneuil Hall to hear protests as the British successively taxed molasses, stamps on documents, and other imports. In 1766 there was a moment of peace: Faneuil Hall saw the selectmen drink to the king's health after the repeal of the Stamp Act. But Parliament soon reasserted its "right" to tax, and successively taxed glass, lead, paint, paper, wine, and tea. In this pre–Revolutionary War period Faneuil Hall hosted fiery debates, impassioned pleas, and inspired oratory about the colonists' demands for justice that later turned into calls for American independence. Here, the Sons of Liberty made famous Otis's purported cry, "Taxation without representation is tyranny."[7] They used Faneuil Hall so often that it became known as the "Cradle of American Liberty."

The British were unmoved. In July 1767 the British cabinet resolved to pass new restrictions on American commerce. "[I]t was determined to raise a farther revenue by imposts, additional to those already existing, and which were, in themselves, sufficiently obnoxious and oppressive. The military force in the colonies was largely to be increased, and the power of the military commanders to be augmented, so as to make them more effective in instruments of putting down oppression."[8] As Faneuil Hall became a symbol of bloodless battles in the war of words it also became "the focal point in the organization of colonial resentment and protest against acts of the British Parliament."[9]

On October 1, 1768, seven British warships with two full regiments of red-coated regulars landed at Long Wharf and marched up King Street. The British government had ordered troops to Boston in response to rioters who had looted and damaged Lieutenant Governor Thomas Hutchinson's mansion. During this occupation—which is how colonists saw it—many Bostonians defied the latest reprehensible act of Parliament—the Quartering Act—and refused to house British "lobsterbacks" in their homes. The British 24th regiment consequently encamped on Boston Common, and the 14th regiment commandeered Faneuil Hall as their barracks. Resentful citizens remarked that the bloodied carcasses of beef hanging in the first-floor market were a symbol of what should happen to the new second-floor residents. The occupation by British troops lasted until they were removed to a Boston Harbor island at the end of 1770.

On the night of March 5, 1770, tensions led some angry Bostonians into taunting a lone British soldier stationed outside the Town House (which had been rebuilt and converted into what is now called the Old State House). Captain Thomas Preston of the British 29th and nine of his soldiers rushed to the aid of the sentry. Without warning and without orders, the gang of Bostonians was fired upon. Five colonists were left dead, including eleven-year-old Christopher Seider and an African American named Crispus Attucks. Church bells began ringing to signal an alarm, and men and boys dashed from their homes. Several British companies of the 29th under Colonel Carr also immediately reported for duty. The throng of citizens on King Street surrounded the British soldiers, teetering on the brink of more violence.

Ordered by Colonel Carr to disperse, the crowd defiantly refused. They insisted that Captain Preston and his men be arrested for murder. Lieutenant Governor Hutchinson and a group of patriots intervened. Working together, they managed to calm the crowd, thus sparing the soldiers' lives. "[H]ad not some gentlemen of influence interposed their good offices, the prisoners would have been torn to pieces before they reached the jail."[10] Once people began to disperse and most of the British troops returned to their barracks, a group of angry citizens battered the soldiers and dragged them to Faneuil Hall. There, Justices Samuel Pemberton, Richard Dana, and Edmund Quincy heard numerous eyewitness accounts of the incident until three o'clock the next morning. Before the night was over the incident was being called the Boston Massacre and the patriot movement had its first martyrs.

The following morning the Sons of Liberty appeared before Lieutenant Governor Hutchinson at the Town House, demanding that all British troops be immediately moved from Boston, out to the harbor island forts. They insisted that the citizenry and soldiers could no longer safely live together. Sam Adams was the spokesman for the group. (He was later portrayed in the bronze statue outside Faneuil Hall as he was supposed to have appeared that morning. He stands resolute, with arms folded, defiantly awaiting Hutchinson's response.)

Captain Thomas Preston sought out two of the most respected trial lawyers in Boston and engaged John Adams and Josiah "the Patriot" Quincy Jr.[11] to defend the British soldiers charged with perpetrating the Boston Massacre. Josiah was a boyhood neighbor and a distant cousin of John Adams.

Upon learning that his son was defending the British soldiers, Colonel Josiah Quincy, who supported the patriot cause, wrote him a scathing letter, in which he insisted that the younger Josiah's participation in the trial would tarnish the family name. "Good God! Is it possible? I will not believe it. I must own to you, it has filled the bosom of your aged and infirm parent with anxiety and distress, lest it should only prove true, but destructive of your reputation and interest; and I repeat, I will not believe it, unless it be confirmed by your own mouth, or under your own hand."[12] But Josiah Jr. reminded his father that a lawyer had an obligation to administer legal counsel in defense of men "not legally proved guilty, and therefore, however criminal, . . . entitled by the laws of God and man, to all legal counsel and aid; that my duty as a man obliged me to undertake."[13] He knew that his reputation was not at stake with the patriots, because the Sons of Liberty had approved his and John Adams's defending the British. "For my single self, I consider, judge, and with reason hope to be immutable."[14]

What made Josiah Jr.'s stance even worse for Colonel Quincy was the news that his elder son, Samuel, was appointed to assist the special prosecutor for the trial. His sons would be on opposite sides. Samuel Quincy had graduated from Harvard College in 1754, in the same class as John Adams, and both had been admitted to Boston's bar on the same day (November 6, 1758). Instead of following the patriots' cause, Samuel Quincy had sided with those loyal to Britain. Even though he was close friends with John Hancock, Sam Adams, and other members of the Sons of Liberty, Sam Quincy had accepted eminent Crown appointments as Barrister and Solicitor-General of the Province. Such were the elements of the patriot-loyalist times during the growing tempest preceding the American Revolution. Brother opposed brother, friend stood against friend, neighbor against neighbor.

In October 1770 Preston's case came to trial at the Superior Court at Faneuil Hall. He was acquitted. In November the nine other soldiers implicated in the Boston Massacre were tried. The brilliant defense mounted by Josiah Quincy Jr. and John Adams during the nine men's traditional English common-law trial by jury saved their lives. Seven of these soldiers were acquitted of the charges brought against them. Two others were found guilty of manslaughter. They were not put to death, however. In open court, their thumbs were branded "M" (for manslaughter) and then they were discharged.

By November 5, 1773, Bostonians were holding the first "tea meetings" at Faneuil Hall. Led by John Hancock, patriots met to discuss the fate of that "baneful weed." "More than four hundred housewives and one hundred and twenty-six young ladies [had] signed an agreement in February, renouncing the use of tea until the Revenue Acts were repealed."[15] On December 16, 1773, in protest to the tax levied on imported tea, a mob disguised as Indians went to Griffin's Wharf, where the cargo ships *Dartmouth* and *Eleanor* were berthed. Anchored nearby was the *Beaver*. Altogether the vessels carried over 90,000 pounds of English tea, valued at £9,000.[16] The masked "Indians" forced the merchant sailors ashore and dumped the contents of the tea crates into the salt water, temporarily turning Boston Harbor into the world's largest teapot. Sam Adams knew that the British would take extreme measures in response to this Boston Tea Party. He also knew that united action among the American colonies was the only way to give the patriots a chance against British strength. He called for a meeting.

The Massachusetts Convention, consisting of deputies from ninety-six towns and four districts in the Massachusetts Bay Province, convened at Faneuil Hall in January 1774. They discussed what they could do when the inevitable increase in British troops arrived.

Both in government circles and among the people, Britain reacted with profound conviction that the unruly and defiant spirit in Boston must be crushed. On March 7, 1774, the king addressed Parliament and accused the Americans of attempting to injure British commerce and subvert its constitution. In response, Lord North introduced the Boston Port Bill, which called for suspending trade and closing the port of Boston. Joint forces of the British army and navy were employed to enforce the embargo. The British navy strictly enforced the resulting blockade of Boston Harbor, which began in June 1774; any travel over water, even from pier to pier or among the nearest islands, was forbidden. Wharves became deserted, warehouses were rendered useless, and nearly all seaport-related business was closed. Boston's only access to supplies was across the Neck that linked the town to the mainland.

Boston was also again immediately occupied by a large force of soldiers. Many infantry regiments, together with three companies of artillery and twenty-two pieces of cannon, encamped on Boston Common. Additional troops reoccupied Faneuil Hall. The Welsh Fusileers encamped on Fort Hill, and several companies of the British 64th were at Castle William (at Castle Island in today's South Boston), where they were keeping most of their powder and other stores. This occupation lasted for the next two years.

In response, the Sons of Liberty, now operating underground, created the Committee of Correspondence to communicate news and opinion that arose from the Cradle of Liberty to other towns and colonies. "During the months between the passage of the Port bill, which closed the harbor to commerce, when not a fishing boat could land, or a gundalow float down the Charles or Mystic with provisions for the distressed people; when contributions of food were arriving from every one of the thirteen Colonies, the committee made their distribution from Faneuil Hall."[17] In less than a year America was at war with Great Britain.

By April 1775 a warning was spread, thanks to Paul Revere and William Dawes, that the British planned to raid the militia's weapons store in Concord (about twenty miles from Boston). Sam Adams and John Hancock were, at that time, hiding in a house near Lexington Common. On that same common the militia waited for the British arrival, knowing that the redcoats would have to pass through on the way to Concord. The shots fired that day—and the eight American deaths— are seen as the official start of the American Revolutionary War. Seventy redcoats died on the retreat back to Boston from Concord, from hit-and-run sniper fire.

As skirmishes continued to break out, relations between the occupying forces and the loyalist and patriot colonists were not helped by British insensitivity. For example, while billeted at Faneuil Hall the British soldiers had organized a theater, sponsored by their Society for Promoting Theatrical Amusements. The performers, who were British officers and local loyalist women, acted out plays that usually ridiculed the patriots. The audience was mostly made up of other loyalists and red-coat regulars. On June 17, 1775, during such a parody, someone shouted from out-side that the British had marched upon Charlestown and that blood was flowing. Most of the audience thought it was part of the comedy at first, and they loudly applauded.

"The audience suddenly heard distant musket shots, increasing to volleys, and doubtless wondered how the stage manager had produced the illusion. An officer appeared in haste upon the stage and shouted that the Yankees were making an attack. It was so natural that the officers in the audience pounded their applause with their swords, and the soldiers clapped their hands, thinking it was part of the play. 'I tell you the Yankees are attacking us. Officers to your regiments,' shouted the man on stage. The musketry increased, and the horizon in the direction of Charlestown was illuminated by burning buildings. The play had a sudden ending. The audacious Yankees from the regiments at Cobble Hill had crossed the mill-dam and attacked the outposts."[18] The battle of Bunker Hill ended in defeat for the patriot militia. About five hundred of their soldiers died, including Dr. Joseph Warren. But they gained the respect of their enemy, who lost over a thousand soldiers in the battle.

Also in June 1775 the Second Continental Congress (with patriots such as John Adams and John Hancock in attendance) met in Philadelphia and created the Continental Army. The army was intended to organize the various rebel militias into readiness to fight the British more effectively. George Washington, their appointed commander in chief, went to Boston in July to assume command of his men. Over the next several months he formed them into disciplined troops, and in March 1776 he set up artillery on Dorchester Heights. Along with the newly arrived American general Henry Knox, Washington and the American army forced the British to take to their ships and evacuate Boston. Washington correctly assumed they would head for New York's harbor, so he left Boston to Knox's command and took a contingent of the army to New York.

The British took with them several portraits from Faneuil Hall: those of King George II, Governor William Sherley, British Field Marshal Conway, and Colonel Isaac Barré. The latter two were missed by the patriots, as they had defended America on the floor of Parliament, greatly aiding the colonists' cause. The rest of Faneuil Hall, however, was left mostly undamaged by its British occupants.

The next several years did not seem promising for American troops, despite early wins and the Continental Army's tenacity. But in May 1778 the American alliance with France was announced, and the tide began to turn. The French helped America toward important victories, and by October 1781 they helped end the war by laying siege to Cornwallis's troops at Yorktown, Virginia, until he surrendered.

Also in October 1781 a French fleet consisting of twelve ships and four frigates entered Boston Harbor, where their crews were honored at Faneuil Hall. "From the newspapers of the time we learn that after dinner seventeen regular toasts were given at intervals of five minutes, each sentiment being accompanied by the discharge of cannon in the square."[19]

In 1784 the American Revolution ended with a treaty signed in Paris (with such names on it as John Adams and Benjamin Franklin). The Marquis de Lafayette, a general in the American army and a close associate of General Washington throughout the war, was entertained that same year at a dinner in Faneuil Hall. A salute was fired outside from thirteen cannon. "As the patriotic toasts were given, a train of artillery under the command of Major Davis fired salutes in Market Square, and during the festivities a portrait of Washington was unveiled amid great enthusiasm."[20] There were reports that the portrait brought tears to Lafayette's eyes.

Sadly, most of the heirs of Benjamin Faneuil and of Peter Faneuil's (now married) sisters had sympathized with the king; they left for Halifax and London during the evacuation of Boston. At about the same time, a patriot mob went to Faneuil Hall and destroyed Peter Faneuil's portrait there. In 1791 the Faneuil family's vacant, looted mansion was confiscated by the new Massachusetts Commonwealth, along with the property of many other loyalists. The government resold it to Lieutenant Governor William Phillips.

The Faneuils had dearly loved Boston but could not relinquish their allegiance to England, the country that had so warmly welcomed them and their fellow French Huguenots years before. Some years later, many of the Faneuils became destitute. They looked forward to returning to America but could not until it yielded, as they firmly believed it one day would, to the superior power of the British Empire.

Despite the family's allegiance, Faneuil Hall retained its name after the American Revolution. Its constant use during and after the war as a center of revolutionary activity had made it a symbol of American independence. Not only had it survived its occupation by British troops, it had hosted public receptions and military banquets for national leaders, orators, war allies, and visiting dignitaries such as the Marquis de Lafayette in 1784 and General George Washington in 1789.

As the attention of Boston turned to building a new city in a new country, Faneuil Hall returned to its primary use as a merchants' market and town hall. The upstairs was mostly used for assessing taxes, poll taking, and town districting, but popular gatherings for celebration and solemn occasions were also held. Boston's black community was granted use of Faneuil Hall in 1789 "for purpose of public worship, one day a week, provided it be on a Tuesday or Friday & in the afternoon."[21]

By the close of the eighteenth century Faneuil Hall's assembly space could no longer accommodate town meetings and the selectmen frequently convened at Old South Meeting House. "In no town in the Puritan Commonwealth were the people more keenly alive to the preservation of their rights and liberties than in Boston. The town meeting was their parliament; the meeting-houses their parliament halls; but they were dependent upon the courtesy of the pew-holders for the use of the houses, when, as was often the case, the town hall was not large enough to accommodate the voters."[22] The selectmen's relationship with the clergy at Old South Meeting House and other churches apparently became strained after a while, as the clergy "became unwilling to admit such large numbers to the free use of their buildings."[23]

The rapid growth of the town also warranted increasing calls for relief of Faneuil Hall's congested market quarters. The demand for merchant space was so strong that selectmen ended their traditional leasing policies and solicited sealed bids for stall rentals. Clerk of the Market Caleb Hayward tried to keep the market stalls orderly and the rules obeyed but the situation was often chaotic. For some fish, meat, and vegetable stands, a roofed shelter—called the Shambles[24]—was erected adjacent to Faneuil Hall in 1791, but it proved to be inadequate. In another effort to enlarge the outside market area, the selectmen expanded Dock Square to include the Town Dock. In 1799, they also appointed a committee to study the feasibility of excavating a cellar beneath Faneuil Hall to create additional merchant space, but nothing was done. Another six years passed before Charles Bulfinch submitted a proposal for enlarging Faneuil Hall to its present dimensions. The cost was expected to be approximately $58,000.

Charles Bulfinch was the son of a wealthy and prominent Boston family who had graduated from Harvard College in 1781, then traveled abroad, studying architecture. He mastered Neoclassical design, which he brought back to Boston and used to construct many new buildings even though the Federal style was still in vogue. As America's first native-born professional architect and one of its earliest urban planners, he was also chairman of Boston's selectmen, a position he held from 1799 to 1818. In 1805, long before "conflict of interest" was a moral or legal issue, the town voted to accept his proposal. Work at Faneuil Hall began under his direction and that of Jonathan Hunnewell, a master mason.

In 1805 Faneuil Hall was widened by adding on to its north side, and another one and a half stories were added to its height. When finished, the enlarged broad-gabled structure measured seven bays in width (previously it had been three), nine bays in length (the same as before), and three and a half stories in height. Bulfinch retained the original design of a ground-floor market with an upstairs public hall, but he expanded the market area under the building by excavating and outfitting the cellar for retail occupancy.[25] The new space allowed the second-floor assembly hall, now

*Faneuil Hall after Charles Bulfinch's enlargement on the right side of the building in 1805,
with an outline showing the size of the original building. The view is looking toward the
west. Note the Shambles situated to the right of Faneuil Hall.*
COURTESY OF THE BOSTONIAN SOCIETY/OLD STATE HOUSE.

termed the Great Hall, to be enlarged too. It now rose to a height of two and a half
stories. Second-floor galleries on the north and south walls rose to meet galleries on
three sides of the third-floor level, which provided seating for ladies to observe the
proceedings. "Women, of course, were not included in the early voting procedures,
since 18th century law limited voting rights to citizens who were white, male, over
twenty-one, property owners and churchgoers. Needless to say, historical statistics
show those stipulations eliminated 90 percent of the population!"[26] The Great Hall
gained several new interior embellishments. Bulfinch described it as "76 feet square,
and 28 feet high, with galleries on three sides upon Doric columns, the ceiling is supported by two ranges of Ionic columns, the walls are enriched by pilasters and the
windows by architraves—platforms under and in the galleries rise amphitheatrically
to accommodate spectators."[27] The attic level provided storage space.

Bulfinch created a grand inside staircase along the eastern wall, allowing a view of the water from the stairs. He also moved the cupola to the eastern end of the roof ridge. These changes made the structure seem closer to the harbor both from inside and when viewed from an approaching ship (a major means of access to the market district). The signature grasshopper weathervane, resting atop the cupola, now stood eighty feet above ground.

The first notable banquet that occurred within the new Faneuil Hall was held on September 5, 1812, when Isaac Hull and the officers of the frigate USS *Constitution* and those of the vessels *President, United States, Congress, Hornet,* and *Argus* were honored. "As in previous banquets, there were seventeen regular sentiments [expressed]. Just why that number should have been selected can only be surmised; possibly experience had shown our fathers that that was a safe number of potations."[28]

In the winter of 1813, Bulfinch slipped on the icy steps of Faneuil Hall and broke his leg. He was confined to his home through the spring, unable to attend to his duties as selectman until he healed.

By the early nineteenth century, thanks to the reopening of maritime trade after the war and the international trade of the 1790s, Boston's commerce was thriving. The Baltimore Clippers, modeled after the speedy French frigates that had helped the United States win the war with Britain and the direct predecessor of the true clipper ships, were efficiently skirting the Eastern Seaboard's waters. Boston remained ahead of New York and Philadelphia as the most important seaport in the United States.

Many outsiders came seeking new fortunes. Between 1790 and 1810 Boston's population tripled and new districts changed the social makeup of the town. The North End, the West End, the South End, and Market Square all took on new cultures and grew in population. Bulfinch's new State House, completed in 1798, had moved the seat of government from the bustling downtown Market Square location to the top of Beacon Hill, which had been reduced from three hills to a single hill and was surrounded, still, by countryside.

Boston's topography remained a deterrent to expansion. Its original peninsula now extended from the harbor to the Neck, over to Noddle's Island in East Boston, and down to South Boston, which had been annexed in 1804. But from the lofty dome of the new State House, to the graceful and noble church spires in the midst of rooftops and chimneys, to the low-lying coastal perimeters crowded with wharves, Boston needed more land to accommodate its growth. The three hills that had once inspired the name *Tramountaine* were therefore razed to fill in the watery coves and marshes that could extend Boston's shoreline. Old Shawmut's majestic elevations were decapitated to allow urban expansion.

The laborious effort had begun years earlier, about 1800, when the rugged South Cove coastline was lined with fill from Fort Hill and Mount Vernon. Between 1803 and 1805, more of Mount Vernon was carted off to develop house lots on the flats at the western foot of Beacon Hill. This created Charles Street. In 1807 Harrison Gray Otis's Mill Pond Corporation began to cut down the central peak of Tramountain to fill the seventy-acre Mill Pond, an effort that took twenty-five years to complete. John Winthrop's two-hundred-year-old "City upon a Hill" slowly became the "City on a Fill."[29]

Many of its original characteristics remained as it grew, however. The crowded waterfront was still full of activity. High above, the wealthy dwelt beneath quiet, spreading elms in fashionable homes. These mansions, with gardens that mingled the scent of roses and honeysuckle with that of salty harbor breezes, sat along the eastern slope of Beacon Hill. The back side of Beacon Hill and the watery marshes of Back Bay were considered rural country until the fill projects eventually changed all that.

Changes in Boston's governmental structure did not come as easily as did the changes to its physical layout. The town seemed to cling to its colonial past so much that the town fathers gained a reputation for their American Revolution–era appearance, in their frock coats and buckle shoes: "[T]hey could still be seen wearing a colored jacket, a flowered waistcoat, short breeches that buttoned at the knee, a ruffled shirt and cravat, all topped with a cocked hat and a powdered tie wig."[30]

The new ways of thinking that followed the adoption of the country's new Constitution did gradually affect even tradition-bound Boston, however. Staunch religious control and rigid political opinions began to ease, and a new generation of Bostonians called the Children of the Revolution began to thrust Boston into a time of free thought and daring discussion.

Then, in the midst of all these changes, Boston was unexpectedly swept by a devastating national economic depression that started in 1820 and lasted in Boston for the next five years. By 1822 maritime businesses had been reduced to such low levels that many regarded Boston as a commercial seaport on the verge of collapse. Throngs of seamen, dockworkers, and draymen were left idle. Still confined by the city's watery borders, the population swelled to nearly 45,000. As unemployment increased, vagrancy and crime multiplied.

Citizens complained to the selectmen about a variety of other issues as well: The town itself was not strapped for funds, but Boston's overcrowded streets had fallen into utter disrepair and were in need of attention. Sewers were backed up and disease was mounting. Household and commercial trash was not being collected. Animal droppings were not being cleaned from the street each day. People wondered if they needed a regulation against the ancient practice of tossing human waste into the gutters, now that the city was so crowded. Street pollution simply was over-running the town.

Until now, Boston had been administrated by its Board of Selectmen and five other municipal boards: the Board of Health, Surveyors of Highways, Overseers of the Poor, Firewards, and the School Committee. The board members were elected annually and they functioned independently from the selectmen and from each other. This governmental structure had been organized around a Boston with a much smaller population and with a manageable number of municipal problems. But now citizens and selectmen were at a loss over which board was responsible for what problem.

The presence of so many problems undermined all efforts by the town fathers to retain control of Boston's government. A controversy arose over whether to incorporate into a city. Conservatives steadily resisted all attempts to change the current form of town government, but the Children of the Revolution argued that the problems of this pocket community had become too complex for such a method of governing.

After a year of intense debate and political maneuvering, on January 7, 1822, the citizens voted in favor of articles of incorporation. On February 23, 1822, Governor John Brooks signed into law the legislative act that granted a charter to incorporate Boston as the first city in the Commonwealth of Massachusetts. On March 4, the town voted to accept the charter by a vote of 2,797 to 1,881.

The charter specified a mayor as a vested chief executive, and an eight-man executive Board of Aldermen. In addition, there would be a Common Council with a mixture of both legislative and executive powers. It would be made up of forty-eight men, four from each of the twelve wards, which were newly established in an effort to represent the areas of the city proportionally. The mayor, the eight aldermen, and the forty-eight members of the Common Council would be elected annually by ballot. The aldermen and the Common Council would be called the City Council when acting as one body. All of the powers belonging to the city would be vested in the mayor, the aldermen, and the Common Council and exercised by concurrent vote. Yet, the five municipal boards remained autonomous.

A city seal was adopted that bore a motto from the Bible's book of Kings: *Sicut Patribus Sit Deus Nobis* (May God be with us as he was with our fathers).[31] On April 8, 1822, the city held its first election and, for the first time, Bostonians independently cast their votes for leaders of the newly established wards. These leaders started to wrestle with the many problems plaguing the new city, such as how to confront the blighted areas of Boston, especially those around Faneuil Hall and Market Square.

In May 1822, John Phillips, a Harvard College graduate and a direct descendent of one of Boston's wealthiest mercantile families, was elected Boston's first mayor. He was also of the same Phillips family that had taken over the Faneuil home in the early 1790s. As a former Suffolk County Court prosecutor and state senator, he was deemed a suitable figurehead to administer the new city. Mayor Phillips, however, had misunderstood the terms of the city charter and assumed that his mayoralty would be little more than a comfortable position for his political retirement. He had expected the new city to govern itself, as the town had, turning to its mayor only for summoning the City Council. Thus, he guided Boston only timidly during its first year as a city. This might have worked if the city had still been small and made up of a few extended families.

Boston, however, had become a diverse city comprising transient strangers, most of whom were hard-pressed by the economic depression, and it was in need of basic bureaucratic change. Phillips did not proceed aggressively enough, and his administration foundered. Boston's independent municipal boards, still officially unaccountable to the mayor and City Council, remained mostly idle, and the citizens became thoroughly disgusted with their elected officials. At the end of his term Mayor Phillips refused to seek reelection, citing his failing health.

When Boston was incorporated into a city in 1822, shipping, marine-related commerce, and other seafaring interests still dominated its congested waterfront, although maritime business up and down the coast had slowed because of the depression. But the docks and wharves did not present a distinguished face to the sea, especially not at the Town Dock and its close neighbor, Faneuil Hall. Any sense of dignity around Market Square had long been replaced by the snap of the whip, the rattle of the wagons, and the clomping of the hooves of horses driven by a multitude of country farmers heading to market in droves. The noise from the boisterous draymen's hoisting of crates of vegetables and sacks of grain to merchant ships added to the chaos. And the results of fishmongers, butchers, and farmers disgorging rubbish into the stagnant waters of the harbor were unsightly. Seagulls screeched as they circled above the swill, while sailboats strained against the sludge to reach berth. The area was labeled "a receptacle for every species of filth, and a public nuisance."[32] It was a daily sight that had remained mostly unimproved for nearly a hundred years.

The Market Square district, an area that had been designated in 1784 as the north, south, and west sides around Faneuil Hall, was considered to be downtown Boston. Just east of the district was the original Town Cove, an inlet choked with five principal finger wharves. Four of the wharves were privately owned and the other, the Town Dock, still belonged to the city. Atop the four private wharves were clusters of tattered shacks, squalid food stands, and dilapidated warehouses. Although the wharf businesses retained some commercial activity, most of the wharves themselves had fallen into serious disrepair, their wooden buildings and piers decaying, the waters below cluttered with derelict and abandoned scows. The only exceptions were Long Wharf and the recently renovated India Wharf, just south of Town Cove.

The sludge-choked mudflats below the wharves east of Faneuil Hall were prevented from being flushed out by the tide. The ancient Mill Creek, once a freshwater stream that flowed down from Tramountain to Mill Pond and the site of John Winthrop's first encampment on old Shawmut, now acted as the central outflow of sewage for the city. The constant stench that hung over Market Square grew worse at low tide. And when the east wind blew in from the harbor, Bostonians throughout the city had to endure its offensive odor. During the summer months it seemed

Facing page: *View of downtown Boston, 1823, looking westward. This illustration offers an overview of the scene around the Town Dock, Faneuil Hall, and Market Square when Boston was first incorporated into a city.* ILLUSTRATION BY GARY M. IRISH, ASAI, 2002.

the worst, and the wealthy found refuge in the country, for it was thought that diseases were caused by bad odors. "In the season of danger the sons of fortune can seek refuge in purer atmospheres. But necessity condemns the poor to remain and inhale the noxious effluvia."[33]

Faneuil Hall's market itself had become crammed with the wares of multiple merchants and its butchery facilities were now grossly inadequate. On the north side of Faneuil Hall a long row of open wooden stands, the Shambles, had been hastily constructed in 1791 to expand the shelter. Consisting of a roof supported by sets of wooden posts, it was now used by fish and vegetable dealers who squeezed together, sharing the rent, which for the whole building was $520 per year. "It was calculated that twenty years changed the whole number of individuals there employed."[34] Vendors in the Shambles were constantly exposed to the elements, which were especially uncomfortable at the windblown waterfront during the long, harsh Boston winters.

The stalls inside Faneuil Hall market were also notoriously unhealthy, largely because they still lacked an adequate water supply. In 1774 wells had been tapped at nearby Dock Square so that Faneuil Hall could be fitted with two pumps, located outside the building. Through the years, though, these old wooden pumps were often in disrepair, so many stall keepers would haul water in buckets from the pumps at Long Wharf. During the enlargement of Faneuil Hall in 1805, little was done to address its water problems, and the Shambles was left intact.

In 1822 an order was passed by the Common Council to help clean up the east side of Faneuil Hall. The order would have effectively altered the eastern facade to extend the beef market, and the entrance would have been relocated. But, although the City Council approved the order, the expansion was never initiated. On the west side of Faneuil Hall cramped mutton stalls remained.

Market Square itself was no better in 1822. Pigsties cluttered a portion of the square, not far from Faneuil Hall. The nearby wharves held chicken crates bursting with livestock, which sometimes got loose. Droves of unruly goats, swine, and geese being herded to market created filthy street conditions. Oftentimes unruly boys added to the frenzy by picking up piglets by their tails and tossing the animals at pedestrian shoppers. Nearby buildings were dilapidated and some were inhabited by vagrants.

The avenues leading to Market Square were narrow and crooked. One of the worst was Roe Buck Passage, a very odd roadway that connected the genteel North End with the wharves. In the course of only a hundred feet, the street turned in three places and its width varied from twenty to thirteen feet. There was a particularly bad blind spot behind Roe Buck Tavern (a downtown tavern of ill repute). This one street, which had been the site of many wagon and stagecoach accidents, had left one child dead and another mutilated that very year. Petitions to straighten and widen Roe Buck Passage had been presented to the selectmen for years, but they could never decide which board was responsible.

On the busiest market days the cobblestoned streets around Market Square were jammed with wagons and jostling masses of people. Some country farmers, after enduring the hardship of traveling great distances, were compelled to take their stand as far away as Court Street, by the Old State House.[35]

In 1822, a major urban decision was made to ease the traffic around Market Square. An ordinance was enacted that restricted draymen, pushcart peddlers, and country farmers from openly plying their trade on city sidewalks. This ordinance also meant that draymen—who not only stevedored the docks and warehouses but also drove wagons led by teams of horses to transport goods from the ship area to destinations throughout the city—could no longer sell goods directly from their wagons. The law restricted their routes as well, limiting their income as a result. It also crippled pushcart peddlers and country farmers who sold from their wagons. Hence, many owners of the smaller stores increased their prices. Instead of presenting a solution to the problems plaguing Market Square, this new law only worsened the situation.

No one denied that the market district needed major change. But introducing order into this chaos seemed impossible. It would take a gifted man to institute the drastic reforms needed to solve so great a problem. That man became Boston's second mayor. Josiah Quincy was a Boston native, a member of the sixth generation of Quincys in America. Also a first cousin of former mayor Phillips, Mayor Quincy had spent half his life in public service and was ready to assume a critical role in a most desperate situation.

3

A Need for Renewal: Josiah Quincy Proposes a New Marketplace

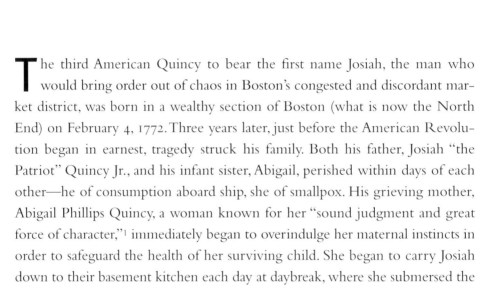

T he third American Quincy to bear the first name Josiah, the man who would bring order out of chaos in Boston's congested and discordant market district, was born in a wealthy section of Boston (what is now the North End) on February 4, 1772. Three years later, just before the American Revolution began in earnest, tragedy struck his family. Both his father, Josiah "the Patriot" Quincy Jr., and his infant sister, Abigail, perished within days of each other—he of consumption aboard ship, she of smallpox. His grieving mother, Abigail Phillips Quincy, a woman known for her "sound judgment and great force of character,"[1] immediately began to overindulge her maternal instincts in order to safeguard the health of her surviving child. She began to carry Josiah down to their basement kitchen each day at daybreak, where she submersed the three-year-old in a tub of frigid water pumped directly from the well.[2] She believed this practice would invigorate his immune system and prolong his life. Whether or not she was correct, Josiah Quincy lived to the age of ninety-three.

Beginning in childhood, Josiah Quincy was constantly reminded of greatness that accompanied his family's name. When he turned eight, his grandfather, Colonel Josiah Quincy, reminded the boy that he was already branded by the significant actions of his forebears. Colonel Quincy wrote, "Besides diligence and application when young, it is indispensably necessary to the forming of a distinguished career in public, that truth shall be the invariable object of your pursuit, and your end, the public good. These are the maxims of wisdom, which I have every reason to think your Great-Grandfather [Edmund],[3] as well as your deceased Father [Josiah Jr.] strictly adher'd to. Though some of them were remarkably distinguished, I indulge the pleasing hope, that by your assiduity and perseverance you will one day equal at least, if not surpass your predecessors in every respect."[4] That dictate had also extended back to the surviving Josiah's Puritan ancestor, Edmund Quincy, who had arrived in America in 1633 and who was descended from Saire William DeQuincey, Earl of Winchester, a surety baron and signatory of the Magna Carta in 1215,[5] whose name was distinguished on that document by the family crest of "seven mascles conjoined."[6]

That Edmund Quincy came to America from Achurch in Northamptonshire, England, in the company of Reverend John Cotton in 1633. That same year Edmund Quincy was elected to the Great and General Court of Massachusetts as a representative. During these first years representatives such as Edmund laid the groundwork for the establishment of many laws and institutions for the Bay Colony. Among these actions was the creation of the first college at Newtowne (later renamed Cambridge). This school later became Harvard College. Representative Quincy was also appointed to a committee by the General Court to secure title to the remainder of the Boston peninsula for the Massachusetts Bay Colony. His role on this committee was to estimate the fair sum necessary to purchase most of Reverend William Blackstone's land, which was situated on the south side of the Charles River mudflats.[7] This forty-four-acre tract of rolling land was bought by the Puritan community for the appraised value of £30 sterling and kept open for common use. Boston Common is still there today, the oldest public park in America.

Representative Edmund Quincy's passionate commitment to public service was part of many family stories handed down 135 years later to his great-great-great-grandson Josiah. At Harvard College, in 1790, Josiah graduated with first honors, the youngest boy in his class, and was chosen English Orator for his commencement, just as his father had been. Immediately after graduating, he began the study of law at the office of Judge William Tudor, a leading member of the Boston bar. Judge Tudor was impressed with Josiah Quincy's competency. While Josiah was still apprenticing, Tudor left the young man in charge of his clients during one of the judge's extended trips to Europe.

When Josiah completed his legal studies in the summer of 1793, he earned his second degree at Harvard, was again chosen to deliver the Masters' Oration at commencement, and was admitted to the bar. The next year, he opened a small law office in Boston. In his first case, he successfully defended a runaway slave.

After the death of his friend Josiah "the Patriot" Quincy Jr., John Adams had taken a personal interest in young Josiah's welfare. He too challenged the young man to go into public life. This was what Josiah's own father had planned to do before his life was cut short, Adams told the young man. He should consider how, instead of aspiring to wealth in the private sector, Josiah could achieve much greater fulfillment through politics.

Adams apparently helped convince his young listener. Josiah could easily have made his way in life without much effort, given his lineage. He had always been taught to look backward, in a family tradition that came close to ancestor worship. But he decided to add his own name to those of the Quincys who had distinguished themselves. Like his father, and his father's father, and his father's father's father, and on back to Saire William DeQuincey, he would go into political life to serve the public.

Now living on Pearl Street in Boston, Josiah was named to his first public office, Boston's Town Orator, a position that had once been held by his distant cousin, John Quincy Adams. On Independence Day 1798, Josiah delivered a brilliant and stirring oration, marked by his youthful enthusiasm, that recounted the principal dangers to the liberties of the new country. "Think you Americans, that the spirits of our departed patriots and heroes, from amid the band of the perfect and just, look not down complacent on the events of our day? Yes, surely; and on their thrones [they] exult, 'These are our children!' "[8] His address to the citizens of Boston from the balcony of the Old State House drew such tears from the audience and attracted so much attention that it was reprinted and distributed in pamphlet form in Philadelphia, then the seat of the federal government. In 1798 he was persuaded to join the conservative Federalist Party, which he saw as representing the American ideal of liberty. He remained an active member in this party until he died.

As a Federalist, Josiah first served in the Massachusetts State Senate, then was elected to Congress in 1804, where he served three two-year terms as a congressman. Upon returning to Massachusetts, he was twice elected Speaker of the Massachusetts House of Representatives, where he established himself as a leading authority on poverty in Massachusetts. By 1822, he was seated as a justice of the Suffolk Municipal Court by Governor John Brooks and had also been appointed by the General Court (the legislature) to chair a judiciary committee to investigate the causes and remedies of poverty in Massachusetts.

At a time when the defense of human rights was barely given consideration,

Josiah Quincy's Pauperism Committee investigated the causes of pauperism in Boston and across Massachusetts. In 1820 the committee concluded that paupers could be classified into two separate groups: those who chose to be indigent and those who were destitute by reason of circumstance. Josiah Quincy concluded that if the "unworthy poor" were not distinguished from the "worthy poor," the contamination would eventually corrupt society. Thus it was the duty of society, his report said, to differentiate between the "vicious poor" and the "virtuous poor" with regard to charitable intentions.

His investigation also emphasized the inhumanity of incarcerating honest citizens who had been victims of the economic depression—especially the children charged with petty theft—in the same jail with hardened criminals because there was only one city prison in Boston and one state prison in nearby Charlestown. At the time, anyone convicted of a crime (including pauperism) within the municipality, regardless of age, sex, color, status, or severity of the infraction, was confined at the Leverett Street jail.

When his report was accepted by the Boston selectmen in 1821, the town voted to establish a debtor's prison in nearby South Boston, and also to replace the failing almshouse, or poorhouse. Although the House of Industry would not be ready to receive debtors to work off their debts for about another three years, Josiah Quincy's efforts to make the public aware of human rights had already begun.

Judge Josiah Quincy's committee report remained true to the convictions he had put into practice on the bench. He was known for giving uncharacteristically lenient sentences to those he saw as true victims of poverty, for he had seen it do little good to imprison a man, woman, or child for an extended term for petty crimes or debt. Yet, for the hardened criminal, he had no such sympathy. His report stated publicly that his principal concern was to protect society, not to rehabilitate the deviant at the expense of the taxpayer.

Local newspapers lauded Quincy's actions and widely publicized his demands for judicial and social reforms. Aligning himself with the pauper's cause not only added to his popularity but earned him the support of honest and hardworking citizens who were casualties of a depressed economy.

Politically, Josiah Quincy remained popular. His record as a concerned public servant and a vocal jurist who sincerely desired a better city led to his election as Boston's second mayor on May 1, 1823. That same day he addressed the assembly at

Faneuil Hall, making two issues clear: He intended to immediately improve conditions around the new city his way, and he planned to remain in office indefinitely.[9] At fifty-one years of age the new mayor stood more than six feet tall—fiercely intense, spirited, sagacious, and eager to initiate the much needed urban reforms—in prime condition to take on the job.

Mayor Quincy quickly discovered, however, that the failures of the previous administration could not be "cured" solely by changing who sat as city's chief executive. The office of mayor had been limited in power by the new city's charter, which had retained too much of the out-of-date town government structure.

Mayor Quincy refused to be called by the title Chief Administrative and Executive Officer unless he could be such in reality. This meant, he was sure, that he had to interpret the city charter as having meant to give the mayor enough executive power to bring all five municipal boards under his control. He "regarded the duties of the executive officer [to include acting] absolutely and exclusively with the character and interests of the city [at heart], studying and undertaking all its rights, whether affecting property, or liberty, or power, and the maintaining [of] them, not merely with the zeal of official station, but with the pertinacious spirit of private interest. The honor, happiness, dignity, safety, and prosperity of the city, the development of its resources, its expenditures, and police, should be the perpetual object of his purpose, and labor of his thought."[10] By assuming responsibility for all vital health and safety issues he could then ensure "that all negligence, carelessness, and positive violations of duty be prosecuted and punished."[11]

Mayor Josiah Quincy, therefore, appointed himself chairman ex officio of every executive committee serving under each of the five municipal boards. By centralizing this splintered municipal authority, he hoped to eliminate individual posturing and give one controlling voice to all decisions. He thereby instilled a new sense of leadership over this city of 45,000 inhabitants, who had endured decades of decay owing to the boards' squabbling over power and blame. This was only the beginning of his new method of governing the city.

When Mayor Quincy learned that four of the boards had complete autonomy in spending tax dollars, he wrote an ordinance that made two major changes: It established the office of Auditor of Accounts, which instituted a new system of financial controls. And it compelled each board to request appropriations from the City Council, where only the mayor and the city treasurer could authorize funds.

Naturally, this ordinance caused dissatisfaction among the members of the socially prominent boards and their elite executive committees.

During his first formal session with the City Council, Mayor Quincy announced that he intended to foster civic pride among the citizens of Boston. He would make Boston a cleaner, healthier, and safer place by first improving the sanitary conditions around the city. Henceforth, he proclaimed, all livestock (fowl, swine, cattle, etc.) being brought into the city that normally would be taken to Market Square would be restricted to Boston Common until the animals were sold or slaughtered. Exemptions would exist for residents, who were allowed to keep cows pastured at Boston Common or near their homes, and for horses, which, at the time, were the only means of transportation.[12] The pronouncement also promised that all streets would be cleaned and household garbage would be collected and disposed of on a regular basis. "In the whole sphere of municipal duties, there are none more important than those which relate to the removal of those substances whose exhalations injuriously affect the air. A pure atmosphere is to a city what a good conscience is to an individual, a perpetual source of comfort, tranquility, and self-respect."[13]

Prior to 1822, the Board of Health had jurisdiction over Boston's streets but only to the point of quarantining infectious diseases and servicing various public health needs. The board relied upon scavengers and country farmers to eliminate filth by carting away household waste and animal droppings to use or sell as fertilizer or as feed for swine. The practice of retrieving manure from Boston's streets and selling it back to the suburban farmers was a highly lucrative business, but it had not kept the streets clean. The streets remained especially contaminated during the hot summer months, the height of farming season, and the time of year when disease spread most quickly from refuse in the streets.

In order to accomplish his promised cleaning of the streets, Mayor Quincy's first step was to accuse the Board of Health of being incompetent and of catering to its patronage rather than protecting the public's welfare. He executed an ordinance that banned tossing household garbage and human waste into the streets. Then the mayor claimed that the health of the city should be managed by a professional who would be directly accountable to the mayor's office. So he created the new office of city marshal to act as chief health officer and to oversee the duties of the city's constables, who would enforce the new laws.

Under the this new structure the city made rapid progress. The requirement of city livestock owners and farmers entering the city limits to restrict their animals to Boston Common left the streets manageable. Teams of sweepers were hired to purge every street, lane, court, and alley—as well as every dock, wharf, bulkhead, and quay—of accumulated debris for the first time in two centuries. A fleet of wagons and teams of horses were purchased by the city; then laborers were hired to remove the heaps of refuse. Quickly, piles of debris that had accumulated over the years were carted away; the nearest property owner, or owners, was billed for the expense of the removal. Within a month the city streets were cleaned of three thousand tons of accumulated sweepings and a dump was established at the far corner of Boston Common.[14]

To pay for this endeavor, Mayor Quincy sold most of the manure back to the city-owned farms. They were charged by the ton and anyone caught collecting manure gratis from Boston Common or the streets was fined. Both scavengers and farmers had to obtain a license to haul away debris if it was unsorted—that is, mixed with material that could be used as fertilizer. The whole expense of Boston's first street-cleaning effort paid for itself by the end of 1823.

To his detractors,[15] Mayor Quincy claimed that paying for his initial goal of cleaning the streets by reselling the refuse had not been planned. The city, he asserted, was not in the business of profiting, but rather of taking back control of its public streets. He pointed out that "[f]or the first time, on any general scale destined for universal application, the broom was used upon the streets. On seeing this novel spectacle, of files of sweepers, an old and common adage [i.e., sweeping out of office; cleaning up government] was often applied to the new administration of city affairs; in good humor by some, in a sarcastic spirit by others."[16]

He also pointed out that, in less than a year, he had successfully justified to Bostonians his claims that the inefficiency of the Board of Health was part of what had been holding back the city from an efficient system. He was not the first to point this out: Prior to Boston's incorporation as a city, the Board of Health had been accused of such corruption that the General Court had added a provision to the city charter that allowed the elimination of this board if the mayor found a legitimate reason. Mayor Quincy used this provision to abolish the Board of Health and place all of its duties under the city marshal. This new law enforcement officer became responsible for Boston's health needs, which included keeping the streets perpetually clean and using constables to enforce the ordinances. The first city marshal he appointed, who also was to oversee the constables, was Benjamin Pollard, a Harvard graduate and a Boston lawyer.

The mayor also attacked the lack of maintenance of the city's sewers. He said they were not being well managed where they were at the time, in the hands of private enterprise, so he brought the entire drainage system under the city's control, overseen by the city marshal (Pollard). For the first time, the neglected sewers were all scoured, unplugged, flushed clear, and restored to flow as designed. This completely eliminated the all-too-prevalent problem of mosquito-breeding stagnant water lying above the sewer drains, especially around the market district. Not surprisingly, Boston's disease and death rates began to decline steadily.

The mayor did not hesitate, either, to undermine yet another board—the Surveyors of Highways, who were responsible for street maintenance. As executive officer of the city, he appointed a superintendent of the streets and gave him jurisdiction over the Board of Surveyors. The superintendent then marshaled gangs of laborers to work nightly at repairing the streets. This was easily done if they waited until after the newly instituted ten o'clock curfew.

By these two gestures, Mayor Quincy furthered the cleanup of Boston's streets. He also gained more needed control over much of the city's governing structure.

Josiah Quincy had learned from his mother the importance of discipline in maintaining good health. As an adult he equated such discipline with high morals, orderliness, and self-respect. He became known for his precise grooming, his gentlemanly behavior, and his cultivated appearance. So, while serving as mayor, unlike many gentlemen of the era, Josiah Quincy arose each day long before the rooster crowed. He spent some time rigorously performing his own form of calisthenics and then plunged into an outside coldwater "air-bath." He then shaved, cleaned his teeth, dressed in the day's clean clothes, powdered his hair, and breakfasted. After gulping a mugful of extra-strong black tea and eating beef and eggs with a greased biscuit for breakfast, he donned his greatcoat (a long caped overcoat) and was out the door by five o'clock, ready to depart on horseback.

At this early hour he was often seen galloping through each quarter of the city, conducting his daily inspection of every street in Boston and either making a checklist of things that needed to be corrected or following up on the state of previously noted problems. In Quincy's Boston, begging was prohibited, vagrancy was banned, and loitering of any kind was forbidden. Soon it became commonplace to observe the mayor apprehending and delivering anyone he considered to be a deviant to the Police Court or to Leverett Street Jail. If property owners cluttered the sidewalks in front of their shops, they would soon receive notice from the city marshal ordering that "they cause said street to be cleared in front of their respective estates forthwith."[17] Upon a second infraction, the mayor personally issued a fine to those who stood in violation.

This hands-on approach to running the city improved the city's physical look. For some citizens, though, such incessant vigilance was unwelcome; it was labeled "officiousness" and "intermeddling."[18]

At his office in Faneuil Hall Mayor Quincy listened to complaints and concerns from individual citizens, who lined up every morning for their turn to be heard. The remainder of his day was spent in long sessions with the City Council or chairing the executive board committees.

Some evenings he gave formal dinner parties for such luminaries as Daniel Webster, the captain and officers of the USS *Constitution* (which was anchored in Boston Harbor), and relatives of the Adams, Hancock, and Phillips families. Other evenings he held executive committee meetings by the fireplace at his home, where his wife, Eliza Susan, graciously received his guests. Occasionally, he would accompany his family to the theater, especially when Shakespeare was being performed.

Sundays were reserved for God and family. He attended the service at Arlington Street Church. Then he managed family affairs and had dinner with his wife and seven children at their home on the corner of Hamilton Place and Tremont Street, overlooking Boston Common. Known for never wasting a precious minute, Mayor Quincy also worked on Sundays when time permitted. He sometimes managed to squeeze in his early morning rounds on Sundays, as well as preparing his schedule for the following week and conducting committee meetings.

Affixed to his desk at Faneuil Hall he kept a reminder that the way to glory is justice. It was an epigraph written by Cicero: *Præclare Socrates hanc viam ad gloriam proximam et quasi compendiariam dicebat esse; si quis id ageret, ut, qualis haberi vellet, talis esset. Quodsi qui simulatione et inani ostentatione et ficto non modo sermone, sed etiam voltu stabilem se gloriam consequi posse rentur, vehementer errant.* Or, "Socrates used to express it so admirably, 'The nearest way to glory—and a shortcut, as it were—is to strive to be what you wish to be thought to be.' For if anyone thinks he can win lasting glory by pretense, by empty show, by hypocritical talk and looks, he is very much mistaken."[19]

As his responsibilities grew, so did Mayor Quincy's pace. One morning while inspecting the city at daybreak he was apprehended by a night watchman for racing his horse and endangering the public within the city limits. He was then arraigned at the Police Court and two witnesses testified to his speeding. When the watchmen learned his identity and prepared to immediately release him, he insisted that they carry out their investigation to make sure that no risk to pedestrians had occurred. He pleaded "Not guilty" but stood willing that judgment should be entered against him and the appropriate fines imposed, "to show that no individual could be placed above the law."[20]

With so many urban problems still awaiting reform, Mayor Quincy focused his attention upon Market Square. He couldn't help noticing, whenever he gazed eastward from his Faneuil Hall office window, the collection of colonial-era structures crammed together. And the docks beyond! "Effluvia," he called the polluted harbor waters and the horrible odor that hung over Market Square, "noxious effluvia."[21]

He recognized the adverse effect the newly enacted city ordinance had upon wagon and pushcart vendors and, by extension, upon Boston's merchants. He knew the farmers and vendors hadn't had enough space even before the ordinance, and he wanted to provide it to them as soon as possible. He was convinced that the only way to do so was to repair the entire market district and expand it, widening streets in the process. The whole city would benefit, he thought. Commerce would have room to grow, Boston's waterfront would be less unsightly, and the city would present a more dignified face to those arriving by sea, a major means of approach to Boston.

Josiah Quincy had no idea, at first, that his proposals would face such steadfast opposition—not only from prominent citizens but from members of the City Council and the state legislature as well. Although it was widely acknowledged that Market Square was desperately in need of renewal, no one else was willing to jeopardize his standing in the community for such a radical idea. Why, nothing on this scale had ever been done before, or even contemplated! And these were not the times to take on financial risk.

A market scene around Market Square, about 1823, decades after the Shambles was erected.
ILLUSTRATION BY GARY IRISH, ASAI, 2002.

Mayor Quincy did not look at the risk; he saw only the future results of the expansion—new jobs, an established location for marketing, a new legitimacy given to wagon and pushcart merchants, and a city that had enough faith in itself to do what had to be done. He wrote of his determination to see it through: "It is not the natural brilliancy of wit and the flashes of imagination (which, by the world, is denominated genius) that are, in my opinion, to be envied. It is firmness of nerve—that strength of mind which capacitates us for intense application and hard, laborious attention—which is the soil where every laurel and every virtue is cultivated with success."[22] He was determined to see it through.

He knew that the best way to go about realizing a grand plan was to first get the approval of the City Council, and also of most of Boston's citizens, and then introduce changes to the plan gradually. Boston's history of decision making, especially in regard to the market district, showed that it did not easily differentiate between progress and lunacy. Idealism, it sometimes seemed to say, was left to fools and madmen. Therefore, Mayor Quincy decided to introduce his solution in phases.

When he was elected, Josiah Quincy had defined his position as mayor before the City Council by stating that he "promised nothing except a laborious fulfillment of every known duty, a prudent exercise of every invested power, and a disposition shrinking from no official responsibility."[23] He displayed this last quality in the courage it took to present his first phase of revitalizing the market district. He addressed the City Council and said that the pushcart peddlers and wagon vendors needed space to sell their wares. He asked that the City Council approve funds to purchase private properties to provide land to begin expanding Market Square. Hoping to allay fears, he cited nearby India Wharf as a prime example of successful waterfront renewal.

India Wharf had been a collection of streets and small independent piers that extended into the harbor from India Street, most of them holding ramshackle warehouses and wooden shanties until 1807. Then, in an ambitious commercial project, a private group of investors converted the property into an efficient wharf system. Designed by architect Charles Bulfinch, India Wharf was extended to 980 feet into the harbor, its streets were widened, and its dilapidated structures were replaced with thirty-two, five-story brick warehouses. Since its redevelopment, India Wharf had engaged ships from India, China, Russia, and the Mediterranean sea trades. In 1823, when Mayor Quincy used it as an example to his Council, it was still considered Bulfinch's most outstanding success and perhaps even the most lucrative maritime venture ever in Boston.

The City Council was not easily persuaded by Mayor Quincy's presentation of his ideas. After much debate the Council appropriated a mere $15,000 for the most obvious need—a new vegetable market to replace the Shambles adjacent to Faneuil Hall. When the new market was completed, the slaughter and sale of meat would be restricted to the stalls inside Faneuil Hall's first floor.

Although Mayor Quincy was disappointed by the limited scope of this makeshift resolution, he did not object to the Council's measure. He waited until he

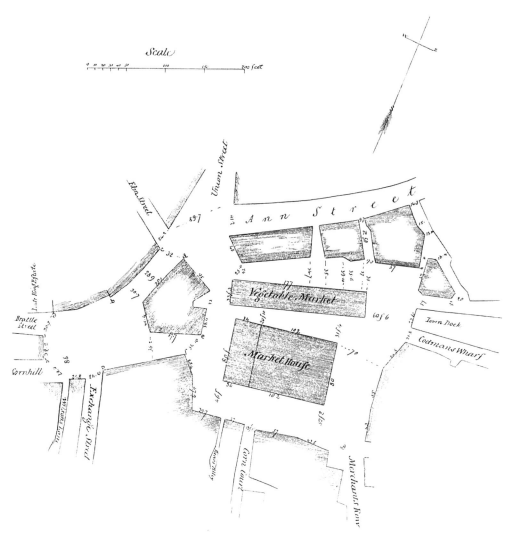

*Dock Square, Market Square, Roe Buck Passage, Faneuil Hall (labeled Market House),
and the Shambles (labeled Vegetable Market). Reprinted from* Hale's Atlas, *1819.*
Courtesy of the Bostonian Society/Old State House.

had a better argument to present them, and he did not initiate the approved small-
scale improvement.

A month later, Mayor Quincy readdressed the issue. He informed the City
Council that he envisioned a more ambitious scheme. The logical solution to the
lack of space in the market district was to do more than replace one pseudobuilding.
They needed to widen streets and extend the district seaward, he said, by filling in

the shore and creating more land. This would maintain the market area's link to its historic waterfront, and it would provide more land for pushcart and wagon vendors, which was sorely needed. He emphasized that if the project was careful to meet the needs of Boston's citizens, the future benefits would almost guarantee that the city's financial well-being was safeguarded. It would then be a straightforward process to convince voters that the expenditures were justified.

His argument continued with specifics on how to explain this substantial development. The city had not spent much of the taxes it had collected while Mayor Phillips had been in office. It was in a good financial position, therefore, to secure the necessary funds from City Bank.[24] An expanded new market district around the already approved new vegetable market would allow more vendors into the same area, and thereby generate competition. This, in turn, would reduce consumer prices.

He noted that the circumstances were favorable for purchasing distressed property at lower prices. He pointed out that the owners of neighboring properties at Long Wharf and the North End would realize an appreciation of value by the formation of new streets—especially if the problems of Roe Buck Passage were finally corrected. It was paramount, however, that the city purchase every private property necessary within the scope of his proposed public works project to ensure success. He concluded by reasoning that $15,000 was insufficient to initiate such a project and petitioned the City Council for additional funds.

Although the City Council denied the additional funds, the mayor was authorized to investigate the possibility of assembling waterfront parcels for future purchase. As part of this implied approval of Mayor Quincy's concept, the City Council assigned the public works project a name: the Extension of Faneuil Hall Market.[25]

Immediately, Mayor Quincy formed an executive committee for the project, naming himself chairman. He appointed seven members from the Common Council and three from the Board of Aldermen and named the new group the City Council Committee on the Extension of Faneuil Hall. The committee was also referred to as the Market Committee. One of its prominent members was an alderman who was noted for being an excellent architect and author, Asher (or Ashur) Benjamin. He would soon play a pivotal role in the extension project.

Asher Benjamin had grown up in the Connecticut River Valley, where he became a housewright's apprentice. In 1797 he published *The Country Builder's Assistant*, based upon his experience of working with Charles Bulfinch. It was the first builder's handbook authored by an American citizen. In 1803 he arrived in Boston and settled in the West End, which was a growing neighborhood on the backside of Beacon Hill. Three years later he penned his second book, *The American Builder's Companion,* which became a standard reference for many tradesmen. In 1808 he designed and oversaw the construction of the Boston Coffee Exchange Building, a structure that rose seven stories and was capped by a distinctive dome. When Mayor Quincy asked him to help design the new market district, Benjamin began work on a master plan for the new vegetable market, widened streets, and the reconstruction of the Town Dock. He worked under the mayor's direction and was assisted by surveyor Stephen T. Fuller and, in an advisory capacity, another renowned architect, Alexander Parris.

Between August and November 1823, Josiah Quincy personally met with every property owner between State and Ann Streets. To each owner he conveyed the message that the city intended to purchase private property in order to provide land for wider roads, a new vegetable market, and adequate vending space for wagon and pushcart merchants. His efforts focused on thirty properties that, taken together, covered 127,000 square feet. These included land and buildings, private passageways, and wharves and wharf rights. (Legal wharf rights—or licensed tideland—were products of laws created by the General Court during the 1640s that gave explicit permission to waterfront property owners to build on or to fill harbor land that fell between the high and low watermarks. Harbor land beyond the low watermark belonged to the Commonwealth.)

   In 1823 there were five principal wharves between State Street and the North End's Ann Street that extended seaward from Faneuil Hall: David Spear's/Greene Wharf; Bray's Wharf; Nathan Spear's Wharf; Codman's Wharf, and the Town Dock (actually a wharf). These wharves had assorted structures built upon them, most of which were leased to tenants. Initially, Mayor Quincy focused upon the vicinity around Bray's, Nathan Spear's, and Codman's Wharves, together with the Town Dock, as the area of expansion. He commented, "[I]t was evidently for the interest of them all that the plan contemplated should succeed, and not be defeated, or post-

Facing page: *Merchants Row, Faneuil Hall, and the five principle wharves (including the Town Dock). Reprinted from* Hale's Atlas, *1819.*
COURTESY OF THE BOSTONIAN SOCIETY/OLD STATE HOUSE.

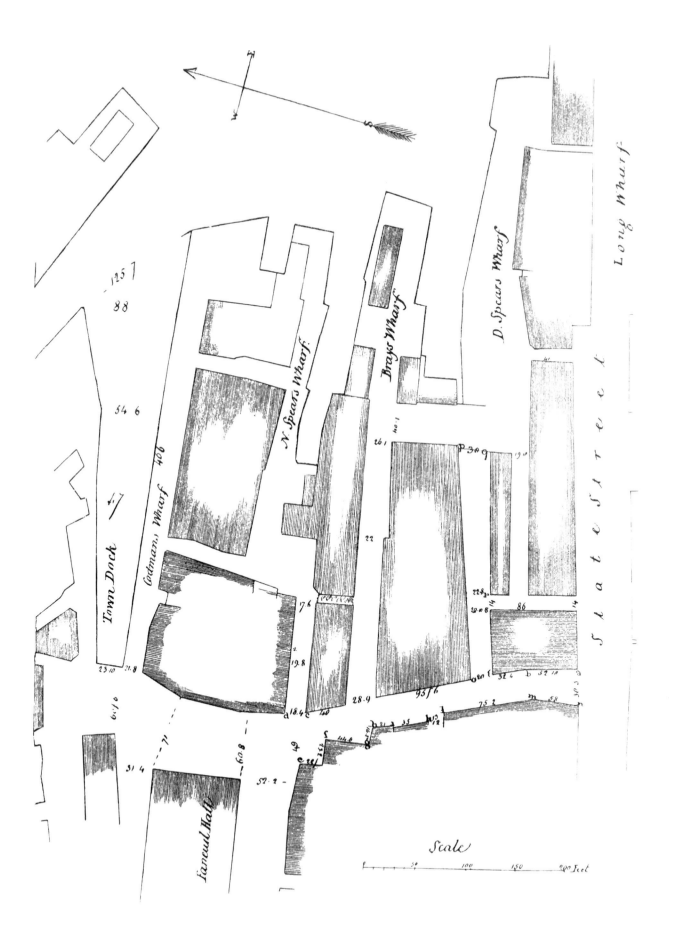

Long Wharf

State Street

D. Spears Wharf

Bray's Wharf

N. Spears Wharf

Godman's Wharf

Town Dock

Faneuil Hall

Scale

0   50   100   150   200 Feet

poned, by the erection of the vegetable market."[26] Some of the owners simply refused to sell, citing the loss of rental income from long-term leases they held. Others were more than willing to negotiate because their properties were in utter ruin. Mayor Quincy shrewdly used the $15,000 budget "as an argument to influence those proprietors to be more moderate in their [sale price] demands."[27] Much of his bargaining had the effect intended. The mayor entered into conditional contracts, far below what some considered "fair price," that would prevent an owner from increasing his demands should the city proceed with the extension project and their former property become more valuable.

Mayor Quincy reasoned that "fair price" consisted of the appraised value of a property based upon its physical condition and the rental income that existed at the time of the appraisal. But many property owners saw this public works project as an opportunity to inflate the value of their property. They spoke of "fair price" as including the loss of years of future income. And they pointed out that some of their existing long-term contracts with renters of their properties could not be broken.

On December 10, 1823, the Market Committee transmitted three options to those owners who wouldn't sell to the city for the project: to combine their properties into common stock offerings, to have their properties valued by independent appraisers, or to establish their own reasonable price and accept the city's reasonable counteroffer.[28] They were given ten days to respond.

By December 20 there was no response that accepted combining the properties into common stock or selling their properties by appraisement. Several of the proprietors, however, expressed their willingness to set their own price—at extremely high prices. The others refused to sell at all, declaring that they had other related business interests around the city that would be harmed by the development. They therefore would neither enter into price negotiation nor discuss the subject any further. In response, Mayor Quincy flatly withdrew the proposals.

Despite this, in less than six months Josiah Quincy held conditional contracts for purchasing most of the properties needed to extend Market Square eastward for half the sum of the owners' initial asking prices. He had negotiated the prices down from a high of about $800,00 to $400,000. These conditional contracts held by the city stipulated "payment of a specified sum by the City of Boston, on or before May 1824 [in exchange for] full title and warranty."[29]

Throughout the time of the mayor's negotiations, Asher Benjamin and surveyor Stephen Fuller were designing and redesigning new building concepts and street layouts under the mayor's supervision, in an effort to maximize space as much as possible and lessen the time needed to finalize the plans after the expected go-ahead was given.

On December 29, 1823, the Market Committee reported to City Council that the prices demanded by some remaining owners were too high and the lack of cooperation by others rendered it impossible to proceed with negotiations. The Committee was now convinced, though, it reported, that the extension project could proceed without jeopardizing the city's investment. To do so, the powers of eminent domain might have to be exercised.

At that time, the city could use eminent domain to take private property only for road purposes, not for a public building project. In response, the City Council said they would be prepared to appeal to the state legislature for "such an extension of the powers of the Surveyors of Highways, as may enable the city to become possessed of such estates in the vicinity of Faneuil Hall Market as the said Surveyors may deem it expedient for the city to possess for the public use, under such limitations, restrictions, and provisions, as the Constitution enjoins, and as regard for the interests of the public, and respect for the rights of individuals shall dictate."[30]

By early 1824 Boston's citizens were still strongly divided on whether the cost of the extension project would cripple the city if it proceeded. Public sentiment had been voiced to the point where the mayor said that "the whole subject should be laid out before the inhabitants of the city for their sanction."[31] It seemed too big an issue to decide only through their elected officials. And he needed to know, before proceeding any further, whether the general public was opposed to the project. The newly incorporated City of Boston returned to its political roots, therefore, and proceeded with a town meeting.

On January 16, 1824, concerned Bostonians convened at Faneuil Hall to hear the mayor's preliminary proposal for enlarging Market Square. At this town meeting, Asher Benjamin unveiled a three-dimensional model of a master plan. Displayed was a long one-story building flanked by two equally long buildings, each of which would be three and a half stories high. All three buildings extended eastward from Faneuil Hall, on land that would exist after more of the harbor was filled in. The buildings would be surrounded by a new system of streets. Mayor Quincy still called the one-story central building a new vegetable market, and he said that its "centre

. . . was to coincide with the centre of Faneuil Hall."[32] It would be a single-story structure about 50 feet wide and 420 feet long, which brought the total square footage to about 21,000—over three times the size of the building the City Council had approved the previous June and more than four times the size of the Shambles. The new market would have a roof supported by a double row of heavy wooden columns. There were no sides, no doors or windows, no protection from the elements other than the roof. Flanking the vegetable market would be two long buildings, which would look like warehouses and hold merchant stores. On each side of the center building, between it and the flanking warehouse/stores building, would be a broad avenue 65 feet wide. On the far side of each warehouse/stores building there would be another access street, each 50 feet wide. The warehouse buildings would be 55 feet wide and about the same length as the vegetable market. They would be built with common brick reminiscent of the row-house-style warehouses at nearby India Wharf.

The immediate reaction of the citizens was predictable. Instead of viewing this as the biggest single development in the history of Boston, one that would solve the market district's space problem for years to come, they deemed it an impractical dream, which they "opprobriously denominated 'the mammoth project of the Mayor.'"[33] The amount of debt it would take to build was even more intimidating than the project's size. People said it would lay the foundation of a city debt "which neither the present inhabitants of Boston, nor their prosperity, would be able to pay."[34] To this latter objection Mayor Quincy responded, "[D]ebt is no more an object of terror than a sword. Both are very dangerous in the hands of fools and madmen. Both are very safe, innocent, and useful in the hands of the wise and prudent. In the case of Faneuil Hall Market, what possible object of rational apprehension can there be in a debt created for the purpose of purchasing a tract of territory wholly within the control of the city authorities?"[35] His clear argument did not win him instant support.

Many people felt that such an ambitious development was better left to private enterprise, which, they said, was more adept at such construction than public officials. Others denied that a new vegetable market was even wanted.

Josiah Quincy was not deterred. He rebutted by pointing out that Market Square was becoming so overburdened by the rapidly increasing population that it was embarrassingly inconvenient. To be useful, any improvement must be essential, extensive, and permanent. He ran through numbers, demonstrating how the cost of new market facilities would be justified by the increasing annual rental income the city would receive from these buildings. And widening Roe Buck Passage and creating new streets, he emphasized, would favorably change the value of nearby privately owned real estate.

His ideas were not received passively.

During the town meeting's heated debate, Mayor Quincy narrowed all concerns down to two questions: whether the extension project should proceed under the guidance of city government (rather than by private enterprise), and whether the City Council should apply to the state legislature for an extension of its powers of eminent domain.

Ultimately, the mayor's rebuttal was effective enough to carry the proposal forward. The majority of those attending the town meeting voted in the affirmative on both questions. "A reconsideration of the vote was moved, but it was negated and the motion was disallowed. The Hall and galleries were full, and it was attended by some gentlemen opposed to the subject, that the actions had been carried three to one."[36]

The vote in the mayor's favor did not keep local newspapers from criticizing the decision. The *New England Palladium* denounced the public works project as fiscally irresponsible. The *Boston Patriot* declared that Mayor Quincy's proposals would inflate Boston's residential real estate market to the point where the poor would be squeezed from affordable housing. Other critics insisted that the scale of development would alter the essential character of Boston at the expense of small businessmen, established small shops, and independent merchants. So far-reaching were Quincy's ideals that some ridiculed his proposal as "Quincy's Folly."[37]

4

Negotiating for a Grand Market

Three weeks after the citizenry approved Mayor Quincy's plan at the town meeting at Faneuil Hall, the mayor and his Market Committee, speaking for the City Council, appealed to the state legislature (the General Court) for an extension of the city's powers of eminent domain. The debates took place during February 1824. Using his skills as a lawyer, politician, and municipal judge, Mayor Quincy told the legislators about the city's desperate need for a permanent functional marketplace and then stated that the city could not provide such an area because certain private property owners were refusing "fair price" offered by the city and demanding unrealistic prices instead.

In rebuttal, Daniel Webster, whom the noncooperating property owners had retained to represent them, addressed the General Court. He argued that "fair price" should include payment for benefits their holdings would generate in the future. It would be unfair, he said, for any municipal authority to take private property at present value when its intention was to increase the property's value through redevelopment. Therefore, "fair price" should be defined as the properties' present value plus the value of *all* future potential benefits. After all, by taking their private property, the city was denying these owners potential future growth as well as earnings. Webster did not attempt to quantify a term limit of that future.

Mayor Quincy responded that the city was trying to establish a public works project that would cover a wide range of real estate uses. These included the use of existing public streets, private lanes, and different forms of commercial property and ownership interests. He stressed that transforming this district from its present assortment of antiquated buildings and wharves into one unified modern development would better this part of Boston. No single owner should be granted undefined future benefits based on this improvement. The court should limit its award for their future benefits to twelve months.

Additionally, he assured the General Court that the city was not in the business of profiting from the future rents of the development. The city sought a broader set of benefits. It would need much of the rents from the development to pay for the cost of the development and for maintaining it without resorting to taxation. Any excess rental income not used for the marketplace would be deposited in the city treasury and used to subsidize other public works projects. Therefore, if anyone was going to benefit from the marketplace's "profit," it would be the citizens of Boston, not the city itself.

Mayor Quincy further argued that the city's powers of eminent domain would be rendered useless if these private property owners were allowed to predicate their property values on unlimited hypothetical future rental income. He insisted that if the opinions of professional real estate appraisers were not used to arrive at what "fair price" should be, municipal judges would become the arbiters. With so many different properties located within the sphere of this one public works project, he predicted, the courts would be inundated with lawsuits and the development would ultimately become stalled or bankrupt.

Lastly, Mayor Quincy cited earlier examples in which these same property owners who were so vocal in their opposition to the city's interpretation of "fair price" had used the city's same definition in their own dealings. The General Court had granted these private investors specific extensions of the laws of eminent domain for their business ventures based, not on future earnings, but on present-use valuation. Therefore, the democratically elected municipal government should logically be the recipient of the same benefits.

In late February 1824 the state legislature passed an act that authorized the city to take land from private owners for reasons other than street extension, but only under a lengthy set of procedures. Additionally, a new definition of "fair price" was established by the General Court that said the property value in future eminent domain cases would be predicated on the physical and financial status of a property at the time of the taking. For the first time, the forced sale of private property necessary for public redevelopment projects was clearly and legally defined. Josiah Quincy had successfully clarified the Commonwealth's method of valuing private property for eminent domain proceedings. Limits had now been set on such private property valuation.[1]

With public support and its new legal authority now in hand, the City Council authorized the Market Committee to borrow up to $500,000 from City Bank. On March 9, 1824, the mayor assembled a subcommittee called the Building Committee and named himself chairman. He also appointed Aldermen David Weld Child and Asher Benjamin and Councilman Eliphalet Williams as its members. Alderman Child was named superintendent and was entrusted to oversee the entire development.[2] As such, the superintendent was given the authority to appoint subordinates and make daily decisions regarding all construction. For his efforts, Alderman Child was budgeted $1,000 per month.

One of the first properties the Market Committee purchased was the historic Triangular Warehouse. The Triangular Store, as it was officially called, was situated at the head of the Town Dock on Roe Buck Passage. It was a curiously shaped building with towers at each angle and a center tower rising above the central slated roof. Each tower had a pointed roof that was capped by a stone ball. The massiveness of its construction spurred conjecture that it was originally used as a fort for the protection of the town or as a British customhouse. It was, in fact, just a warehouse erected by London merchants in 1700. In March 1824 the city bought the Triangular Warehouse and "all rights of passageway and the use of Town Dock"[3] at the appraised value of $15,000.

In April 1824, most of the private property owners who were under conditional contract with the city through the end of 1823 were paid in cash for their properties. By the end of the month, the City Council appropriated additional funds to pay off all the remaining conditional contracts before their termination in May 1824. Some of those who had refused to sell their properties in December 1823 reapproached Mayor Quincy to set a price, now that the city was empowered with extended eminent domain authority.

During this same period of time, Mayor Quincy continued to expand the scope of the development while negotiating with more property owners around the perimeter, using tactics that were clever, persistent, and timely. Once the approximate dimensions of some of the new streets had been drawn out on the master plan, the

*The Triangular Warehouse, officially called the Triangular Store, was situated
at the head of the Town Dock on Roe Buck Passage.*
COURTESY OF THE BOSTONIAN SOCIETY/OLD STATE HOUSE.

city was in a position to take land by eminent domain for street expansion through
the Board of Surveyors of Highways. When he encountered an individual who
adamantly demanded an unrealistic price, he agreed to meet that price—on the condition that their property would be reassessed for taxes at the agreed-upon sale price
if the development did not proceed. Fearing that their asking price might be used to
their disadvantage if the public works project failed, many an owner renegotiated his
price downward.

Attacks against Quincy's public works project continued, from a cross section
of citizens. But in May 1824 Josiah Quincy and all incumbent aldermen were
reelected without measurable opposition. Bostonians had known about the mayor's

project for nearly a year, and the election made it apparent that most voters now approved of the development. With the confidence of the citizens behind them, the mayor and the City Council were encouraged to proceed aggressively with the development and even increase its proportions. It had been one long year since Josiah Quincy had convened the Market Committee to find a solution for the problems plaguing Market Square. Now the most daring construction project undertaken to date was being born. Quincy's younger son, Edmund, recalled that, after the project proved its value, his father was often greeted at public gatherings by attendees respectfully rising and breaking out into applause.[4]

The city began negotiating with the owner of Codman's Wharf and other wharves at "fair price," as defined by the General Court. The Market Committee voted "that the Mayor be authorized to offer to the Reverend John Codman payment in full for his estate bounding on and all his rights in and adjoining the Town Dock the sum of Seventy five thousand dollars."[5] In June 1824 Codman, together with a group of proprietors, agreed to sell their combined properties to the city for the aggregate price of $286,000. Of this price, $100,000 was for the wharf itself.

Yet, some still held out for more money and claimed they were entitled to a greater price for their property because of their essential location within the development and because they owned such a large percentage of the land needed. Some attempted to inflate their price by using fictitious buyers as leverage: "I now tell you, as a man of honour, as a gentleman, and what I am still more pleased to say as a friend, that if you wish the property, the former it is known that you will give the sum before proposed—110,000 (dollars), the better for I cannot warrant for a moment the ideas of the gentlemen who are interested in this property."[6] The mayor's standard response was: "[T]he readiness of the city government and their willingness to settle the price by three persons mutually to be chosen . . ."[7]

Mayor Quincy discovered that a number of the properties listed to uncooperative property owners were in arrears on tax payments; some had not been paid since as far back as the end of the American Revolution. As a result, Boston instituted some of its first actions in demanding payment of back taxes under penalty. The sale price of such property might be vastly reduced by taxes due, or the property might be lost entirely for back taxes of the owner, or owners might be sent to pauper's prison. Where there were multiple owners of a property so threatened, the mayor sometimes received a flood of letters denying part ownership. One such denial stated, "We further certify that we did not pay to said Codman nor did we collect from him [nor] from any tenants any part of the taxes on said wharf stores for the year 1824 [so demanded]."[8]

In June 1824 the city began issuing promissory notes for the purchase of various properties in the vicinity of the planned development in lieu of cash. Labeled FANEUIL HALL MARKET STOCK, the first certificates were issued to the heirs of Samuel Parkman for the "fair price" of $55,000. These fifty-five certificates were each valued at $1,000. Each would bear 5 percent annual interest—the interest to be compounded and paid on a quarterly basis—and each was redeemable in twenty years. The certificates of other properties purchased by promissory note varied according to the property's value and the circumstances argued by the owner. For instance, Mary T. Arthorp's property was bought for $5,700 in notes: five certificates were issued for $1,000 each and one for $700, all at 5 percent interest, payable in five years. Samuel Learned sold his property for $30,000, to be paid by fifteen $1,000 certificates at 5 percent, payable in five years, plus fifteen $1,000 certificates at 6 percent, redeemable in one year. Overall, the interest paid ranged between 5 percent and 6 percent. The terms of the notes varied from one to fifty years. The face value of the certificates ranged from $100 to $100,000. In the case of Codman's Wharf, the Reverend John Codman was paid one certificate for $100,000 at 6 percent interest, payable in thirty years, which included "fair price" for his property, lost rental income, and relocation expenses.[9]

On June 12, 1824, after securing an additional six properties—including Eustis Wharf by Ann Street—Mayor Quincy notified all remaining tenants and owners on all wharves to vacate their premises within thirty days. Construction was about to begin and $20,000 of appropriations would be used to tear down wharves, construct the principal bulkhead, excavate the enclosure, and lay hollow wooden drains.

On July 2, 1824, the City Council authorized the rerouting of Mill Creek outflow into the harbor and the relocation of the waterfront bulkhead to enclose the expanded area. The Boston and Roxbury Mill Dam Corporation was engaged to build the new bulkhead along the easternmost perimeter of the proposed landfill. At the same time, the stone contractor Abner Joy constructed the new ten-foot-wide granite conduit, which turned the course of Mill Creek away from its previous route, taking it, along with drainwater sewer outflow, some 400 feet seaward into Boston Harbor.[10]

By mid-July 1824, the mayor reported to the City Council that the Committee had "been able to effect so nearly the purchase of the whole circle of territory necessary for the city to possess, without resort to the exercise of the powers granted by the Legislature; that they have deemed it expedient in all cases to yield to the reasonable, and in some, to the extreme, demands of proprietors, rather than resort to a compulsory process."[11] The owners of one crucial property—Nathan Spear's Wharf—however, refused to deal with the city. It was situated at the very heart of the development.

On July 22, 1824, the City Council authorized the extension and widening of the two main avenues from 50 to 80 feet. At the same time the City Council also notified the owners of Nathan Spear's Wharf to submit all their demands at a formal hearing before the Council. On the appointed day, the Spears not only refused to appear before the City Council but "uniformly declined all negotiation concerning their interest in the contemplated sphere of improvement, and . . . any proposal of sale of it to the city." They also stated that their "purpose . . . was fixed and unalterable."[12]

Because the boundaries of the master plan were still not finalized, the Spear issue was left temporarily unresolved. The occupants of the wharf were simply ordered to vacate their premises while Mayor Quincy turned his attention toward Long Wharf, instructing the Market Committee to "request, that the Proprietors of the Long Wharf will sell to the City, at a fair price, all this land and flats, lying to the North and East, of a line extending along Bray's Wharf (so called) in the direction of the front line of Parkman's building to the circular line."[13] With enough purchases made, construction could begin in earnest.

Word was spread by handbills of the need for laborers to haul earth for the new landfill. Individuals who owned tipcarts, heavy wagons, or stone trucks were hired, as were truck companies with their own fleets of heavy wagons and stone trucks. The city marshal reassigned some city laborers from the street-cleaning detail to the new construction site. Dozens of idle draymen and seamen suddenly found new employment, too, in this first phase of construction.

The remaining portion of the original Town Cove was to be drained and prepared for the new development. Over time, cartful by cartful, this tedious process of "land remaking" was accomplished. Half this area consisted of wharves and old structures built upon earlier landfill and the other half of polluted waters. The wharves and buildings were torn down, the polluted waters were drained, and their garbage and sludge were disposed of.[14] Once the new bulkhead was in place, harbor waters could be held back and the area could be drained of all remaining seawater and silt by buckets and pumps. The reclaimed land was cleared all the way down to its upper layer of Boston blue clay (hardpan), which is where the heavy stone foundation of the vegetable market would soon rest.

By July 29, 1824, additional land purchases allowed the proposed vegetable market and flanking warehouses, which had been about 420 feet long in the proposal, to be lengthened to more than 500 feet. The Market Committee formally adopted a new ground plan, and Alderman Asher Benjamin was instructed to redesign the larger vegetable market by enclosing all its sides and adding a cellar. The originally planned open vegetable market was now transformed into a general market house intended to sell every provision. It was still, however, only one story high.

By August, the initial underground drain installation was prepared along the north side of the construction site by Zachariah Fish, who laid hollowed pine logs with plugs provided by Daniel Adams. A local newspaper reported that "the first operation, for locating and building this Market-House, commenced on the 20th of August, 1824, by staking out the ground for the same. . . . Shortly after, the razing of the old buildings, the filling up of the docks, and other work were simultaneously entered upon."[15] The perimeter staked out for the new market house was planned for a 500-foot-long single-story wooden structure. Its center would still be aligned with the center of Faneuil Hall, for aesthetic reasons.

New properties only recently purchased were added to the scope of the overall development. These included David Spear/Greene Wharf (but not Nathan Spear's Wharf, which the city had yet to negotiate), some properties by Long Wharf, and part of Bray's Wharf.

As the scope of the extension project grew, so did the design of the market house. On September 6, 1824, "The Committee in the subject of the elevation of the market house reported that they preferred to have the lower floor, not more than six inches above the sidewalk, and the market house to be I story higher."[16] (In other words, the building would now be two stories, and the first floor would be about six inches above the sidewalk.) Asher Benjamin responded to the change by producing a scale model of the new market house. It was designed to be built of stone instead of wood, and was described as "one story high with cellars and about 520 feet long."[17] The next day the City Council sanctioned plans for a two-story market house with cellar, built with stone, by appropriating $75,000 for its construction. The City Council also unanimously agreed with the mayor that the northern boundary of the project should not be restricted by Mill Creek, as was first contemplated. It was decided to purchase a number of the finger wharves in the North End, beyond Eustis Wharf, in order to eventually extend the bulkhead all the way to the North End section of the city.

From the beginning it had been the intention of the Market Committee to determine a method of minimizing costs. By September 1824 it was becoming clear that, instead of the city's building the flanking warehouse/stores and renting out space to merchants, as had been considered earlier, it would be better for the units to be financed by those who would use them. Individuals could buy the land their unit would be on (sometimes termed a *footprint*), construct their unit in accordance with the city's overall plan, and pay property and other taxes (inventory, income, etc.) through their businesses. On September 10, 1824, the Committee voted "relative to the sale of the buildings on both sides of the new market house, and to the plans of those buildings [to] recommend [that] authority . . . be given to make sale of the store lots, on the North side of the said new market house."[18] And on September 13 the City Council granted the Market Committee authority to conduct a sale of lots along the north side of the proposed market house. The city would auction these individual lots of land (footprints) where each unit within the building would be erected. Although the number of individual lots and the formal design for the range of stores as a whole had not yet been prepared, Mayor Quincy still envisioned an integrated complex of uniform stores forming a single long warehouse building, like those at India Wharf.

With the Town Dock officially closed during the chaotic demolition around Market Square, merchants in nearby shops attempted to conduct normal wharf business without it. Buildings and wharves already purchased were being torn down, while some tenants and owners remained in business, paying rent now to their new landlord, the city. Roe Buck Tavern, for instance, was kept open by its former owner, who would now pay rent to the city until the time came to tear the building down.

Other store and shop owners stayed open, too, also paying rent to the city until they were ordered to vacate. The city would then reimburse them for lost business and relocation costs. Landlords were also reimbursed for lease surrenders—money they would have received for the remainder of the term of their leases—to a maximum of twelve months.

Few tears were shed over the loss of many of these old buildings when they disappeared forever, especially the nefarious Roe Buck Tavern. Shanties, hovels, shacks, wharves, rooming houses, and warehouses—even the mysterious old Triangular Warehouse, which had stood for over a hundred years on the north side of the Town Dock—were torn down to make room for the sweeping changes that lay ahead. Remarkably, a few old buildings nearby, like the Old Feather Store, which had been built about 1680, escaped demolition.[19]

In September 1824 Alderman Asher Benjamin met privately with Mayor Quincy and reported that he was having money problems. He could no longer afford to spend so much of his time designing and redesigning the buildings on his alderman's salary. He didn't resign from either the Market or the Building Committee, but he did recommend that the committee look for a new architect. He endorsed his mentor, Boston's new leading architect, Alexander Parris.[20] Prior to this time, Parris had lent his expertise to the overall birth of the project only in an advisory capacity—such as overseeing Stephen Fuller's surveys and positioning of buildings, and preparing warehouse drafts with Asher Benjamin—because Mayor Quincy had primarily relied on Benjamin's architectural experience.

Parris had previously implored the Market Committee on two occasions to be granted general oversight of the project because he was concerned that if annually elected public officials were in charge and if they were voted out of office, this exciting new project might suffer. His second letter to the Market Committee stated it this way: "[E]specially when the parties who have the control are subject to annual changes, such as our Municipal Authorities, (of which you have the honor to be members,) . . . an agreement or appointment should be made with some person to be continued on the work until its completion, to see your improvements carried into effect."[21] The argument was heard and acted upon. None of the politician-builders wanted such a large undertaking to suffer, should any of them be voted out. Parris was engaged as the city's appointed architect for the project.

Alexander Parris was born in Halifax, Massachusetts, in 1780. A year later his

Portrait in crayon of Alexander Parris (1780–1852) by W. E. Chickering, c. 1845.
Parris was employed as the architect for Faneuil Hall Market and the flanking warehouse/stores
on North and South Market Streets. Another well-respected Boston architect, Asher Benjamin,
served on Mayor Quincy's Market Committee and provided earlier drawings for the project.
Courtesy of the Bostonian Society/Old State House.

parents relocated to the Maine frontier at Shepardfield (later renamed Hebron). The next year Parris's father was killed by a falling tree and his mother returned to Halifax. At age sixteen, Alexander Parris began his career as an apprentice under Pembroke housewright John Bonney. Spurred on by his mother's widowhood and the need to support his family, he worked hard enough to be made a journeyman by the time he was nineteen. By the age of twenty-one he had advanced to the level of carpenter and builder. Following the War of 1812, Alexander Parris moved to Boston and practiced civil engineering and architecture. He lived in Boston's West End, where many of his neighbors were housewrights, masons, hardware dealers, builders, and emerging architects, among them Asher Benjamin. He built various seawalls and bulkheads around Boston Harbor, drafted building renderings, and designed row houses. During his first seven years in Boston, he gained considerable experience in granite construction and established links with local artisans. His personal style of architecture moved toward economical and functional forms that employed large pieces of hand-hammered granite.

For three years he served as Charles Bulfinch's executive of construction during the building of Massachusetts General Hospital. By the time Bulfinch departed for Washington, D.C., in 1817 to begin work on the U.S. Capitol, Parris was well positioned to replace him as Boston's premier architect. By 1824 a significant aspect of Parris's reputation was the achievements he'd made in engineering his projects, especially with the use of granite. His sense of design was based on the Greek Revival movement. With his highly respected background in engineering, his interest in Greek Revival, and his experience under Bulfinch, Alexander Parris was a perfect match for Mayor Quincy's vision of a grand market house.

Parris's first assignment for the city was to lay out the northern warehouse/store lots for sale. At this time, the broad avenues on either side of the market house were given their new names: North Market and South Market Streets.[22] Also named was Marginal Street, a new road that extended from Long Wharf across the harborfront bulkhead to Eustis Wharf.

Parris also began redesigning the market house itself, and he enlarged it. On September 14, 1824, the Market Committee voted, "That the enlarged plan of the improvement of the market now drawn by Mr. Parris, be projected, upon the principle of two stories in front . . . that there shall be two stories through the whole length of the new market house . . . that the lower main story be drawn at an elevation, not higher than fifteen feet, and the upper at an elevation not higher than ten feet . . . that the lower floor of the market house be at an elevation of not more that fifteen inches above the sidewalk . . . that the length of the market house be extended at the Eastward to the full length of the stores . . . that the Building Committee be instructed to prepare grand plans and elevations of the buildings and market house, and also the conditions of sale of the store lots. . . ."[23]

On September 21, 1824, the Market Committee set terms for the first auction, for the twenty-five lots for the northern warehouse/stores, two of which were separated from the other twenty-three by a section of Merchants Row that had formerly been part of Roe Buck Passage. The individual stores would have deeds of purchase mandating nearly identical architectural constraints for each building. "That each purchaser shall effectively box-out the sea water, against his lot, as soon as the cellar walls are built; and in case of neglect or refusal by any proprietor, it shall be lawful for any other proprietor of a lot, to apply to the Mayor and Aldermen, who after notice to such delinquent purchaser may authorize any of said proprietors to box the same; and such delinquent shall be held to pay for the expense with interest, and the bills in case of delinquent shall be submitted to the Mayor and Aldermen, whose decision thereon shall be final and this shall be inserted among the conditions of sale."[24] Also, the conditions included that no bid be less than $7 per square foot, the terms at 10 percent in cash with a bond secured by a mortgage payable at any period not exceeding thirty years, at 5.5 percent per annum. The purchaser would be required to build, on or before July 1825, a four-story unit according to plans and specifications being prepared by architect Alexander Parris. (In the final plans, this height changed to four and a half stories.)

Two days before the auction, the city sold the two lots separated from the rest of the planned northern block. They were on ground that had recently held the Triangular Warehouse. Each lot contained about 2,500 square feet and they were bought by Samuel Hammond and Nathan Faxon for a total of $32,000. The deeds of sale required that, when erected, these two buildings should match the architecture of the planned northern warehouse/stores, except that they would not be attached to each other. They would be separated by a narrow passage named Conduit Alley. Hammond and Faxon did follow the plans they were given, but because the northern warehouse/stores were still being planned, some design differences ensued.[25]

On September 29, 1824, the first public auction was held at Faneuil Hall and a preliminary design model of the range of warehouse/stores was displayed. Some of Boston's most prominent merchants attending included the textile importers Amos and Abbott Lawrence. These brothers' manufacturing interests created the Merrimac River Valley city that still bears their name—Lawrence, Massachusetts. Of the remaining twenty-three staked lots, seventeen were sold on that day.[26] All of the lots, covering 30,037 square feet, netted the city $303,483.77. The average selling price was about $10 per square foot, a figure considered incomprehensible at that time. According to Mayor Quincy, the auction "greatly increased the popularity of the plan and sanctioned its success."[27]

Between the time the previously purchased properties were owned by the city and the time they were vacated to be demolished, rental income brought in $2,458.42 to city coffers, and interest from these monies deposited in the bank earned $471.28. Thus, the initial revenue derived from all lots sold amounted to $306,413.47.[28] The auction was reported in the local newspaper as follows: "The lots of Land for Stores, connected with the extension and improvement of Faneuil Hall Market . . . were sold in Faneuil Hall (the day being rainy) on Wednesday last, by Mr. Coolidge, of the firm Coolidge, Poor and Head. The lots were 26 [sic] in number. Prior to the sale, Lots No. 1 and 2 were sold to Mr. Samuel Hammond. (to whose land they adjoin) at private sale, for $20.83 [sic] cents per square foot. The others were sold at auction without reserve. The company filled the Hall, and much interest was expressed for the sale. The public cry is that the purchasers are crazy in giving such prices; but it must be observed that the purchasers are among our very shrewd men, and usually know what they are about as well as their neighbors."[29]

When Parris was formally engaged as the architect, the market house design was far from complete in all its details. Encouraged to expand the market house by the success of the September auction, he extended the building to its final length of 520 feet eastward from Faneuil Hall (535 feet including the porticos on each end) and redesigned it to be built of white granite. In less than three weeks, Alexander Parris had completely altered Asher Benjamin's design of the market house and was improving the design of the northern warehouse stores. As Josiah Quincy and his Market Committee constantly altered the designs, Parris refined his architectural renderings with each change, eventually adding columns and a dome. On October 5, 1824, "Mr. Benjamin presented a plan of elevation of the new market house dated

Portrait in oil of Gridley Bryant (1789–1867) by an unknown artist, c. 1825.
Bryant, along with Abner Joy and John Redman, supplied most of the granite for the
market house. Bryant also supplied granite for the Bunker Hill Monument.
COURTESY OF THE BOSTONIAN SOCIETY/OLD STATE HOUSE.

17th. Sept. 1824—in which the lower floor is two feet ten above the pavement—the lower apartment fourteen feet high—the upper eleven feet high."[30] Given the brief time span in which he redesigned the market house from a single-story wooden and two-story stone structure to a raised two-story granite edifice complete with columned porticoes and a central domed pavilion whose ground floor would be above street level, it is evident that Alexander Parris had extraordinary talent.

Not only did Parris bring his architectural proficiency to the development, he also brought excellent workmen and managers like Gridley Bryant, the stone contractor. Bryant reported to Mayor Quincy that the amount of white granite needed to build the market house could only be obtained from quarries north of Boston. The quarries in the vicinity of Westford and Chelmsford, Massachusetts, which he said he had used in some of his other construction projects, could provide the required amounts of white granite. The closer quarries at Quincy, Massachusetts, were already engaged in preparing the granite for the Bunker Hill Monument. They had only enough stone immediately available to build the market's foundation. Gridley Bryant and his associates, Abner Joy and John Redman, who were the stonemasons on several of Parris's prior commissions, were hired to start assembling the market house foundation atop the prepared ground of Boston blue clay.

In order to keep the market house from settling into the newly filled land, Parris was careful to design the foundation to distribute the extreme weight of the building evenly. When constructed, the pyramid-like granite foundation, which ran the entire length of the building, was much wider at the base than at the top, where it accepted the blue granite cellar (supporting) walls, the cellar floor, and the outer white granite block walls of the market house. The blue granite used in the foundation was quarried in Quincy, Massachusetts, and transported by barge down a makeshift canal in Quincy and across Massachusetts Bay by sloop to Boston Harbor, where it was unloaded at the construction site.[31]

Because about eight feet of the foundation was below the mean high tide level, the workmen laying the foundation worked at low tide, in muck. Once the foundation walls were built, waterproofing could begin. It was done in the usual way of that period. The cellar was waterproofed by filling the boxed-out space between the foundation stones and the backfilled earth with wet clay, a cumbersome process necessary to keep basements dry at waterfront locations. Thereafter, workmen were presumably drier.

In November 1824 lumber from Maine began arriving by the shipload. The schooners *Washington, Dove, Fair America,* and *Lavinia* and the sloop *Jones Hale* transported massive quantities of wood for the timber framing of the first floor of the market house. This lumber and other supplies were received on a temporary wharf, Lumber Wharf, and stored until needed.[32]

Since extensive lengths of rope were required during nineteenth-century con-

The pyramid-like foundation design of the market house
(looking from the east end of the building).
DRAWING BY GARY M. IRISH, ASAI, 2002.

struction, the Boston Cordage Company was engaged to provide abundant quantities of hemp rope.

By the end of October 1824, the mayor reported to the City Council that the original intention of widening Market Square beyond Butler's Row could now finally be realized, except for the intransigence of some of the property owners of Nathan Spear's Wharf, which was at the very center of the master plan. Following the death of Nathan Spear (which probably occurred just before the project got started), ownership of Spear's Wharf land had been divided into eighteen parts. Four had settled with the city since June and been issued promissory notes at the appraised value of the property for their proportionate share of ownership. Eleven others were still undecided, but three heirs, representing only three-eighteenths of the property, adamantly refused to sell their portions of the property to the city or even submit to arbitration. Given that the property had realized a substantial increase in its value after the first auction, they wanted to benefit along with the city and sell at second-auction prices.

A frustrated Mayor Quincy said that because of them "it was not possible to place the centre [line] of the Market house in coincidence with the centre [line] of Faneuil Hall, without crossing [their] property, almost in its whole length."[33] His disgust was enhanced by the fact that, on September 30, 1824, the day after the first public auction, he had received a letter from those same three heirs in which they had said they did not intend "to stand in the way of city improvements," and declared their "willingness that their lands should be embraced in the plans adopted, and sold with the city lands, they receiving their portion the average of the sales so made."[34] Presumably they had changed their mind after seeing what people had been willing to pay for North Market footprints. The outraged mayor reported that he had refused to acknowledge this letter and, instead, turned his attention to other matters, which included paying off all remaining conditional contracts necessary to widen the master plan to the south, to Butler's Row. He was not about to allow these private individuals to profit at the public's expense.

Searching for an alternative means to obtain this parcel, the Market Committee recommended employing the extended powers of eminent domain. The City Council, however, was hesitant to exercise its new authority, fearing that a lengthy and expensive legal challenge against these untested powers might ensue. Although Nathan Spear's Wharf had been vacated, torn down, and removed during the summer, the greater percentage of deeded rights was still held by the remaining heirs of the Spear family.

By December, the postponement of obtaining the Spear property so jeopardized the progress of the development that an alternative solution was needed. Determined to outmaneuver the Spear strategy, Mayor Quincy and his Building Committee publicized a substantially altered master plan that called for broadening

South Market Street and abandoning the idea of situating the new market house so that its center aligned with the center of Faneuil Hall.

In this new plan, the South Market Street lots were moved south seven feet and the entire market house was moved north fifteen feet, so that the north wall of the market house lined up with the north wall of Faneuil Hall. This increased South Market Street from 80 feet to 102 feet and, sadly, reduced North Market Street from 80 feet to 65 feet. A defensive Josiah Quincy later described this loss of symmetry as "a circumstance often mentioned with regret, as a mistake, by those ignorant of the obstacles which rendered the present relative position of the market house expedient."[35]

On December 18, 1824, the mayor laid before the Market Committee his "plans of an enlargement of South Market Street, and extending this plan of improvement so as to include all the properties as far as Butlers Row."[36] He also said that "among the circumstances which had a tendency to accommodate and restrict apparent tendencies to the growth of the city of Boston, was the narrowness and crookedness of its streets, and its want of great spaces and wide public squares for the accommodation of the business of the citizens."[37] Once the Market Committee approved of this new plan, the City Council also sanctioned Mayor Quincy's recommendation and instructed his Building Committee to relocate the market's foundation walls accordingly. Under the new plan, the location of the Spear property now stood in the path of the newly widened South Market Street, not the market house itself. This put their old wharf within the bounds of the Board of Surveyors of Highways. Now this crucial property could be legally taken by the preestablished powers of eminent domain for street extension. No new legal ground needed to be tested in court.

When the Spear heirs learned of this maneuver they were outraged. They claimed that harmful injustice had been done to them. They felt entitled to the increased value of their real estate created by the city's public works project. Now their "fair price," like others whose property had been taken by the Board of Surveyors for street extension, was equal to the value of their property when originally appraised.

The new owners of the northern warehouse/store lots were also furious when they learned that North Market Street had been reduced from 80 feet to 65 feet. They considered such action contrary to the faith pledged by the city at the time of sale, and they threatened a class-action lawsuit.

Inundated with protests from the Spear attorneys and the North Market owners, the aldermen questioned the legitimacy of the mayor's reasons for repositioning the market house. They strongly suggested he reconsider moving the market house back to its original position and pay the Spears what they demanded. The mayor did not back down.

On the evening of December 24, 1824, a determined Mayor Quincy convened an emergency session of the City Council to address all concerns for widening South Market Street. He began his delivery by restating the importance of the public's desire for great squares and wide public spaces, which were more vital to the citizens than the demands from certain private property owners. He reminded the City Council how the congested conditions of downtown Boston would be permanently alleviated by this grand new avenue. He continued by reasserting that the creation of Marginal Street across the waterfront bulkhead would provide a new principal route for the businesses between the North End and State, India, and Broad Streets. As such, the previously planned width of South Market Street would be too narrow for the anticipated influx of carts, trucks, wagons, and teams of horses coming from the direction of both Marginal Street and Market Square. The union of the widened South Market Street with both Marginal Street and Market Square would easily accommodate this heavy traffic, though, and it would also provide one great open area by the waterfront to assemble.

The members of the City Council were eager to adjourn for the Christmas holiday and were disgruntled at having to remain late into the evening. Their dissatisfaction was compounded by the fact that Mayor Quincy, who abstained from all forms of alcohol, had yet to state anything new to convince them to accept the new plan to widen South Market Street to 102 feet.

Then, in closing, Josiah Quincy reminded the members of the City Council of the extreme pains and great expense the city had taken to assemble the acreage needed for the current development. More important, if the growth of the city should warrant a future expansion of the market house, then their sons and grandsons, their own "prosperity," would not have to contend with the complex problems and pains of acquiring private property that their city fathers were presently enduring. There would remain open at least one wide, grand avenue to accommodate the expansion of the entire south wall of the market house if it was ever needed. Or, the wall of the market house that ran along South Market Street could be moved over thirty feet the entire length of the building and line up with the south wall of Faneuil Hall while South Market Street remained open as a wide avenue. In essence, it would be a gift for the generations to come.

This last argument swayed the members of the City Council. They agreed with the mayor's observations and voted unanimously to permanently widen South Market Street to 102 feet and reduce North Market Street to 65 feet in width, for the benefit of future generations. Finally the Spear property could be legitimately seized at "fair price" for street extension, disallowing its owners from profiting from the city's public works project by selling at the price set at the second auction, planned for March 1825.

Mayor Quincy was now a in position to fully execute his grand scheme because the last legal hurdles of the extension project had been overcome successfully. He had not even once had to resort to the yet-untested extension of the city's new powers of eminent domain.

Hip, hip, huzza!

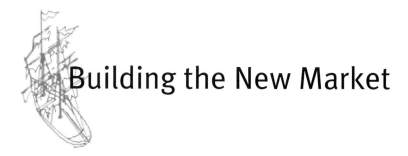

Building the New Market

By January 1825 legal titles to all of the private properties were finally held by the city. Boston's boldest municipal development to date was completely under way, having implemented unprecedented policies for public and private land development. The open competitive bidding for warehouse/stores land parcels and the architectural design controls and the deed restrictions on the use of these properties[1] had never before been executed on such a grand scale. These policies resembled today's private condominium controls, and they proved to be essential initiatives for the uniform renewal of the market district.

The City Council appropriated $150,000 for construction of the market house and scheduled it to be completed by the spring of 1826,[2] the same time the warehouse/stores were required to be completed and open for business. Josiah Quincy worked tirelessly to deliver the extension project—on time and on budget.

He sent out a clear signal that he would not tolerate any further distractions from even the most cunning self-interests. He sought to accomplish 100 percent of his ambitions by reminding everyone involved that they shared one agenda—to finish all construction in record time. Gradually, the project's former nickname—"Quincy's Folly"—changed to a new one: "Quincy's Market."

But as the foundation walls of the market house and most of the North Market stores were finished, as cartfuls of dirt and gravel were delivered for both backfill around the foundations and fill for the new streets, the owners of the northern warehouse/stores remained dissatisfied. They were uneasy over the fact that, after they had made their investments, North Market Street was officially reduced in size by fifteen feet. If that could happen, what was next?

Some of these owners proposed that the market house be widened to eighty feet so that South Market Street would be narrowed to nearly the same width. Others went so far as to demand that "the cellars of the market house, which was now, through its whole length, finished and walled, . . . be taken up and removed, so as to coincide with the centre of Faneuil Hall."[3] In response, "the Committee communicated their determination to proceed with the market house according to the present location and dimensions, unless the City Council should expressly direct [the] removing [of] the cellar walls and erecting the market with the centre coinciding with the centre of Faneuil Hall, and [then] only on this condition: that the proprietors of the north block of stores consent to pay all expenses consequent on such removal."[4] That decision by the Market Committee put the matter to rest, and work proceeded on the off-center market house.

On February 7, 1825, Asher Benjamin abruptly resigned as alderman after filing bankruptcy.[5] Josiah Quincy recalled Benjamin—and his participation on the Board of Aldermen—as "one of its most active and talented members, whose practical skill, scientific acquirements, experience, and great judgment, as an architect, had largely contributed to the success and extensiveness of this important improvement, as he had been, in every stage of the building of the new market house, joined in council with Alexander Parris, the employed architect, in devising and improving its original plan."[6] A week later Mayor Quincy appointed Alderman Caleb Eddy to replace him as a member of the Market Committee.

That same month Alexander Parris submitted renditions of the market house and flanking warehouse/stores in order to establish the amount of granite that would be needed for all three buildings. White granite would be used for the outside walls of the market house and for the front facing of the North and South Market buildings.[7] The Building Committee authorized Gridley Bryant to travel to the quarries at Westford and Chelmsford, to procure the necessary granite and begin floating the rough-faced white granite down the Middlesex Canal so that it would be in Boston by spring 1825.[8]

During the early nineteenth century, the Middlesex Canal provided a faster and smoother alternative to the ox-drawn wagons that traversed the rocky and rutted roads of eastern Massachusetts. Two horses, one on each side of the canal, pulling a packet boat (barge) along the canal, could draw as much as twenty-five tons. The same amount of granite being pulled overland would have required eighty yoked oxen. By this method large allotments of granite could be more easily shipped from the North Shore and as far away as New Hampshire, if needed.

The granite used was from a quarry owned by the Tuck and Reed Company, and was transported down the canal by quarryman Charles Hollis. When it arrived in Boston it was taken "to its terminal at 'Charlestown Mill-pond,' thence across the river to the dam where now is Causeway Street, and through its gates into the 'Boston Mill-pond.' From this they were taken by the old 'Mill Creek,' now covered by Blackstone Street, to the Town Dock, near Faneuil Hall."[9] From the Town Dock, the stone was dragged into the construction site on skids pulled by oxen or hauled in mule-drawn stone carts with labor provided by convicts from the Massachusetts State Prison in Charlestown.[10]

As the granite continued to arrive, the city prepared for its second major auction—for the South Market lots. Held at Faneuil Hall like the first one, it took place on March 31, 1825. It was again conducted by auctioneers Coolidge, Poor and Head.

By this time many shrewd Boston investors were eager to buy lots and erect stores within the city's new market district. The response was so enthusiastic that several investors who had purchased lots at the September auction expressed interest in owning additional lots within the South Market range. Many notable people bid for lots there as well, among them shipping tycoons Samuel and Enoch Train of the Train Packet Line and proud owners of the *Flying Cloud,* the fastest clipper ship of its era; Robert Gould Shaw, one of Boston's earliest millionaires; noted investors Israel Thorndike, Charles Torrey, and Samuel Hammond; and William Phillips, father of Boston's first mayor, John Phillips, and benefactor of Phillips Academy at Andover in partnership with his nephew, Mayor Josiah Quincy.[11]

A newspaper reported that the "lots laid out on the street south of the new market house were on Thursday sold at auction. The attendance of our fellow citizens on the above occasion was very general, and the best evidence of their public spirit, and the utility of the Great Improvement, is to be seen in the sums the lots were knocked off for."[12] The twenty-two[13] lots of the South Market range of warehouse/stores, covering an area of about 33,865 square feet, were sold for an aggregate sum of $403,195.00. The highest price paid was $21 per square foot; the lowest was $10, establishing a greater land value than was expected.[14] The success of these sales assured the owners of the North Market stores that their investment in this development was sound, despite the narrowing of North Market Street.

On Wednesday, April 27, 1825, after nearly two years of planning and negotiating, according to city records, Mayor Quincy deposited a leaden chest in the cornerstone of the market house. The chest contained, among other things, original plans of the area, which showed the Town Dock as it appeared before development and after—with its new market, streets, and stores overlaid with dotted lines; a colored map of the city; the City Charter and the Rules and Regulations of the City Council; a list of the officers of the city and of the wards for 1824–1825; twenty-two newspapers published during the preceding weeks; eight copies of Caleb Snow's *History of Boston*; and a case of coins and currency from the American Revolution. There was also a fifteen-ounce silver plate on which was inscribed: "Faneuil Hall Market, established by the City of Boston. This stone was laid April 27, Anno Domini, MDCCCXXV, in the forty-ninth year of American Independence, and in the third of the Incorporation of the City."[15]

Mayor Quincy assisted in lowering the large block of granite into position at the market house, and he "acclaimed the market to be an ornament to the city, a convenience for its inhabitants, a blessing to the poor, and accommodation to the rich, and an object of pleasure to the whole community."[16] (Coincidentally, the granite cornerstone of the Bunker Hill Monument, designed by architect Solomon Willard, was also laid in 1825. Although both structures were built with granite blocks, the market house was completed and occupied within sixteen months, while the Bunker Hill Monument was still under construction sixteen years later.)

Once construction of the South Market stores commenced, many of the individual sites that were situated on dry land needed their foundations excavated. The Market Committee purchased much of this excavated dirt and used it as fill for new public streets. Some of these streets included Marginal Street, which was extended from State Street across the eastern bulkhead directly to a new unnamed street, one of two streets that now formed the northern and southern boundaries. The entire length of Roe Buck Passage was widened to thirty-five feet and, after it was straightened, incorporated into Merchants Row as the project's western boundary. A passageway was created near the southern boundary and renamed Butler's Row for Peter Butler, who once owned a warehouse at that location. The following week Alexander Parris reported to the Market Committee that when the Old Mill Creek had been redirected along the northern boundary as a ten-foot-wide channel during the summer of 1824, a surveying error had occurred. The conduit came too close to the North Market warehouse/stores building. As a result, the owners laying the foundation walls at the seaward end of the North Market stores were forced to gradually narrow the width of the building to avoid running into the underground conduit.[17]

Between the summers of 1825 and 1826, all three buildings of "Quincy's Market" were constructed concurrently. The market house and the new public streets were built by contractors, independently hired laborers, and state prison convicts— all engaged by the city. The flanking warehouse/stores were constructed by the various private owners, who employed their own builders and workmen. Many workers on the project were specialized laborers, craftsmen, artisans, independent contractors, and subcontractors.[18] At that time hard work, long hours, and low pay were the rule of the day. Except for holidays, a working man toiled from sunrise to sunset all year long, six or seven days a week, depending on his observance of the Sabbath. The single-day holidays included Washington's Birthday, Independence Day, Thanksgiving Day, Christmas Day, and April Fast Day, "a day of fasting, humiliation and prayer."[19] There were no paid vacations.[20]

The principal contractors who built the market house included Lazel-Perkins and Company; Daniel Hastings II, who supplied the multiple window components; and Levi Brigham, who prepared door and window woodwork that would take nearly a year to mill. At the time, windows were usually assembled at the site, within a wall opening, so there were separate invoices for window frames, window mullions and muntins, window dressings, window sashes, windowpanes, window glazing, window oiling, window painting, window weights, window ropes and pulleys, window hardware, and window cleaning. Smith Cobb of Portland, Maine, contracted to provide the extensive lumber needed for the market house. (He had begun delivery in November 1824 on various schooners and sloops.) Henry Wood prepared the dimensioned stone (stone shaped in accordance with the architect's measurements). The ironwork contractors were Adams and Safford; the coppersmith, Charles Tracey; the principal landfiller, Thomas Tilden; and the Boston Soap Stone Company was the builder of the fish benches and meat-cutting counters.

Marketing, during this time, was transacted amid chaos, mostly to the west of the construction area—at Market Square and inside Faneuil Hall and around the Adams Square area. Spectators became transfixed at the sight of nearly four acres of existing land and more than three of newly filled-in harbor, all of which was being developed in this one integrated public and private project. With gravity-defying feats of engineering, long before the age of steam power, the cumbersome granite blocks and wooden timbers were hoisted into place by the Boston and Roxbury Mill Dam Corporation.

After dark the construction site was fenced off and guarded till dawn by night watchmen. This prevented vagrancy, theft, and vandalism. Through the night, the buildings and streets were illuminated with candles or with lanterns fueled by whale oil, their flames ignited by steel and flint.

As construction of the market house became more complex, the city engaged an independent surveyor to verify completion of all construction phases and measure components so that the Building Committee could be assured that the dimensions, quantities, and weights included in their contractors' invoices were accurate. Also, the city began selling back parts of properties previously purchased but not finally incorporated into the project. These properties were located near the northern boundary. They were resold at a profit with the stipulation that any old buildings still on them be torn down and rebuilt to match plans and specifications that would be provided by architect Alexander Parris.[21]

The Market Committee[22] advertised in the *Columbian Centinel* newspaper for bids to supply the market house construction with 600 casks of lime and 600 tons of sand for mortar. Robert Robbins was awarded the contract to provide these materials; he also provided horsehair for plaster and cement. The Committee also advertised for proposals to paint and glaze the outside of the market house's many windows.

Teams of horses and mules were bought by the Market Committee and hired out to private companies as the work intensified and horses needed replacing. Carting earth and hoisting stone remained the most intense work, and the city continued to advertise in the *Columbian Centinel* for more laborers.

The Market Committee voted to start reducing the city's debt. They would use some of the new cash from the second auction to pay down some of the purchase certificates given to private property owners.

Other decisions were made to build a model merchant's stall in the market house for public examination; to contract for stone coving on the best terms; to increase the size of the brick sidewalk on the north side of the market house from fifteen to thirty feet; to lay a brick basement floor; to install copper throughout the building as the means of carrying water from the roof; to build four staircases, all on the south side of the building; and to sink a well and reservoir capable of containing 300 hogs-heads[23] of water in South Market Street. The Committee also voted to commence paving portions of North and South Market Streets as well as Marginal Street with Belgium block, a large, imported street stone, when the brick sidewalks were completed. And the Market Committee voted to hang all of the doors inside the market but voted against having the interior horsehair plaster walls painted. Fireplaces were spaced every seventy-five feet.

The Market Committee decided where to position different types of merchants—near or far from the fireplaces, depending on whether heat would benefit or detract from the sale of their goods.[24] An advertisement called upon "all dealers in meat, vegetables, fish, fruit, and generally all articles sold in the market, who wish to obtain stalls, in the new market, to send in their names to the Mayor, specifying the square feet of floor, they would wish to occupy and for what objects, the location they prefer, the manner in which they intend to have the same fitted up, and whether they wish for a cellar connected with their stalls."[25] The Market Committee also made recommendations on how the interior should be subdivided. "That the fish market be finished according to the Building Committee with the stalls, adjoining the walls, whetstone dado, and tables. That the ground floor of the market house be divided in the following manner. The first section . . . be appropriated for mutton, lamb, poultry and other small meats. In the second, third and center sections for beef and pork . . . or either . . . In the Westerly half of the fourth section for butter; fruit and early vegetables. The Easterly half of the fourth section, and the fifth section for vegetables. The sixth section for fish."[26]

Month after month the Market Committee approved payments of streams of invoices. Additional costs included settlements of properties purchased, referees (mediators) paid in cases relating to properties purchased, and damages sustained because of surrendering leases; legal services in examining titles to properties, serving notices, copying and drawing deeds, and attending meetings as referees; purchasing of remaining lots of land, private ways, and alleys; advertising; night watchmen; surveying; agents representing the proprietors; and Jedediah Blanchard's bill of rum for the workmen, $54.90.[27]

When it became apparent that Marginal Street would not be completely extended to the North End in time for the market's opening, the Market Committee recommended to extend a small bridge spanning the seaward end of Mill Creek and build a temporary street from North Market Street to Eustis Wharf. Although the Marginal Street extension would not be completed for another eight years, there were already plans to increase the length of the bulkhead at a northeast angle into the North End and demolish the wharves behind the bulkhead.

The marketplace development demonstrated large-scale granite architectural techniques more significantly than any other local, state, or national project of that era. Parris had all three buildings constructed with an unprecedented amount of large structural pieces of granite that yielded dramatic simplicity. This was accomplished through an emerging method of construction, often referred to as the trabeated[28] method, which employed granite posts and lintels to create a higher percentage of wall area opened to windows while remaining structurally sound. This style was first used by Charles Bulfinch when his designs called for unobstructed wall openings. Josiah Quincy must have smiled when he read the growing number of positive articles being published about the project.

In an article entitled "A Visit to the Metropolis," written during the summer of 1825, a correspondent for *Boston Monthly Magazine* noted, "A new market is now erecting on an extensive scale, and will be an ornament to the city." Although the market house was only partly completed, the writer went on to say, "[T]he taste, decision, and independence is, of Mr. Quincy, their mayor, who is a man of mind."[29] And in the fall, a New York City newspaper noted its appreciation of the stone used by calling it "that very fine building material . . . all white, or light gray granite from the Merrimac River region." The paper also gave a glowing description of the market house, "obtained . . . from Mr. Alexander Parris, the architect," by declaring, "We consider the edifice, with extensive improvements on both sides of the street, as objects worthy of particular attention, and honorable not only to the City of Boston, but indeed to the United States."[30]

The market house itself incorporated simplicity and strength in a five-part composition that could be traced back to ancient sources. It consisted of the two ends fronted like temples, the long, arcadelike east and west colonnade wings, and the domed central pavilion, which was the largest and most ornate element of the design. The porticoes on each end, consisting of four monolithic tapered columns that supported a triangular pedimented gable, resembled the ancient Parthenon in Athens.

By using solid granite columns Parris avoided the typical stacked circular stone blocks that were sometimes derided as "piled-up grinding stones." Parris later described the columns as "three feet and six inches diameter at base, two feet and ten inches at neck, each shaft in one solid piece, twenty feet and nine inches long with a capital of Grecian Doric. Each column weighing approximately fifteen tons. The columns support a pediment, the tympanum of which has a circular window for ventilation."[31]

These monolithic granite columns, erected at both ends of the market house, were quarried in Westford "with Charles Hollis hewing granite for the pillars of the Market House in Boston from huge boulders found in the north part of the town."[32] One person recalled details on how they were quarried. "I have heard from eyewitnesses the story of the teaming of these columns, eight in number, from the northeasterly part of Westford to Boston by teams drawn by twenty [*sic*] yoke of oxen."[33] And another said, "Persons are now living here who remember to have seen those pillars drawn by oxen through the town on the way to Boston. That was before the existence of railroads."[34] (These sources are probably referring to oxen pulling the granite between the quarry and the Middlesex Canal.)

The shallow dome at the center of the building was modeled after one of the greatest surviving classical buildings in the world, the Pantheon in Rome. This mix of Greek Revival with traditional Roman architecture represented an emerging nineteenth-century architectural trend called Neoclassical expression. Parris's use of the barest structural elements was his reaction against the (American) Federal style of architecture, which was characterized by slender forms and detailed ornament. When completed, the stone construction of the market district was labeled the "Boston granite style," as a particular expression of Boston's emerging commercial architecture.[35] A local newspaper hailed this "new style of building" as "combin[ing] convenience with solidity and proportion: discarding unnecessary show and decoration."[36] Suddenly Boston's architecture had entered its own "stone age."

The market house that was earning such public attention had been constructed this quickly only through constant supervision by Mayor Quincy. By early summer

1825, wooden staging surrounded the market house up to the roof, but the granite construction had come to a halt. The stone contractors claimed that the Westford quarries had yet to excavate the solid granite shafts for the columns and they could not proceed any further with construction. Mayor Quincy acted on his dissatisfaction with the situation. At a meeting of the Market Committee it was voted "that the Mayor notify Abner Joy, John Redman and Gridley Bryant of their noncompliance with said contract, and that their bonds are forfeited; among other things, particularly in this, that the 15th of June has elapsed and the whole of the work up to the intervals of the second floor is not yet complete; and that the City of Boston, took to them for all damages to which they may be entitled in consequence of this, and every other failure."[37]

On August 9, 1825, Alderman Child, superintendent of the Building Committee, and another committee member were dispatched by Mayor Quincy to the Westford quarries "for the purpose of examining the stock and workmanship of the columns intended for the new Market House."[38] Upon examining the situation, the Committee members discovered that not all eight had yet been quarried and that one was defective and therefore rejected.[39] Child sent a letter to the mayor, reporting that "5 of the columns are now done or nearly so—including the objectional one, and 4 will be forwarded immediately for the west end of the market portico."[40] Records note the "rejection of the granite columns [*sic*] by Messrs. Oliver and Boies, [and] concurrent of the defect, specified and stated in Mr. Child's letter on the 11th of August" and that the good columns had "the appropriation of this Committee."[41]

The first four granite columns arrived at the market (by way of the Middlesex Canal; they were then dragged to the site) less than two weeks later, on August 20, and a new contract was made with Warden Thomas Harris of the state prison in Charlestown, under the prison's Stone Works Program, whereby the convicts were engaged to come to the worksite and assist in spinning the columns. Stonemason Henry Dyling oversaw the lathelike process of their boring, spinning, grinding, smoothing, and dressing the columns. On October 22, 1825, the four columns for the east portico were delivered (again by way of the canal), and the lathing process continued.

Once the granite walls began rising to the second level, the market house took on the nickname "the Bull Market," in reference to the intended sale of beef inside, but it was also commented that even a stampede of bulls would be unable to knock the building down. On September 28 the Market Committee voted "That the Building Committee cause the necessary number of Bull's Heads for the ornament of the Market House to be contracted for, forthwith."[42]

The market house's interior sections were consistent with plans of a two-story English market plan dating back to late-sixteenth-century England, but the scale of the construction was unprecedented. The first-floor colonnade ran east-west and was 512 feet long and 14 feet high, with a 12-foot-wide center aisle. Each side of its center aisle was lined with comparatively slender wooden tapered Doric columns. In the middle of the length of first floor, the colonnade opened out into a square pavilion. This pavilion was designed as a market hall; it had larger stalls than those in the wings, which were used to receive and prepare goods sold in those stalls.[43] The wings of the colonnade (each about 217 feet long) opened off the pavilion, providing space for retail merchant stalls.

Most of the spacious second floor above the east and west wings was left unfinished. Above the first-floor market hall, the second floor had an elegant rotunda capped by the dome. (The dome wasn't visible from the first floor in Parris's day.) The rotunda would be used for assemblies.

From the beginning, Parris intended to give customers a view of the length of the colonnade without the usual obstruction of bulky wooden columns, stacks of heavy bricks, or masonry load-bearing walls. To do this, he sectioned off vendor stalls between and slightly behind each set of columns in each wing, and he left the central pavilion uncluttered. Upon entering the market house from its porticoes, buyers would receive a strong sense of perspective, for as they looked down the unobstructed aisle, the columns would seem to recede into the distance. How to support the weight of the colonnade, however, was a problem.

Parris probably puzzled over how to keep this feeling of spaciousness and still keep the cellars open enough to be functional. Since merchants needed space there for preparing their wares and storing extra goods, Parris did not want to crowd the cellars with bulky brick arches to support the first and second floors. Brilliantly, he decided to partially suspend the colonnade from timber trusses, which would run the entire length of the colonnade ceiling, on opposite sides of the aisle.

He designed sixty columns on each side of the aisle (120 columns in all). Forty-eight of these, twenty-four on either side, would each conceal a single, solid

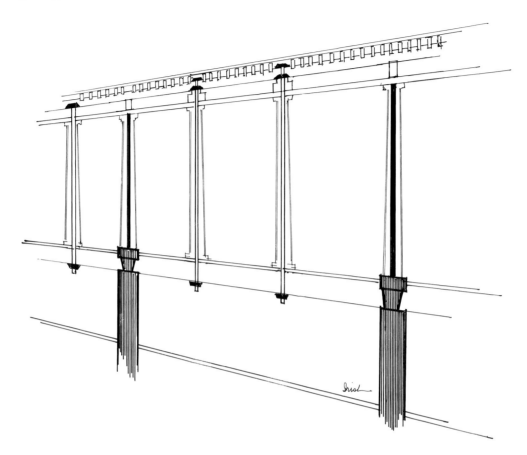

Transverse section of the market house wing and its colonnade's longitudinal section, showing the solid cast-iron compression columns and suspension tension tie-rods before renovation. DRAWING BY GARY M. IRISH, ASAI, 2002.

cast-iron compression post[44] within its wooden casing. Resting atop masonry supports rising from the cellars and up through the colonnade floor, these posts would support the timber trusses running overhead the length of the colonnade and, in turn, support the weight of the second floor. This system would provide stability that was more aesthetically pleasing than the usual bulkier support systems of the times.

The remaining seventy-two wooden columns would also be hollow. They would conceal iron tie-rods, each fifteen feet long, which would attach to the overhead wooden trusses, run down through a hollow column and through the colonnade floor, and be bolted into a cross beam on the underside of the aisle. There would be one such support beam stretching from each of these columns to its facing column. The iron tie-rods would cradle the weight of the colonnade aisle from one side to the other. The combination of iron posts and tie-rods would support the trusses above while suspending the aisle below—fashioning the colonnade into a long bridge within the market house. Parris must have been proud of his imaginative engineering solution to the problem of how to support the colonnade. It resulted in comparatively spacious cellars and a completely open first-floor interior.

The cellars would be raised so that they rose about three feet above ground, giving the market house more height than a two-story building usually had. The sections of cellar between the masonry supports for the colonnade's compression posts were rented out to merchants, each accessed by a single half-height door that led outside. A steep stairway of twelve steps approached each of the cellar doors from the outside, then continued on down to the cellar space. These half-doorways along the length of the market house were interspersed with similarly sized windows.

The most remarkable feature of the market house was the central pavilion and its large double dome, sheathed with copper imported from London[45] and topped with a glassed-in cupola that held a lantern. This section of the market house transformed the building into much more than an ordinary commercial building. Parris's inspiration for the dome came from the circular one on Massachusetts General Hospital, which he had designed under Charles Bulfinch and completed in 1814. The market house dome, though, was oval to reflect more closely the great length of the building.

The pavilion section was approximately one-seventh the size of the whole building—74 feet long and 55 feet wide—but it appeared larger. Its north and south facades had rough-surfaced granite on the first level but dressed and embellished granite on the second floor, which held the rotunda. There were five arched windows at the north and south sides of the rotunda; the middle window of each set was slightly larger than the other four.

Inside, under the dome, the second-floor rotunda's bare plaster walls were designed to naturally urge one's focus upward, at the richly ornamented rosettes and rectangular coffered panels that covered the inner dome up to the small opening that revealed the glassed-in cupola atop the outer dome. Further accenting the scale of the dome and its beauty, the rotunda's large arched windows invited sunlight to brighten the pavilion.

The double dome itself was spectacular. Parris engineered the inner and outer

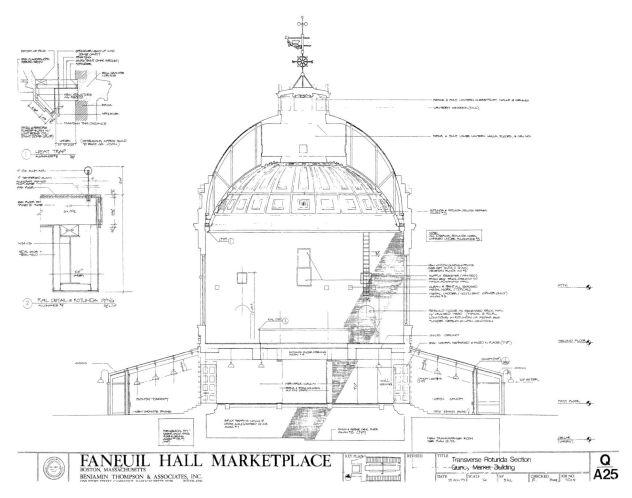

Plans prepared by Benjamin Thompson & Associates for the reconstruction of the pavilion and dome of the Market House in 1975. COURTESY OF JANE THOMPSON.

domes to give the impression that the inside opening of the domed ceiling descended a considerable distance below the opening of the outer dome. In fact, though, they were separated from each other by only a few feet.

In planning the dome, Parris utilized a technique named for its sixteenth-century inventor, Philibert Delorme (sometimes spelled de l'Orme). The Delorme method consisted of using artificial beams as wooden ribs to support the dome. Short lengths of pine planking were laminated in three layers with horse glue, dowels, or spikes to form a light structural beam. These laminated beams were then cut and assembled into rounded fifty-foot arches that acted as vertical ribs for the dome's frame. There were seventy-seven ribs on the external dome, and the internal dome had forty-eight. Laminated framing avoided the need for heavy wooden timbers, allowing the overall weight of both domes to be reduced.

In order for the dome to be evenly supported, Parris had the outer dome mounted on an eight-sided sectional wall built above the rectangular granite pavilion's outer walls. The inner dome was hung from the outer dome by seventy-seven wooden hangers, which were the only structural links between the two domes. The inner dome rested upon a tension ring that received the weight of its vertical ribs but, in doing so, pushed that weight back into its arches, up through the wooden hangers, and into the ribs of the outer dome. The weight being forced into the outer dome was added to the overall mass that gravity pulled down onto the supporting octagonal sectional wall. Hence, the entire weight of both domes was distributed along the sturdy granite pavilion walls.

The elliptical dome, measuring 70 feet by 50 feet, dramatically capped the pavilion with a complete sheath of copper. The dome's oculus (opening) was forty-six feet above the second floor. Through it, an observer in the rotunda could view both the outer dome and the windowed cupola that sat atop the outer dome. This cupola was sometimes called a lantern, for it did indeed hold one, which shone out into the night. Above the cupola, at some point in time, a weathervane in the shape of a bull was added.[46]

At the time there were hardly any tall buildings in Boston, so most people would view the dome only from the ground. From that vantage point, the dome appeared circular, not elliptical, and it was not the main design aspect that helped the market house dominate the larger warehouse/stores on either side. Domination from this viewpoint was achieved by the market house being positioned so that its ground floor was higher than that of its companion buildings, and by its templelike style elements. When viewed from the water, however, which was an essential approach to the market district, the dome attracted attention to the shorter market house. Parris's market house dome was not only effective and beautiful, but also unique to this country at the time and remains so to this day—the only remaining example of a double elliptical dome of Delorme construction in America.[47]

The finished market house was a colossus for its day: 535 feet long (including the porticoes) and 50 feet wide, containing nearly 54,000 square feet on its two floors above the raised basement. The colonnade suspension system, the elliptical dome design, and the solid granite columns had no known precedent anywhere in America and were marvels to both the layman and the professional builder. It was an intent of Parris that the market house dominate the market district. He used many design features to accomplish this, since it was flanked by taller buildings. The market house was positioned on an aboveground foundation, its main floor about three feet above the ground level of that time.[48] Access to the interior market level came from ascending a flight of granite steps at either one of the porticoes or (as far as is known) at one of the pavilion's side entries. This contrasted with the belowground cellars of the warehouse/stores buildings, which were reached by fifteen steps, and their ground-level first floors. The building's dome, its colonnades, and the way its columned porticoes deeply shadowed the comparatively simple entryway also gave the illusion that the market house was a Roman temple. This illusion was intentional, for temples are more imposing than simple commercial buildings like the larger flanking warehouse/stores.

The main approach to the market house was through its ends—which had their four equally spaced solid granite columns, their two arched windows, and their unadorned pediments each with a single central oculus—or through the doors on either side of the stately pavilion. (In the early days, lanterns were attached to the two outer columns of each portico.) Approach to the store units of the flanking buildings was through simpler entries, unit by unit (like a row house). The market house ends with their weighty porticoes certainly caught the eye when compared with the larger, wider ends of the warehouse/stores buildings, which were simpler by far, with comparatively flat wall surfaces and standard, rectangular windows.

Parris added to the dominating look of the market house in other ways too. Because of the building's raised foundation, the windows of its first floor, the floor most likely to catch the eye of the observer, were almost at the same level as those of the second floors of the warehouse/stores. Parris designed these market house windows to be arched at the top, and taller than the arched windows on the second floors of the facing warehouse/stores, so that the tops of the windows on each building aligned with each other. (With the exception of the rotunda, the windows on the other floors of all three building were rectangular.) The warehouse/stores were simple and elegant, while the market house was truly grand.

In late 1825, when the units of the North Market warehouse/stores were nearly finished and the market house and the South Market stores were progressing, Caleb Snow wrote the following in his *History of Boston* (published by Abel Bowen). "[T]he project, which exceeds them all in boldness of design, in promise of publick benefit, and in energy of execution, is that which is now approaching to its accomplishment in the vicinity of Faneuil Hall Market."[49] By February 1826 Abel Bowen, also the publisher of his *Boston News-Letter and City Record,* commented, "However wild the scheme may have been originally considered when the projectors of the New Market submitted a plan to the public, the greatest opposers have become completely convinced on the necessity and wisdom of the plan. We can well remember when the bare idea of a stone edifice of the huge dimensions of the New Market, associated with the thought of making half an acre of land for its site, would have been as novel as a tangible castle in the air; but, it is already accomplished, and it will remain to the remotest generation, a stupendous monument to the energetic inhabitants of a city, preeminently distinguished for its wealth, patriotism, and enterprise." Despite his high praise, he went on to say, "We were at one time disposed to criticize the proportions of this superb structure, and point out those defects which are the most conspicuous; but, on mature deliberation, we are fully persuaded that the appearance of the whole, when completed, will present a very different aspect, and then our remarks will be more particular and extensive. We would merely, however, ask the question, would it not have been better to have three stories, and would it have not been more symmetrical to have wider doors and higher stories?"[50]

By March 1826 it was clear that finding enough of the right stone for the market house was problematic. The stone contractors reported that the quarries in Westford and Chelmsford had reached the point where the massive underground glacial boulders they had been using were exhausted at those locations. Although there was enough granite for smaller pieces, the large white granite pieces needed to complete the market house east- and west-wing walls would have to be quarried from the ledge.[51] The additional time and manpower needed to access the ledge meant that the market house would not be ready to open in May, along with the North and South Market buildings, which were on schedule, ready to open at about that time.

Mayor Quincy became more dissatisfied with his stone contractors. At once, he dispatched two Building Committee members, one of whom was Building Committee superintendent David Weld Child, to travel throughout New England to

locate some matching white granite. Three weeks later they arrived at the U.S. naval yard under construction in Portsmouth, New Hampshire. There they discovered large blocks of white granite that had been recently shipped from the North Shore quarry sites in Chelmsford, Lowell, and Cape Ann.[52]

By April 1826 Mayor Quincy had contacted the naval authorities in Portsmouth, who allowed the Market Committee to purchase their large blocks and slabs of white granite for completion of the market house.

Once the requisite granite was ready to be shipped, Mayor Quincy again contracted with the state prison at Charlestown for labor. This time, guarded convicts would sail to Portsmouth, retrieve the granite, and deliver the stone to Boston via this faster but more expensive means of transport.

A short time later, Gridley Bryant and the other stone contractors were notified that their bond was being called for the second time, and the additional costs incurred for purchasing from a secondary source and for employing the convicts for delivery would be deducted from their contract. Not only had the stone contractors failed to deliver the promised amount of granite, but Mayor Quincy had been forced to pay others to find alternative sources and to deliver the white stone.[53]

The convicts had already been put to work turning the stone columns. After they delivered the blocks from New Hampshire, they were put to work dressing the stone—preparing much of the exterior rough-faced granite to a smoothed and finished state—for such uses as granite coving (recessed designs chiseled out of the stone). Such hand-hammered embellishment was used throughout the market house, especially under the (outside) eaves of the roof. The coving for the eaves was created like most of the other coving: first the rough granite block was reshaped into a right angle to form the cornice, and then it was coved to embellish the design. The roof eaves pieces were chiseled, smoothed, and dressed into precise pieces in order to create a cambered appearance.

In designing the North and South Market buildings, Parris faced architectural problems by not planning a pair of simple row houses with some individuating design feature to separate each unit. His goal was to give the facades a unified look along

Facing page: *View of the market buildings during construction, October 1825.*
Illustration by Gary M. Irish, asai, 2002.

*Measured drawings by Architectural Heritage, 1968, of Faneuil Hall Market, 1826.
Left, elevation of west portico and part of west wing, No. 1 South Market Street;
right, elevation of part of west wing, No. 3 South Market Street, showing an
entrance to the market level.* COURTESY OF ROGER WEBB.

their lengths while simplifying their ends, which were a mere one-tenth of the
buildings' long sides. Ultimately, Parris designed a unit-by-unit motif, which was
repeated along the length of both the North and South Market buildings. He created a series of wide openings, which were especially appropriate for the first-floor
storefronts, and used large elements of granite to help contribute to the uniformity
of the design. On each side of the length of the market house, across the street, stood
the simple windowed granite facade of a warehouse/stores building. The contrast set
off the market house because of its comparative complexity.

The completed North and South Market buildings were four and a half stories
high. A street-level vaulted passageway went through the center of the range of
stores, so a person could get from the rear of the stores to the market house without
walking the length of the building.

Thanks to the granite posts and lintels (the trabeated construction method), the North and South Market buildings' granite facades displayed an unprecedented reduction in the percentage of wall area closed in by stone. Instead, about half the front wall area displayed doors and windows. The repetitiveness of these openings gave a simple unity to the buildings and also resulted in a dramatic increase in open space. (The side and rear elevations of the buildings had a more traditional spacing of windows in the brick walls.) The arched windows on the second level of the

Measured drawings by Architectural Heritage, 1968, of North Market building, 1824.
Left, *front elevation of one store unit, North Market Street;*
right, *rear elevation of one store unit, on what is now named Clinton Street.*
Courtesy of Roger Webb.

North and South buildings' front wall were also trabeated in structure, their rounded window heads shaped by granite posts and wide lintels. (Their arches were at the same height from the ground as the market house's first-floor window arches.) Most individual stores were four openings wide and four levels high. Since there were twenty-three units in the North building and twenty-two in the South building, the length of each facade was unified by nearly a hundred openings at each level. There were no architectural features to distinguish each store along this repetitious facade, but there was a parapet rising between each unit at the gable roof level that culminated at a chimney. A single window dormer extended from the center of each roof section between the parapets. Inside, each unit was separated by an interior brick party wall that aligned with the roof parapets. These walls contained individual fireplaces that provided heat to each level of each store.

There was, however, a slight variation between the size of the units. The central unit (or store) in each building was five, rather than four, openings wide. This accommodated the arched passageway through the stretch of stores. The first and third stores from each end were slightly broader than the rest. The lengths and breadths of the two buildings also differed: the North Market building was 520 feet long and 50 feet wide and the South Market building was 530 feet long and 65 feet wide. The wider South Market building, which was expanded after the purchase of the last private properties along the south border, had an extra stack of windows at its gabled end.

Because all forty-seven[54] stores were privately owned, occupancy of both buildings began occurring intermittently between late 1825 and the spring of 1826 as individual construction was completed. Both buildings contained a variety of merchants who utilized the ground floor with its with decorative storefront for retail or wholesale business. They initially used upper floors for warehouse storage and small offices. They either used their basements or rented them out to needful market house stall merchants.

When individual stores opened to the public, most warehouse merchants sold dry goods. A sampling included feather merchants, candle makers and lamp oil vendors, brass and copper dealers, tanners and sellers of leather goods, tobacconists, cobblers, vendors of curiosities, and sellers of West Indies goods. There were also pewter shops, upholstery and clothing stores, and fashionable boot and shoe shops.

∽

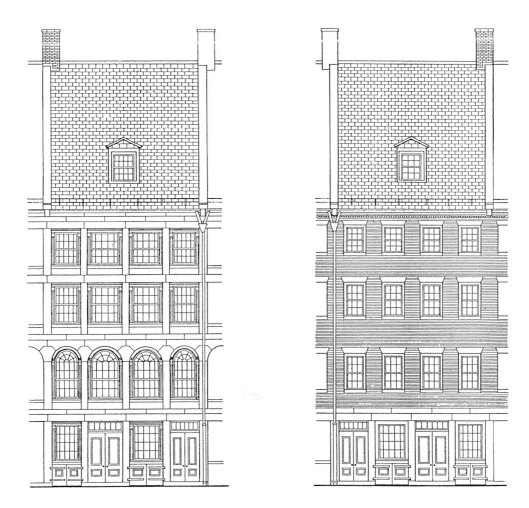

Measured drawings by Architectural Heritage, 1968, of South Market building, 1825. Left, front elevation of one store unit, South Market Street; right, rear elevation of one store unit, No. 16 of what is now named Chatham Street. COURTESY OF ROGER WEBB.

The two parcels sold prior to the September 1824 auction now had a freestanding building on each lot, separated from each other by Conduit Alley. These two struc-tures, situated west of the North Market building (and north of Faneuil Hall), were started before Parris finalized the plans for the North building. They employed the same trabeated granite facade system as the warehouse buildings. But each structure was eight bays wide and had a high hip roof instead of a gable roof with a window dormer.

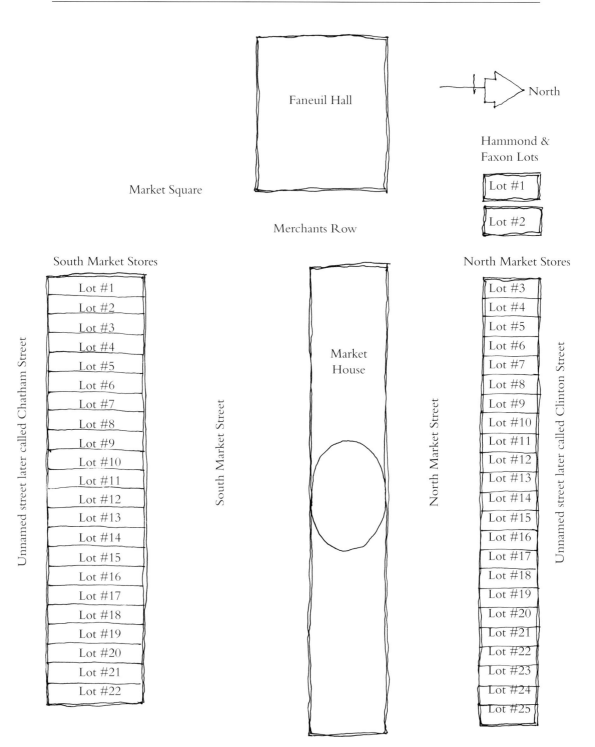

Faneuil Hall

North

Hammond & Faxon Lots

Lot #1

Lot #2

Market Square

Merchants Row

South Market Stores

North Market Stores

Unnamed street later called Chatham Street

South Market Stores
Lot #1
Lot #2
Lot #3
Lot #4
Lot #5
Lot #6
Lot #7
Lot #8
Lot #9
Lot #10
Lot #11
Lot #12
Lot #13
Lot #14
Lot #15
Lot #16
Lot #17
Lot #18
Lot #19
Lot #20
Lot #21
Lot #22

South Market Street

Market House

North Market Street

Unnamed street later called Clinton Street

North Market Stores
Lot #3
Lot #4
Lot #5
Lot #6
Lot #7
Lot #8
Lot #9
Lot #10
Lot #11
Lot #12
Lot #13
Lot #14
Lot #15
Lot #16
Lot #17
Lot #18
Lot #19
Lot #20
Lot #21
Lot #22
Lot #23
Lot #24
Lot #25

Unnamed street later called Marginal Street and later renamed Commercial Street

Before the public works project was completed, thirteen institutions, associations, and private investors contributed funds toward its development. By August 1826, when the last of the buildings—the market house—was opened, the balance of the Faneuil Hall Market stock certificates pledged to previous private property owners had been paid. By the end of the year only City Bank and some private investors remained as stockholders. The thirteen construction and permanent loan lenders included City Bank, the United States Bank, the Provident Institution for Savings, the Massachusetts Bank, the Manufacturer's Mechanics Bank, the Merchant's Bank of Salem, the Fire and Marine Insurance Company, the Suffolk Insurance Company, the Boston Athenaeum, the Bunker Hill Monument Association, the Funds of the Boston School Committee, the Charitable Fire Society, and private investors.[55]

The entire marketplace complex elicited much comment; it was called innovative even before Alexander Parris's drafts were converted into finished buildings. This use of granite posts and lintels was not Boston's earliest trabeated construction, but it certainly was the most conspicuous. The technical achievement of shaping solid granite shafts into smooth and tapered unpieced columns stimulated the public's imagination; published descriptions were careful to provide precise dimensions. The three new buildings that had created approximately 400,000 square feet of new commercial space had also pioneered the use of hand-hammered pieces of granite larger than any used before in New England. The granite was fashioned either into blocks for load-bearing walls or into longer posts and lintels. This repetition of trabeated construction did more than create consecutive, uniform openings for large windows and doors. It set a precedent for future granite construction, and was later observed as a prototype for skyscraper schematics one hundred years later.[56]

By midsummer 1826 the new market house—"Quincy's Market"—was nearly ready for occupancy. The slate-covered gable roof was finished and the hand-wrought copper gutters were installed. All of the multipaned window sashes were glazed, oiled, and painted. The remainder of the streets were covered with bricks, granite slabs, Belgium blocks, and cobblestones. By the time the new market house was ready to be opened, the City Council voted to essentially terminate Faneuil Hall as a market and restrict its use to city offices and a public meeting house. A limited

Facing page: Forty-seven auctioned lots, Fall 1824–Spring 1825.
DRAWING BY GARY M. IRISH, ASAI, 2002.

Faneuil Hall, including the southwest corner of the market house. View is looking toward the northwest. This illustration also clearly shows the Hammond and Faxon buildings just north of Faneuil Hall and the market house, west of the North Market building. Reprinted from American Magazine *2, no. 2 (October 1835), 55.*
COURTESY OF THE BOSTON ATHENAEUM.

number of retail dry-goods spaces on the first floor would subsequently replace the butchers.

During the three years it took to develop the marketplace, Mayor Josiah Quincy clearly presented himself as a municipal leader whose sole objective was the betterment of Boston. Once the grand public works project was completed, his goal to eliminate the chaos around Market Square was more than realized—out of the grim came magnificence. Between 1823 and 1826 he doggedly pursued every aspect of the development by being bold, decisive, and fearless. He showed a talent for knowing when to let things pass and when to press for essential goals. More than a public servant, he was a bricks-and-mortar mayor who was involved in every detail of the project's inception, planning, and completion. Without such hands-on leadership, the Extension of Faneuil Hall project would have never got any further than its proposal. "From the beginning to end, Mr. Quincy was the soul of the enterprise; never discouraged, indefatigable, freely incurring personal responsibility when it was necessary to further the object."[57]

The print's caption reads: "Boston, Faneuil Hall from the east in 1825 by John Stobart."
The date is incorrect since Faneuil Hall Market was not yet completed in 1825. The caption
should read: "Faneuil Hall Market as seen from Boston Harbor when completed, 1826."
Courtesy of Maritime Heritage Prints, Boston, Massachusetts.

Faneuil Hall Market Is Born

Now almost finished, the new market house, between its flanking warehouse/store buildings, more than replaced and expanded the simple Shambles and the overcrowded stalls in Faneuil Hall. The new market buildings on the seven and a half acres the city had developed sat in stately elegance, waiting to support trade. The new, wide streets waited for their first pushcart and wagon vendors, their first crowd of customers. In 1826 the birthplace of Boston was ready to present to the sea and to its citizens an architectural statement of confidence and pride in the city's ideals.

The warehouse/stores were open, as scheduled, by the spring of 1826. The market house, because of the slowdowns in the delivery of granite, planned to open midsummer. But on August 7, more distressing news came in. The Board of Aldermen received a communication from the proprietors at Long Wharf asking leave to have the bulkhead fixed, "in consequence of the bulging out of a part of the sea-wall, recently erected, from the yielding nature of the foundation."[1] This "bulging" at the bulkhead by Long Wharf apparently caused a safety concern by Marginal Street (the street running along the waterfront) and since this was the route the proprietors at Long Wharf were using for access to the market house, opening was delayed until late August.

During these last weeks before the market house opened, however, time was not lost. The docks became lined with chests of teas and spices, hogsheads of rum, bales of cotton, casks of molasses, and other goods imported to Boston by the new merchants. And the stores in the flanking "equally splendid" North and South Market buildings were already doing business, "stocked with supplies from all over the world, its market stalls offering tex-tiles, fabrics, spices, and household wares of every description."[2]

On August 11, 1826, just before the market house opened, an auction of lease bids was held for the stalls not already leased by nineteen former Faneuil Hall stall merchants; each lease would be for the term of one year, transferable only upon the approval of the Market Committee. These terms held less security than the owner-ship opportunities at the warehouse/stores, but the change from the cramped market quarters at Faneuil Hall to the comparatively oversized market house stalls caught the interest of merchants from around the city. Eager purveyors—former Faneuil Hall merchants and new lessees combined—leased the first-floor stalls for a total of $20,000, and the cellars, which now had zinc-lined oaken Eddy chests to keep pro-visions cool, were leased for a total of $5,240. At the end of the year the city's first-year income of $25,240 was applied directly to the project's outstanding debt. The new merchants in the market house who bid for this desirable stall space in August 1826 included Thomas Livermore (stall no. 27), William Hovey (stall 32), Leonard Whiting (stall 18), Joshua Horn (stall 19), Like Forbes (stall 20), Samuel Gay (stall 21), Eben Davis (stall 22), Frederick Weld (stall 23), James Dugan (stall 24), Benjamin L. Summer (stall 25), Bordman Williams (stall 26), O. M. Gale (stall 28), Jared Allen (stall 29), Daniel Chamberlain (stall 30), Thomas Hill (stall 31), Nathan Robbins (stall 33), George Phipps (stall 34), Abel Babcock (stall 35), and F. J. Ripley (stall 36).[3]

On August 19, a local newspaper carefully boasted that the newly built, almost open, market house had been finished "without the intervention, we believe, with-out a single accident, or occurrence, affecting human life. . . . It will be two years, to-morrow, since this extensive and noble work was first commenced; and it is now understood, that the Stalls are ready, and will be occupied on Tuesday next, when the whole market business will be transferred within its spacious walls."[4]

On August 25, the day before the market house was scheduled to open, an India Wharf merchant dispatched a letter to his sister stating, "Put on your best bib and bonnet, then there be ready to take the first stage, so as to be in the city by noon, so as to pass the afternoon in viewing the North and South Market streets and which is the market of all markets on the Globe, which by the by, is to be opened tomorrow on the 26 inst."[5]

Before the market house was ready to be opened to the public, the building had to be officially named. On August 7, 1826, at the request of the City Council,

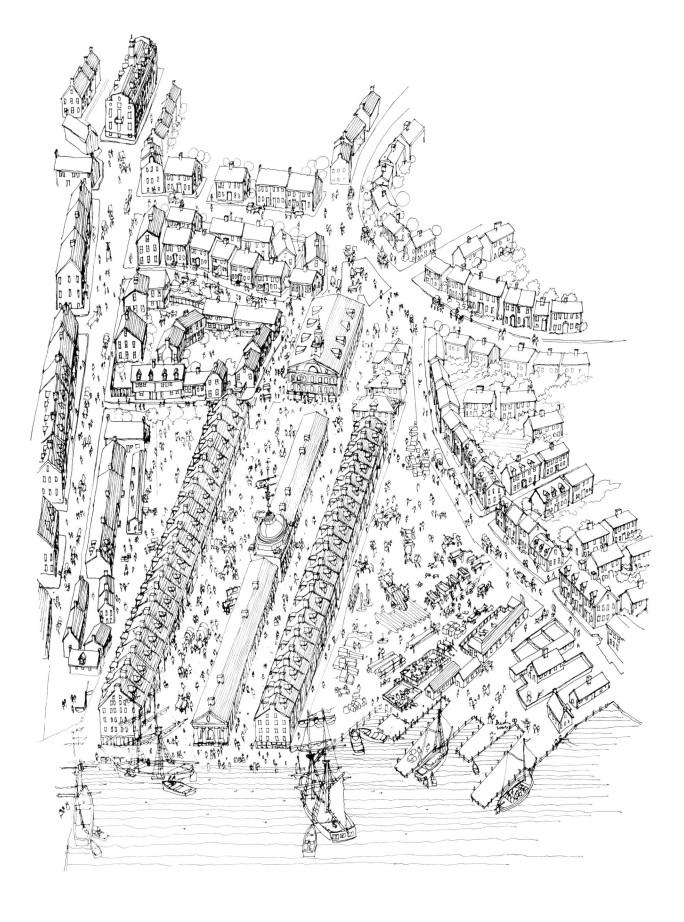

Mayor Quincy read the following prepared statement citing historical continuity and the city's obligation to name the market house accordingly: "The great object of Peter Faneuil, Esq. was to *locate a market* in the vicinity of the Town Dock. For this purpose his donation seems to have been made, and it seems to be due to his memory and to the generosity, which distinguished his original donation, that the market established in that vicinity should be known by the name of 'Faneuil Hall Market'— and that this name of this building called Faneuil Hall shall continue appropriated to that building; This name was given to that building in 1742—and it appears only to be necessary that it should be declared by the City Council that the market established in the new building recently erected to the Eastward of Faneuil Hall shall be known by the name of Faneuil Hall Market—and that a vote similar to that passed [later] in 1761 [to permanently rebuild Faneuil Hall after the destructive fire] be also now passed by the City Council."[6] In response, the City Council voted: "Resolved: That as soon as the new Market House shall be finished and ready for occupation, the Mayor and Aldermen be authorized and empowered to cause a market to be opened therein; to be known and called by the name of the 'Faneuil Hall Market.' "[7]

Early on the morning of Saturday, August 26, 1826, although some of the final exterior construction work was not yet finished, the market bell rang at Faneuil Hall to signal the opening of the new market house. Crowds waited in the rain and fog outside, eager to see what awaited inside. With no opening ceremony, no decoration other than roses and oxeye plants adorning the east and west porticoes, the market house doors opened to the public at the appointed hour.

The only noted event was a scramble among the merchants to have the first sale; Paul Wild from Quincy, Massachusetts, was the successful merchant who served the first customer a leg of lamb.[8] The contented patron purchased his meat from one of the colonnade's 128 stalls where vendors sold mutton, lamb, veal, poultry, venison, or pork. Four stalls sold butter and cheese. Others sold vegetables and fruits, breads and pastries, fish and shellfish. Some purveyors blended their wares, selling salted, smoked, and cured meats. Still others offered a variety of household sundries such as flowers and seeds. Forty-five stalls were reserved for butchers who sold cuts of "honest beef."

Facing page: *View of the completed market buildings, August 1826.*
ILLUSTRATION BY GARY M. IRISH, ASAI, 2002.

After the market house was opened, the *Columbian Centinel* reported, "Faneuil Hall Market was opened on Saturday last. At a very early hour all the stalls were occupied, and filled with the best products of the fields, orchards, gardens and slaughter-houses of our rich vicinity. The stall holders appeared to be highly satisfied with their accommodations, and notwithstanding the abundance brought to market, a very large proportion of it was sold during the day. The avenue of the hall was thronged from morning till night, and many visitors from other parts of the Union expressed much gratification in witnessing the extent and arrangement of this noble institution."[9]

"In the weeks following the opening, the new Market District immediately became congested with the restless energy of bustling crowds as thousands of people poured into the marketplace every day. Faneuil Hall Market was kept very busy and everybody seemed to be in a great hurry to buy the best foods available while they lasted. It also became very noisy outside, with boisterous people, neighing horses, and screeching wagon brakes leaving any chance of quiet for the late evening. But nobody complained because the noise and congestion was a sign of great success."[10]

With Faneuil Hall Market now open for business under its official name, Bostonians, who often prefer to call things other than what they are officially named, acted as though unaware their new market house had a permanent designation. In gossip and asides during its two-year development, those who had derided it had called it "Quincy's Folly." However erroneously, Bostonians now simply called the marketplace "Quincy Market." Mayor Quincy was both honored and amused to have the market house popularly named for him. But he was a man of strong principle who had never approved of allowing mythology to stand in place of factual history within his beloved city of Boston. He always referred to it as the market district or as Faneuil Hall Market.

By November 1826 all of the final exterior construction work was finished on the market house, and the Market Committee finalized all bookkeeping and accounting. They agreed to pay the balance of Alexander Parris's architectural fee—$2,500,[11] paid in increments—but voted to penalize stone contractors Gridley Bryant, Abner Joy, and John Redman nearly $12,000 "and cancel the contract on the part of the City, so as to discharge them from all responsibilities on account of their failures."[12] This left a balance due them of $5,134.80, which the city paid. On November 9 the

Lithograph of Faneuil Hall Market, delineated by John Andrews, published by Andrews and Abel Bowen in conjunction with John and William Pendleton in May 1827. This view was no doubt inspired by Abel Bowen's 1825 view looking toward the west. Andrews, however, introduces two tiers (second and third floors) of round-headed windows in the flanking warehouse facing North Market Street, whereas there is actually only one (second floor). It will be recalled that Bowen in his view eliminated round-headed windows altogether. The seal of the city is below the caption, which might suggest that this was an official view of Faneuil Hall Market.
COURTESY OF THE BOSTONIAN SOCIETY/OLD STATE HOUSE.

superintendent of the Building Committee reported to the City Council that, "all bills and accounts for erecting it, the labor, material and services were paid and the whole concern in a state to be closed."[13] A week later, Mayor Quincy reported to the City Council that the total development cost of the marketplace had reached $1,141,272.33, although everything of a financial nature had proved to be "successful."[14] Of this total cost, $532,797 was recovered from the sale of the lots; additional income from sales of personal property, private property resales, and sales of adjacent lots beyond Eustis Wharf had reduced expenditures by an additional $224,270. The

Engraving of Faneuil Hall Market, delineated by Hammatt Billings, engraved by G. E. Wagstaff and John Andrews, reprinted from Josiah Quincy, A Municipal History of the Town and City of Boston *(Boston: Little, Brown, 1852), frontispiece. The view is looking toward the west. The engraving was probably commissioned especially for the book. Billings captures the bold proportions of the market house with as much success as any artist, perhaps in part because he was also an architect. The original steel plate for the engraving is now in the collections of the* Boston Public Library. COURTESY OF THE BOSTONIAN SOCIETY/OLD STATE HOUSE.

final net expense of the entire project totaled $384,205, when it was originally expected to be no less than $500,000.[15]

Mayor Quincy further reported that the cost of the market house itself was kept within its initial budget of $150,000—it had cost a total of $149,158.75.[16] He indicated that the rental income from the new market house was "adequate to pay, forever, the interest of the debt . . . created."[17] Additionally, the mayor proudly stated that the Market Committee had never taken any credit for paying "for paving streets, opening the Roe Buck Passage, and a street to the Long Wharf, for the general accommodation of the citizens, and particularly those in the North section of the city; nor for any common sewers, reservoirs, pump and well; nor for land thrown into the street to widen Merchant's Row, in front of the new market house and South range of stores. All these, though properly chargeable to the general funds of the city, have been paid [for by] those [benfit]ing from this improvement, and all more than equivalent for any marketable value existing in the dock and square above alluded to, previous to its commencement."[18]

Mayor Quincy continued the Market Committee's final report by saying, "This noble improvement had been completed, not only without any addition to the present taxes or burden to its citizens but also without the possibility that no [*sic*] addition can ever, hereafter, be made to the taxes or burdens of the city, by any of these proceedings and, on the contrary that it has augmented, in no [*sic*] considerable degree, the real and productive property of the city."[19] He concluded by stating, "The success of this undertaking is chiefly attributable, first, to the unshaken firmness and unanimity, with which every succeeding City Council, since its commencement, have pursued and enlarged the original design. —Next, and above all, to the favor with which at an early period it was received by the great body of our fellow citizens in Faneuil Hall, and the encouragement and confidence which they have extended to this Committee, in every stage of its progress."[20]

On November 20, 1826, the Common Council read and accepted the report, then ordered that the same be printed in all newspapers and that seven thousand pamphlets detailing all accounts be distributed to the city's inhabitants.

Finishing streets around the project continued over the next several years. Initially, the city incorporated into the development about seven and a half acres of ground gained—of which nearly four and a half acres were left in the public domain under the market house and within the six new streets. These streets changed names over the years between 1827 and 1834, as intersecting and nearby streets were extended, created, and named or renamed. In 1828 the northern boundary that had been laid out in 1824 (the street north of the North Market building) was named Clinton Street and the southern boundary (the street south of the South Market building) was named Chatham Street. Marginal Street was renamed Commercial Street. By 1830[21] the replacement for the Town Dock was finalized, and City Wharf extended out from the east bulkhead along Commercial Street. Between 1829 and 1833 Commercial Street was extended all the way into the North End. Also by 1830 the last of the lots created in the vicinity of Ann Street further reduced the overall marketplace development cost. A new street, previously called Second Street, was renamed Fulton Street in December 1832, and Creek Street was renamed Blackstone Street in 1834.

During construction, requests had been made to the Market Committee to lease the east and west wings of the second floor of the market house for exhibitions. The City Council had considered occupying its entire second floor with offices, using the rotunda for public assemblies. But now city government decided to remain housed in Faneuil Hall and leave the second floor unfinished until the most profitable and effective use could be determined. In November 1826 the second floor, in a mostly unfinished state, was leased for about three months to its first tenant. The New England Society for the Promotion of Manufactures and Mechanic Arts exhibited and sold American manufactured goods and mechanical inventions. After its initial exhibition, the society petitioned the City Council to use the building again during the summer of 1827, when the space would be finished.

In addition to that rental, the Massachusetts Charitable Mechanic Association held its first fair of domestic manufactures and mechanic arts in the spring of 1828. To facilitate crossing busy Merchants Row, a temporary pedestrian overpass was erected between Faneuil Hall and the market house. People could ascend the stairs on either side of the street and cross safely. The same bridge for foot traffic was also installed during each of the triennial exhibitions that followed.

Later, the Ladies' Fair convened in the east wing of the market house, where Sarah Josepha Hale, an editor and the author of "Mary Had a Little Lamb" and other publications, organized the ladies of the nation to raise funds to help complete construction of Bunker Hill Monument. During the weeklong event the ladies raised more than $30,000 through the sale of crocheted and knitted apparel, homemade jams and jellies, and other handmade accessories.

By now Faneuil Hall Market had become widely popular and one writer described the market scene as follows: "The interior of the Market has always been a scene of attraction to visitors, and a model of its kind. Admirable system and order prevail. Here are sausages in festoons; roasting pig that would have made Charles Lamb's mouth water; vegetables in parterres, and fruits from every clime. Here one may have fish, flesh, fowl, or good red herring. The countenance of those who seek

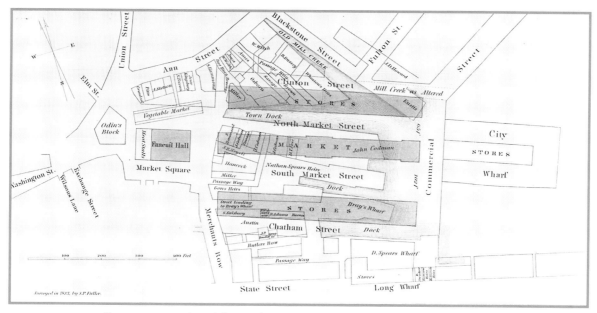

Survey presentation of the Market District, 1852, entitled "Ground Plan of the Market House, erected in 1826." Drawn by S. P. Fuller for the City of Boston.
COURTESY OF THE BOSTONIAN SOCIETY/OLD STATE HOUSE.

their daily food before the stalls is stately. The poor women lingering over the coveted joint far beyond her slender purse is jostled by the dame who is [*sic*] given carte blanche to her purveyor. What quantities we eat!"[22]

While merchants sold a variety of foodstuffs from the stalls inside the market house, the wagon and pushcart vendors were permitted to stand outside, in the adjacent streets, without any charge. Soon it could be observed that "during the busy season it was not an uncommon occurrence to have from 300 to 400 teams on the market limits and adjacent streets, with the produce of suburban farms for sale."[23] Buyers and draymen and farmers with wagons again had the space to sell as they saw fit. Country farmers also discovered that market purveyors were more than willing to purchase all their wares at wholesale. In time, many farmers simply delivered their produce to the storekeepers and the stall merchants rather than spend the day selling retail from their wagons.

While market house merchants sold only foodstuffs, stores within the North and South Market buildings sold all types of merchandise, but mostly dry goods: W. S. Baker sold raw oysters plucked from the harbor beyond the docks; snuffs and cigars were sold wholesale as imported West Indian goods; seasonal clothing, leather goods, hats, and fur wear were sold too. Scattered among the other stores were businesses with strange names such as Fender Maker and Fancy Wireworker, Fired Stoves and Grates, and Bell's Paste Blacking Warehouse. According to his sign, Ozias Gillett sold SEGARS upstairs at 37 South Market Street; and Clark, Brewer and Son sold snuff from a nearby store. Several sail and awning makers ran businesses from the upper floors of the North and South buildings, in close in proximity to the waterfront.

The Hammond and Faxon buildings had a variety of occupants, such as the Franklin Hotel, which remained at the same address until 1856, when it moved around the corner to 24 North Street. Later the Hammond and Faxon buildings housed four tenants in close quarters: the Quincy Market House Hotel, Hovey and Company (another venue for William Hovey), George W. Almy's Clothes Warehouse, and the Agricultural Warehouse and Seed Store.

A small eatery opened on the second floor of the North Market building in 1826. Soon after, the eatery was purchased by three investors: Eldridge Park, who owned a nearby livery stable; John Durgin, a merchant whose family had been in the

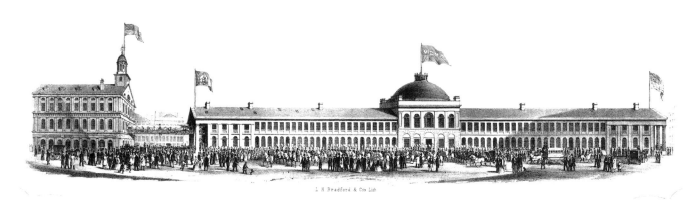

Lithograph poster advertising the Eighth Triennial Fair of the Massachusetts Charitable Mechanic Association, published by L. H. Bradford and Co., Lithographers, 1856. This is perhaps the most detailed and accurate likeness of both Faneuil Hall and Faneuil Hall Market ever published. The temporary second-story bridge facilitating pedestrian traffic between the two buildings can be seen. This bridge was erected for most of the Mechanic Association's fairs, then disassembled and stored after the fair closed for the year.
COURTESY OF THE BOSTONIAN SOCIETY/OLD STATE HOUSE.

restaurant business since the early 1760s; and Durgin's associate, John Chandlier. The eatery was renamed Durgin Park and it served meals mostly to market men and sailors on its long planked tables. Within two years both Durgin and Park died and Chandlier, who continued to operate the eatery, refused to change its name. Over the next sixty-five years, John Chandlier expanded first the menu and the food proportions and then the space he occupied. In order to accommodate the ever-increasing number of patrons who wished to dine elbow-to-elbow with market men and sailors in the maritime tradition, he expanded his dining area to the upper floors of his unit (which had been used for storage), and he also bought two of the adjacent stores and broke through the brick party walls to expand his property.

At the end of 1828, after serving six consecutive one-year terms as mayor, Josiah Quincy was defeated by Harrison Gray Otis. Upon leaving office, Mayor Quincy noted, "The novelty of the office, the diversity of opinions relative to its powers, extensive public improvements, and many new institutions, had rendered his administration one of peculiar trial and difficulty."[24] In January 1829 Josiah Quincy was elected the fifteenth president of Harvard College, where he presided until 1845.[25]

In 1830, city government moved its administrative offices from Faneuil Hall to the Old State House (the Town House that had been rebuilt in 1748). Thereafter Faneuil Hall's upper rooms were used mostly for public celebrations, eulogies, military drills, receptions, and balls honoring distinguished visitors such as President Andrew Jackson and Lord Ashburton.

In 1832 the City Council attempted to rectify a growing confusion between the uses of Faneuil Hall and Faneuil Hall Market. When Charles Bulfinch had redesigned Faneuil Hall in 1805, he had named the greatly enlarged public gallery there the Great Hall. When Alexander Parris designed the new market house in 1824, he denoted the rotunda in the pavilion as the Great Hall. As a result, the Great Hall of Faneuil Hall and the Great Hall of Faneuil Hall Market were often mistaken for each other. In order to correct this situation, and possibly to pay tribute to former mayor Quincy, the Board of Aldermen debated renaming the rotunda Quincy Hall. But after a year of deliberation the proposal was voted down. Thus, neither the market house nor its Great Hall was ever officially named for Josiah Quincy and the confusion about which Great Hall was meant remained. (This inability to make a decision over something to do with marketing seems strangely in keeping with Boston's history of having trouble with decisions about its market structures. It may be kept in mind that 1832 was less than a hundred years after Faneuil Hall was built, thanks to a private person's initiative to overcome voter disagreement.)

During the next fifty years, the Board of Aldermen received a number of petitions to rename Faneuil Hall Market "Quincy Market," since that is what Bostonians had been calling it since at least 1832. But no official action was ever taken to rename it. For the remainder of the nineteenth century, when all three buildings were being referred to collectively, they were called "Faneuil Hall Markets," "the markets" or even "the market-place," but officially they remained Faneuil Hall Market and its North and South Market Street warehouse/stores.[26]

Over the years the marketplace changed with the times. Within five years of the opening of the marketplace, store units in the North and South Market buildings were resold. Some units were merged by taking down the supporting party walls between units and installing overhead cast-iron beams and vertical solid iron Lally columns for support. Market house merchants eventually added awnings along the sides of the building, to expand their market areas.

In 1834 the Mercantile Wharf Corporation purchased the land created by filling in the old wharves north of Commercial Street, beyond Eustis Wharf, and built Mercantile Wharf. From this new wharf the corporation erected three finger wharves and named them Baltimore Wharf, Philadelphia Wharf, and Eastern Packet Wharf. Within ten years another new wharf was built at a right angle to the end of Long Wharf, forming a T, and the three Mercantile finger wharves were extended farther into the harbor, almost meeting the T-shaped wharf. Together, they nearly choked off the waters that led to City Wharf and the marketplace, leaving City Wharf inaccessible to larger ships.

In 1838 the *New York Daily Advertiser* carried a story entitled "A Trip to Boston," in which the writer stated, "We boast, and justly, of our Philadelphia market-house, or rather of our street market-houses; but Boston goes far ahead of us in this matter. I question much whether there is any building of the kind in the United States at all comparable to Faneuil Hall Market. I was particularly struck and delighted with the cleanliness of the stalls, and more especially with the meat benches. Of a Saturday night, when the Market is lighted with gas, it presents an animated and cheerful appearance. It is crowded almost to suffocation by mechanics and other manual laborers, who, with a portion of their week's earnings in hand, are buying, for their wives and children, a few Sunday luxuries. The show of fruits, flowers, and vegetables in this Market is exceedingly beautiful, and not without picturesque effect. In short, the Bostonians may well be content, yea, proud of their market, both in reference to the convenience and beauty of its arrangements, and the excellence of its consumable supplies."[27]

By 1840 a building boom was under way in Boston, and many local builders, architects, and engineers sought permission to use Alexander Parris's models, drafts, plans, and notes on the marketplace as reference for their own projects. None of these could be found at the city offices, however. A year later, William S. Rowson, who had worked as a draftsman under Parris, stepped forward and produced what he said was a copy of Parris's original plans. There were obvious inconsistencies, however, which would lead one to believe that Rowson had drawn his plans from memory, not from Parris's originals. For example, Rowson's plan is labeled "Quincy Market, Boston, Mass., U.S.A.," when, in fact, Parris named the buildings "the new Faneuil Hall Markets." Rowson's drawing had ten doors in each extending wing, but only eight doors actually existed. Parris had labeled the rotunda under the dome "the Great Hall," and Rowson's plan referred to the rotunda as "the Great Room." The second level was actually divided into the rotunda and the east and west wings, but Rowson's floor plan shows that each wing was divided into three separate halls. Perhaps by 1841, the second level had been subdivided into these halls.[28] These plans are valuable, given the fact that all of Parris's work on the project mysteriously disappeared.

In 1842 the city transferred management of both Faneuil Hall and Faneuil Hall Market to Clerk of the Market Daniel Rhodes. He was charged with collecting rents, upholding regulations, and monitoring horse-drawn traffic. Demand for merchant space in Faneuil Hall Market, now located at the epicenter of Boston trade, increased steadily each year.

Twenty years after the marketplace's opening, the city's annual financial statement included comments that its development had completely paid for itself from rentals generated from market house vendors. "Instead of . . . a mistake on the part of Mayor Quincy, the building of the market is the only business operation in which the City of Boston has ever engaged which has proved a financial success."[29] In

Wood engraving entitled "Faneuil Hall Market scene, the day before Thanksgiving," delineated by John H. Manning, and published in Gleason's Pictorial Drawing-Room Companion, 6 December 1851. The text discussing the scene reads as follows: "The reader will need no hint from us to enable him to translate the expressive picture; it tells its own tale of promise as to what is to cover the tables of the good citizens on the following day of domestic jubilee."
COURTESY OF THE BOSTONIAN SOCIETY/OLD STATE HOUSE.

other words, the market house, its adjacent streets, and City Wharf were now considered to be a "gift" to the citizens of Boston.

It wasn't only the finances of the marketplace that engendered appreciation. The market house architecture also proved to be an unexpected model for the emerging nineteenth-century railroad depot. The Maine and Worcester railroad depot in Portland, Maine, and the Boston and Maine railroad station in nearby Haymarket Square were both modeled on the market house. Soon there were also depots in its style in Providence, Rhode Island, and Salem, Massachusetts.

In September 1852 the Board of Aldermen decided to sell City Wharf because of its inaccessibility to larger ships. Josiah Quincy, now retired from the presidency at Harvard, implored the aldermen to retain city control of the property, citing the wharf's importance for smaller ships to the rest of Boston Harbor. Over his objections, the sale proceeded, so Josiah Quincy purchased City Wharf for $411,000 at auction. He then offered to transfer his ownership back to the city if the aldermen would pledge to maintain the wharf and keep it open to the public. The aldermen refused his gesture. Josiah Quincy retained title to City Wharf until his death in 1864.

By about thirty years after the marketplace opened, it was clear that Josiah Quincy's bold plan to build a "mammoth" market district had not been bold enough. With the swell of Irish immigrants, Boston grew to about 500,000 residents. The district again needed more room. In 1853 many store owners at the North and South Market buildings sought to increase the height of their units. Led by Abbott Lawrence, the petitioners appealed to the Board of Aldermen for relief from their deed restrictions, which prohibited any alterations to the exteriors of individual units. Two years later, they were granted permission to alter the facades and to build additional stories on the roof as what they termed full-shed dormers, "provided the owners of all stores would assent thereto."[30] The way had been paved for a variety of building alterations that would diminish the beauty of Parris's granite architecture. By 1866 mansard roofs had begun appearing on additions on the stores at the western end of both the North and South Market buildings. Parris's uniform roofline was no more.

The market house, too, was suffering from use. By 1853 awnings and signs were apparent on the outside walls. And in 1855 the Board of Aldermen entertained a proposal to enlarge the market house by "the addition of two stories, and by widening about seventy-five feet in length of each of its two ends, so as to make them equal in width, and similar in style of finish to the central portion of the building."[31] Pressured by the need for additional space, they used the 1805 enlargement of Faneuil Hall as a legal precedent for such a dramatic alteration to the market house. The Board of Aldermen instructed the Committee on Public Buildings to "procure plans and carry into execution the improvements, provided the cost of said improvements does not exceed $100,000."[32]

The proposal was subsequently defeated with assistance from the city solicitor, who argued in favor of retaining Alexander Parris's original design. "[I]t will appear

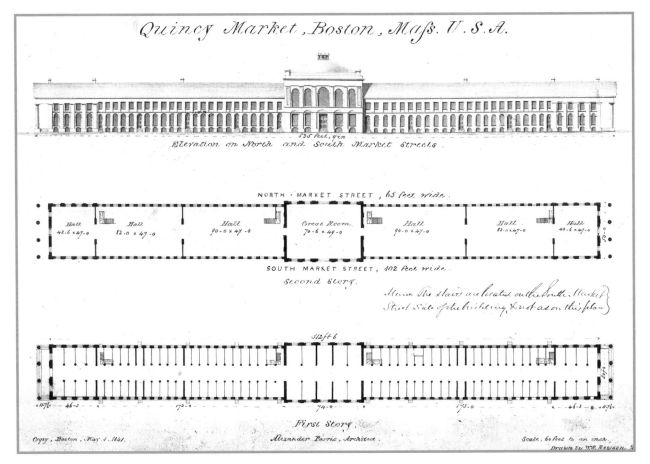

A copy of Alexander Parris's 1824 plans and elevations of Faneuil Hall Market prepared by William S. Rowson, May 4, 1841. As the original Parris drawings were no longer available, this is a most significant document for the study of Faneuil Hall Market. Rowson was a draftsman in Parris's office and probably drew his plan from memory. In 1841 he exhibited drawings and cityscapes at the Third Triennial Fair of the Massachusetts Charitable Mechanic Association, which was held, appropriately enough, on the second floor of Faneuil Hall Market.
COURTESY OF THE BOSTONIAN SOCIETY/OLD STATE HOUSE.

that the plan and elevation of the market house, as it now stands, were adopted by the City Government, at that time, with much deliberation; that all propositions for changes therein were steadily resisted, that the purchasers of lots in both North and South Market Streets bought them with the expectation and understanding that such a building as stands there, and no other, should be erected. Upon these facts, I cannot escape from the conclusion that they established a contract, implied at least between the City on the one hand, and several purchasers of lots in North and South Market Street, and their assignees, on the other hand, that the Market should be built of the dimensions corresponding to the plan and elevation before mentioned, and that it should continue so."[33] The market house was kept to its original size.

The marketplace did take advantage of one unforeseen asset, however, during this time of needing more space—an asset resulting from the unwillingness of the Nathan Spear heirs to sell their wharf to the city back in 1824. By having repositioned the market house off center from Faneuil Hall and by having widened South Market Street to 102 feet, Boston's first grand boulevard now offered priceless room for the growing number of street vendors, vehicles, and customers surrounding the thriving business of the market house.

Also in 1855 the City Council renamed Market Square "Faneuil Hall Square." At that time, shipping traffic along the waterfront had reached its apex, and new wharves were built for the steamships Boston was attracting. More overseas shipping was still coming to Boston than to its ever-competitive seaports of New York, Philadelphia, and Baltimore.

That same year the city expanded its geographical boundaries in all directions, as newly arrived immigrants settled in many different neighborhoods. Many market house merchants shifted their sales from retail to wholesale in response. City records stated that "the Market is now remote from the center of our population, and . . . most of our citizens prefer to patronize provision stores and markets more convenient to their dwellings."[34] This shift did not change the need for more space in the marketplace, however.

For the first time, private investors submitted an offer to the Board of Aldermen to purchase Faneuil Hall Market for an undisclosed sum, presumably because they realized how much money the rentals brought in. The aldermen, recognizing the need of keeping a central wholesale market within the city limits, refused the offer. The city's previous action not to enlarge the market house and this subsequent refusal to sell it established an unintentional precedent for future preservation.

In 1862 the Ames Plow Company, sellers of agricultural hardware, took possession of rooms on the second floor of the market house and hung a colossal sign over the east- and west-end porticos, obscuring the simplicity of Parris's unique granite architecture. At the same time the Boston Produce Exchange moved into the room under the dome and closed off the rotunda to the public. With the Ames Plow signs detracting from the Greek temple look of the building and a private business co-opting the rotunda space, it was now obvious that city controls over the use and appearance of the market house had slackened. From this time forward, the city allowed tenants to disfigure the outside walls with advertising signs and to reconstruct parts of the market house for their individual needs.

This trend had begun even sooner at the warehouse/stores. Both private users and public authority seemed to have lost sight of keeping the marketplace proud, elegant, and orderly.

After the Civil War, food sales at the market house became largely devoted to beef—both wholesale and retail. Livestock from Canada, New York, and the western states was shipped to the stockyards at Brighton, Massachusetts, where the cattle was slaughtered and shipped to the market house. Although this concentration of meat wholesalers and retailers had not been planned, it created the impression of a monopoly. Public hearings were held, and Boston residents testified to "a very general feeling of dissatisfaction . . . with the present facilities for marketing, and with the prices charged for the principal articles of consumption."[35] A study was commissioned, and its report revealed that the market merchants actually had lower prices than competitors elsewhere in the city, and that prices were consistently below those of Albany, New York, and Philadelphia.

In November 1872 the Great Fire of Boston spread from the harbor to Washington Street. It destroyed a total of 776 buildings spread over sixty-five acres in the city's old colonial business district. The markets in the vicinity of Faneuil Hall were spared destruction, but the marketplace's downtown address lost its prestige. The city's "downtown" was rebuilt farther away from the harbor area, in the vicinity of Boston Common and nearby Washington and Summer Streets. Victorian-style designs and nineteenth-century high-rise buildings replaced much of incinerated colonial Boston.

The docks were still being used, however. And in a quest for yet more waterfront land, the city continued to fill in and build around the water. As Faneuil Hall Market and its flanking warehouse/stores had been built on new land between the harbor and the once dockside Faneuil Hall, now the market buildings were separated from the harbor on whose edge they had once stood. By 1872 new buildings

On August 26, 1876, a grand celebration was held to mark the first fifty years of the market house. Here we see a part of the procession that moved through the market house and on to Faneuil Hall. Note that, by this time, signs and awnings were being put on the outside walls of the market house, and the harborfront to the east of the market house was already being filled in and built upon. COURTESY OF THE BOSTONIAN SOCIETY/OLD STATE HOUSE.

stood between the market buildings and the water, and the extended waterfront had a new street, Atlantic Avenue, running alongside the harbor, roughly a quarter of a mile away from Commercial Street. South Market Street was extended to intersect with Atlantic at a harbor defense wall called the Barricado. Part of this project was to fill over City Wharf, parts of Long Wharf, and the Mercantile Corporation's finger wharves so that new streets and buildings could be erected in their place. Quincy heirs, who had inherited City Wharf from the mayor, relinquished the quay under the city's powers of eminent domain. Once Faneuil Hall Market was situated approximately one-quarter of a mile from Boston Harbor, few recalled that it had once been a waterfront reclamation project.

On August 26, 1876, during the nation's centennial celebrations, a semicentennial ceremony was held to mark the fiftieth anniversary of the opening of the market house. Unlike its unceremonious opening on a rainy day in 1826, Faneuil Hall Market was decorated with an extensive display of colors representing nations from around the globe. Two colossal American flags nearly covered both entries of the market house, and all along the colonnade, suspended above every stall, were red, white, and blue banners or streamers, and bunting covered with the stars and stripes.

The grand celebration began with a four-hundred-person procession led by Brown's Band. The parade moved through South Market Street, Merchants Row, State Street, and Commercial Street before entering the eastern end of the market house and traversing the long colonnade to the western portico. The procession then crossed to Faneuil Hall, where another six hundred invited guests were seated for a banquet in the Great Hall. Before the ceremony concluded, Governor Alexander H. Rice stated, "It is not often that any man in any community, or in any country, has so illustrious a record as that which clusters about the memory of Josiah Quincy. All that is illustrious and sagacious as a magistrate, all that is profound as a scholar, all that is patriotic as a self-denying citizen, and wise as a statesman, all that is sagacious and prudent in a business man, he possessed in the highest degree."[36]

The celebration did not save Faneuil Hall Market from being used without regard for Parris's and Quincy's intent. In 1877 the Bunker Hill Monument Association held the last public exhibition on the second floor of the market house. Extensive changes ensued in the following years. The second-floor rotunda and two extending wings were partitioned into offices that were rented to a number of smaller tenants. When the Boston Produce Exchange united with the Commercial Exchange in 1885 and became the Chamber of Commerce, the rotunda was divided into conference rooms. After the Ames Plow Company left the market house in 1909, the Chamber of Commerce divided its second-floor west-end space into twenty-two general offices. The Chamber also created a large assembly hall for stock market quotations in the rotunda and several private executive offices on a new mezzanine floor, which had a rectangular light well, surrounded by a balustrade, built up under the dome.

On November 17, 1879, the area just beyond Dock Square, to the north of Faneuil Hall, was named Adams Square. Sculptor Ann Whitney created a bronze statue of Samuel Adams to be placed there. A distant cousin to President John Adams and outspoken hero of the American Revolution, Sam Adams was positioned with his arms defiantly folded, his back to the sea, keeping a watchful vigil upon his native city.[37]

At the marketplace, seed stores and agricultural warehouses appeared in greater numbers, and produce vendors began appearing in the North and South Market buildings, replacing many first-floor dry goods shops. Some of these produce merchants retained retail stalls inside the market house but others expanded into the wholesale business within their individual stores. "In the fruit and vegetable departments of the market, there are many large and prominent dealers, in both the wholesale and retail departments. To name them for any special character or enterprise would be to name them all."[38]

By now, the market men had gained a reputation for being a jovial, boisterous, and generous group of men who maintained good order and decorum. "The dealers in Faneuil Hall Market have always been most liberal contributors in cases of public calamity as well as to our local charities, which they are constantly invited to aid; for more than twenty years they provided poultry, vegetables, etc., every Thanksgiving for the Soldier's Home in Chelsea in sufficient quantities to furnish them with two weeks supply."[39]

By 1880 the principal merchants of the market house had total annual sales reaching $20 million. They included pork and cut-meat vendors J. P. Squire and Company, C. H. North and Company, and Hiland, Lockwood and Company; beef trade merchants J. V. Fletcher and Sons, J. D. Pringle, Harrison Bird and Company, Ebenezer Holden and Sons, Sanderson, Morse and Company, Severance and Haley, Crosby, Simonds and Kimball; mutton and veal purveyors L. B. Hiscock, L. M. Dyer, Melvin, Williams, Frost and Hilton, who together dispensed from fifty to one hundred carcasses per day; butter and cheese merchants Chamberlain and Company, Hovey and Company, Crosby Brothers and Company, Doe and Chaplin, Morse and Darling, George H. Tinkham, and D. M. Oliver and Company, who together represented some of the more prominent vendors in local and world export; poultry dealers Swan and Newton, Russell Brothers, Lawrence and Company, Robbins, Dunbar, and others who represented the largest dealers in New England; and seafood merchants William Prior Jr. and Company, Johnson and Burns, Walker and Reed, and Knowles and Sons, who all received their supplies not only off the coast of New England but also from as far south as Florida, the interior lakes and rivers, and even from California and the Pacific coast.[40]

By the turn of the twentieth century, the utilitarian steamship had replaced the graceful sailing ships. The status of Boston as a prosperous seaport began to decline significantly with the introduction of numerous railroad lines and the appearance of diesel-powered motor vehicles as means of overland transport. Instead of retrieving goods from the nearby docks, the market teamsters traveled farther and farther from the waterfront to get to the railroad depots in their bulky horse-drawn enclosed wagons.

Newer methods of achieving cold storage replaced the conventional use of block ice. Quincy Market Cold Storage, which initiated refrigeration by means of expansion of cold brine, built a facility near the marketplace in 1882. And the Eastern Cold Storage Company, incorporated in 1898 and located nearby, used the process of direct water expansion to preserve perishable goods. Consequently, marketplace merchants could now ship goods around New England and to distant parts of the country. Food supplies were exported domestically as far as the West Coast and internationally to the British Isles, especially Liverpool and London.

Yet, goods for purchase at the market house remained abundant, too, where anyone could purchase "a pound or a hundred quarters of beef; a pound of sausage or a thousand dressed hogs; a peck or a thousand barrels of apples; a pound or a ton of butter; a dozen oranges or a hundred boxes; a pound or a cargo of fish, fresh or salted; in fact, all and everything required for our sustenance can be secured, in large or small quantities."[41]

Around 1910, electrical lighting fixtures replaced the market house's nineteenth-century gas lighting, and electric refrigeration replaced older methods. The original brick floors inside the colonnade were replaced with oak flooring, and new plumbing was installed. Even though Faneuil Hall Market remained primarily a destination

Facing page: *A busy scene around the market house, 1857.*
Drawing by A. B. Shults. Wood engraving reprinted from Harper's Weekly, *1857.*
Courtesy of the Boston Public Library.

Crowded North Market Street looking west, toward Faneuil Hall Square, 1880. On the left is the market house; on the right is the North Market building. A corner of Faneuil Hall can be seen in the left background. Courtesy of the Bostonian Society/Old State House.

to buy food, the market house also evolved into a popular tourist destination. "Among the many places of interest to which the visitor to Boston is attracted, there is none more popular than Faneuil Hall Market, which, because of its close connection with Faneuil Hall, has become not only a land-mark but a source of pride to our citizens. The sight of three or four hundred wagons loaded with fruits and vegetables, and arranged in a neat orderly manner—the horses having been sent to stables in the vicinity; the competition of the farmers in their efforts to sell their produce; the hustle and hurly-burly of the purchasers who represent the commission dealers, hotel and provision stores, as well as of the poorer classes who are looking for bargains and an opportunity to buy something cheap, is a sight well worth the time of any person who has it to spare."[42]

Crowded South Market Street looking west, 1880. The South Market building is on the left; on the right is the market house; Faneuil Hall is in the background at right.
COURTESY OF THE BOSTONIAN SOCIETY/OLD STATE HOUSE.

Its tourist appeal was not enough to save the marketplace district from collapsing back into the chaos that had characterized Market Square in 1823. Once again, the streets were jammed with masses of horse-drawn wagons and barrows and push-cart peddlers and now, also, motorized vehicles. Adding to the congestion were the hourly deliveries of fresh meats, fish, and produce. Around the market house the stacked crates, barrels, and uncollected piles of trash worsened the scene. It seemed that the once proud buildings were slowly being transformed into a display of commercial indifference. A person viewing the tattered awnings and the tasteless mix of merchant signs would find it impossible to imagine what the district had been like only eighty years before.

When the city's principal fish pier business relocated from the remaining parts

Plan of Boston Proper (the 1795 land of the town of Boston),
showing changes in streets and wharves by 1895.
COURTESY OF THE BOSTONIAN SOCIETY/OLD STATE HOUSE

of Long Wharf to South Boston in 1914, a signal was clearly sent that the market house would not carry its grand nineteenth-century reputation into the twentieth century. Although some seafood merchants remained at the market house, the relocation of many marine businesses to South Boston took away much of the local fishing trade.

The downward trend for the marketplace was hastened by a tragic fire on May 9, 1925, inside the market house. The *Boston Daily Globe* carried the headline: 17 FIREMEN INJURED AS FLAMES SHOOT OUT FROM QUINCY MARKET. The blaze broke out on a Friday evening in the east wing and nearly fifty stall merchants escaped injury as fire swept through the building. Within minutes of the first alarm the streets became crammed with spectators, among them the outgoing mayor, James Michael Curley. The newspaper reported that it was "a spectacular fight" to bring the flames under control and that the fire had caused an estimated $150,000 in damage.[43] The following summer, the east wing was rebuilt and the second floor was again subdivided into a series of offices. More than a year after the fire, on August 26, 1926, the *Boston Daily Globe* carried a small notice nearly hidden among the general advertisements that read: QUINCY MARKET—100 YEARS OLD TODAY. The notice made little mention of the market house's centennial anniversary except to say, "Celebration postponed till September 14–17, because so many officials and others are on vacation."[44]

In September 1926 the centennial celebration began with a band concert followed by tours led by guides costumed in early-nineteenth-century dress. The highlight of the tour was the "Iron Hat" exhibited in the chambers of the Boston Fruit and Produce Exchange on the second floor: "A sign told visitors it was worn by the Mayor [Josiah Quincy] at the opening of the market. One curious person tried to

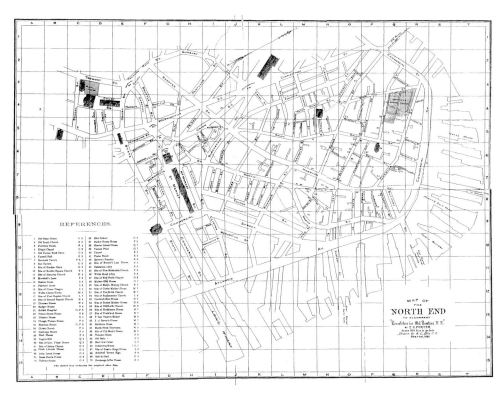

Map of the North End section of Boston showing the distance of the markets from the new waterfront by 1887. The original shoreline is indicated by dotted lines.
Reprinted from Reverend Edward G. Porter, Rambles in Old Boston, New England *(Boston: Cupples, Upham, 1887).*

View of the west end of the market house as seen from Merchants Row, 1880.
COURTESY OF THE BOSTON PUBLIC LIBRARY.

put the silk hat on and then the joke was out. It was really an iron hat, a replica of bygone days."[45] The centennial celebration concluded at the Copley Plaza Hotel, where a banquet was held to mark the occasion. Newly elected Boston mayor Malcolm E. Nichols said of the market house, "It has been a blessing to the community since its establishment and has always been a center of community interest."[46]

For various economic, social, or political reasons, few eating establishments at the marketplace endured. Cottrell's Dining Room first served meals at 16 North Market Street from 1880 until 1888, then moved to 42 North Market Street for two years, and then to 4 North Market Street for about three years. Five years later Cottrell's permanently closed. The Little Market Lunch operated at 2 South Market Street between 1925 and 1930 before becoming a victim to the Great Depression. For a while, Patten's Restaurant operated out of the nearby Hammond and Faxon building, which had been merged into one building many years before, when Conduit Alley had been eliminated. Patten's then moved to South Market. Only Durgin Park restaurant continued to serve food uninterrupted at the marketplace from the time of its opening in 1826.

By 1930 Boston was no longer a major seaport but rather a destination for goods transported by railroad. Even though an extension of the United Freight Railroad Company was located near the market district, rail served the outer-city food distribution facilities better than it did the warehouses deep within the narrow, congested streets of downtown Boston. The Great Depression didn't help the area, either. The warehouses along Commercial, India, and Long Wharves became empty

A busy corner in the market district, 1930. The view is looking north on Merchants Row.
COURTESY OF THE BOSTON PUBLIC LIBRARY.

of their traditional users, so they began housing such tenants as small manufacturing companies or storage firms less well-suited to those nineteenth-century buildings. Many once-thriving Boston Harbor wharves were deserted and left to rot.

Since the marketplace was no longer a principal location to distribute goods from downtown, the city's income from the area's food sales, stall and store rentals, and taxes from real estate and inventories decreased. City agencies, therefore, began cutting the budget for maintenance and repairs at the market house. As vacancies and lower rents spread through the privately owned North and South Market buildings, owners, too, were left without rental income to pay for upkeep. Many individual stores deteriorated. Some were even abandoned.

In 1933, under reelected Mayor James Michael Curley, part of the marketplace development was demolished in an effort to link downtown Boston with East Boston (a fast-growing city neighborhood). Curley's ground plan did not include preserving Faneuil Hall Market and its warehouse/stores. The Hammond and Faxon buildings just north of the North Market building were torn down, allowing North Street to be widened in order to allow access to one of the first underwater tunnels in the country. (The East Boston Tunnel, subsequently named the Sumner Tunnel, was the first of the tunnels Boston still uses to link these parts of the city.) At the time, Patten's Restaurant still occupied the ground floor of the Hammond and Faxon buildings; it relocated to the South Market building.

In 1935 the market house dome, which had been declared to be in need of major repairs, was rebuilt as a project of the federal government's WPA (Works Progress Administration). The dome was partially reclad with copper on the outside, and inside, it was reinforced enough to support a suspended ceiling, which, when installed, completely obscured Parris's adornment of rosettes and coffered panels.

By the late 1930s only ten of the forty wharves built during the nineteenth century remained along the waterfront. They were in hazardous states, their timbers, piles, and planks decaying further with each passing year. Sargent, Lewis, Commercial, Central, Long, and India Wharves still held some original structures, but most were now either abandoned or used only marginally. According to a 1935 survey conducted by the Greater Boston Chamber of Commerce, 90 percent of the waterfront district was now vacant and taxable real estate valuations had declined by nearly 30 percent. "With the falloff of international trade, and the decline of shipping during the Depression years, the port of Boston fell into a critical state. Along the

Merchants Row, which runs between the east side of Faneuil Hall (left) and the west end of the market house (right), looking toward the north, 1900. This is one of the last photographs that clearly show the Hammond and Faxon buildings (center), which were designed by Alexander Parris in 1825 to fit the styles to be used on the market house and on the North Market and South Market buildings. In 1933 these two buildings were demolished to widen North Street and create an entry for what would later be the Sumner Tunnel.
COURTESY OF THE BOSTON PUBLIC LIBRARY.

bridges that ran from Commonwealth Pier to Atlantic Avenue the piers were rotting, the pilings crumbling, the timbers warping, the metal corroding."[47]

The economic downturns caused by the Great Depression and the financial hardships carried through World War II only served to heighten Boston's disregard for its all-but-forgotten downtown waterfront. What assets the city had it used else-

Aerial view of Adams Square and the markets looking toward the east, 1929. The statue of Samuel Adams and Faneuil Hall are in the foreground, in front of Faneuil Hall Market. Note how the north wall of the market house aligns with the north edge of Faneuil Hall as a result of the land controversy in 1824 between the City of Boston and the heirs of the wharf's owner, Nathan Spear. Photography by Aero Scenic Airviews.
COURTESY OF THE BOSTON PUBLIC LIBRARY.

where. For more than thirty years not a single substantial new structure was built along the harbor. Many warehouses, particularly those adjacent to the North End, were eventually destroyed by fire. Other original buildings were gradually torn down because they were abandoned, or seen as obsolete or as prime targets for arson. The foundation holes left by many of these historic buildings were filled in and black-topped, and this process slowly altered the landscape of the once proud waterfront district.

After World War II, the population shifted to the suburbs. No major produce was being farmed within ten miles of Boston, so even city people were forced to look beyond the city for fresh-grown foods. Widespread vacancy now defined the marketplace buildings. Streets that had been crowded with the hurly-burly of horse-drawn wagons and pushcart peddlers were now used by refrigerated diesel trucks, which spewed polluted exhaust upon the remaining merchants. The white granite walls of the market house and the white granite facades of the warehouse/stores that had not yet been covered over or removed for "better purposes" now became blackened with soot.

In 1948 the Massachusetts Department of Public Works initiated the Master Highway Plan for the Boston Metropolitan Region, which included an inner belt expressway and the elevated "Central Artery." Snaking its way through Boston between North and South Stations, the Central Artery made a tight turn at the east end of the North Market building and included an access ramp from the market district. This elevated "green monster" severed the waterfront district from the rest of the city it once served. It also, in a sadly appropriate way, darkened the neglected area below its path and filled it with the hollow buzz of vehicles passing it by.

Two years later, the U.S. Department of Agriculture probed conditions at the deteriorating market house and found the colonnade and stalls to be incurably obsolete, inefficient, and unsanitary. The study reported that the market house still housed half of Boston's wholesalers but that its food handling was double the average cost of other wholesale markets around the city. The USDA recommended that the city establish a new food distribution center in nearby South Bay and close the market house.[48]

At about this same time, the last remaining merchant who had leased stall space since 1826 left the market house. For more than 120 years, Hovey and Company, purveyors of butter and cheese, had remained at the marketplace, first as a retailer until it closed its retail business in 1948, then as a wholesale distributor operating from a North Market store until 1950, when it left for the suburbs.

Part of the decline of the market district had to do with how Boston was coping with its (lack of healthy) growth. During the mid-1950s, it became apparent that Boston's reluctance to erect towers was part of the reason why the city was lagging behind other American cities. This reluctance was partly due to late-nineteenth-century zoning laws that restricted new buildings to the same, or lower, height as

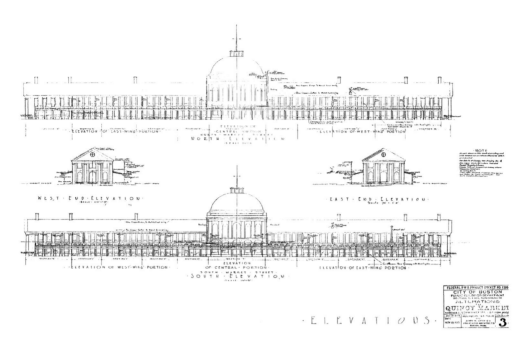

*The oldest surviving plans and blueprints of the market house. These were drawn
for the City of Boston, 1933 and 1934.* COURTESY OF DEPARTMENT OF NEIGHBORHOOD
DEVELOPMENT, BOSTON PUBLIC FACILITIES DEPARTMENT.

those already built. These laws were partly the result of the lobbying of old-family
real estate interests in the city's commercial market. They had objected to taller, more
modern buildings that would deprive their own shorter, older structures of the precious city light, thus undermining their value. But the laws were also there because
insurance companies and fire departments had considered high-rise buildings a
menace since the Great Fire of 1872. Slowly, Boston began to see that other cities
were forcing them to leave the past behind.

The market operators didn't help fend off the decline, either. They had not
shifted focus as population and business areas changed. By the mid-1950s the marketplace was generally considered a nuisance. Most of its original vendors had moved to
other quarters beyond downtown and the remaining merchants had failed to provide
enough variety of wholesale or retail goods to keep business thriving.

As the city ownership of the market house and the private ownership of the
North and South Market buildings allowed the marketplace to deteriorate, the citizens' historical appreciation of the area's architectural significance began to fade. The

marketplace was seen simply as obsolete, serving no profitable purpose in the modern world. Any thought of preservation, with its endless reconstruction process, was considered an impractical burden on the city's taxpayers. The old market district, then, slowly evolved into a blighted area.

The waterfront district reached its nadir when, in the early 1950s, the buildings of Charles Bulfinch's elegant India Wharf were demolished for a parking lot. Given that India Wharf had been seen as a prime example of historic commercial revitalization (it had been part of Mayor Quincy's presentation to get approval for building his own marketplace) and given that Faneuil Hall Markets had become less useful and more neglected in this Boston struggling with the present, many Bostonians assumed that the buildings of "Quincy's Market" were the next to be torn down.

7

Quincy's Market: Decline and Survival

By the 1950s what had once been a model of forward-looking urban planning was now a dank collection of modified warehouse/stores that gave off the unsettling odor of rotting fish, flesh, and fowl from uncollected trash. Market men in their blood-spattered smocks still carried sides of beef through its streets, but now no one cleaned up the trails of blood and the gobs of suet they dropped along the way. On any given day the remains of produce, meats, and other foodstuffs lay strewn across the gummy asphalt that now partially covered the old brick and cobblestone streets. With few merchants left to protest to city officials and with little attention by city sanitation crews, rats moved in, in droves.

Faneuil Hall itself was old enough and had hosted enough history in Boston's eyes to merit being preserved as a historic landmark. It could also still be used for retail sales on the ground floor and assemblies on the second. The marketplace, though, seemed more valuable for its land than for any of its buildings, especially the warehouse/stores along North and South Market Streets.

Alterations begun in 1855, when the Board of Aldermen eased deed restrictions on architectural changes, had gone unregulated for nearly a century. Thanks to the haphazard building and rebuilding of the store units, the once pleasing line of Parris's sturdy gable roofs was now a mishmash of full-shed dormers and flat-roofed additions. The original black slate shingles sat alongside inexpensive asphalt shingles and tarred patches. Much of the

144

once-uniform granite facade was now covered over—or completely removed and replaced—with pressed metal, colored plastic, vinyl, aluminum, mismatched bricks, or other makeshift materials. These changes were more than just unappealing. Poor-quality workmanship and inadequate maintenance had allowed the elements to ruin much of the interiors. Timbers were rotting and the basements were flooded. Some of the store units had even been partially or totally torn down. Of the original forty-seven individual stores in the Hammond and Faxon and the North and South Market buildings, forty-three remained and less than 10 percent were occupied.

Conditions at the market house, which had fewer tenants each year, were no better. Basement meat-cutting rooms were grossly unclean and subject to tidal flooding because the original wet-clay waterproofing for the foundation was no longer effective. The building was lit with bare lightbulbs; the plumbing was obsolete. There was no central heat and much of the cooling equipment was on direct current, which caused intermittent blackouts when overloaded. The walls along the colonnade were caked with years of unwashed grime and soot. Some of the columns were cracked, exposing the tie-rods or compression post within. The ever-present sawdust that covered its floors, a reminder of bygone days, was no longer kept fresh. It lay in bloodied, soggy, moldy clumps throughout the building. Prospects for the building's use as a market in the future appeared doubtful.

While some business continued at the market house, many of its merchants, seeing no future at the downtown marketplace, had moved to larger and more efficient locations. Some had relocated to city neighborhoods such as South Boston, Dorchester, Roxbury, and nearby Newmarket Square, or to some of the closer suburban areas like Chelsea. Others had become part of regional chains or national concerns that took over more and more of their own procuring, preparing, and even packaging. The importance of the independent city food merchant had diminished, thanks to a new suburban catchword: *supermarket*. Despite cheaper rents at the marketplace, the cacophonous hordes of merchants with their wagons and barrows and pushcarts and trucks quieted. Semitrailers and refrigerated trucks rumbled by on the Central Artery but rarely had business to do in the market district. More and more of Mayor Quincy's and neighboring market district buildings were being boarded up.

The market district wasn't the only city area in trouble. The decade also saw other city businesses flee to suburbia. As noted Boston historian Thomas O'Connor indicated, "Downtown industrialists were merely following the national trend when

A historian of singular distinction, Walter Muir Whitehill was affectionately known as "Mr. Boston." Between 1955 and 1976, Walter Muir Whitehill raised public awareness of the importance of saving Faneuil Hall Markets.
COURTESY OF THE BOSTON ATHENAEUM.

they located their new electronics firms and high-tech agencies outside the city, along the approaches to Route 128[1] and closer to the younger work force that had moved to the suburbs during the fifties. But this major relocation of human resources and capital investment cast further doubt on the ability of the downtown area to recover its financial viability and confirmed the prevailing image of the city's schizophrenic economic culture."[2] The financial district, which was just outside the market district, was still thriving, as were insurance companies, which had built closer to the Back Bay. The masses of daily commuters who filled these and other office buildings by day, however, quickly retreated to their homes in the suburbs by night. They had no desire to buy food while in town. Of all the purveyors who had been on Faneuil Hall Market property in 1826, only Durgin Park remained.

Surprisingly, some Bostonians were found to have a sentimental attachment to the markets. The first announcement of their historical significance came from the historian and director of the Boston Athenaeum, Walter Muir Whitehill. He tried to get the mayor and the Boston City Planning Board to agree, commenting as early as 1955, "Bostonians still buy their victuals straight from the carcass, without the dubious embellishments of cellophane. The historical continuity of life in Boston is nowhere more genuinely represented than in the stalls of Faneuil Hall Market. Today, as always, the butchers who man the stalls are reliable men, jealous of their reputation for furnishing goods of high quality, and proud of their location."[3] But city officials like the presiding mayor and members of the Planning Board were not impressed enough by the markets' historical significance because, at the time, urban renewal was focused on the demolition of whole districts or buildings that encompassed whole neighborhoods such as the West End.

Yet it was apparent to Whitehill that the markets had reached a critical point in their long history. He pointed out that even the barbarism done to their architecture had failed to completely obscure their original appeal. If time and tradition meant anything to native Bostonians, he said, the buildings should be saved and brought back to life. The only thing worse than their wretched appearance was the public indifference toward their present condition. His voice went largely unheard for some time. The historians who agreed with Whitehill were also unsuccessful in getting the attention of city officials or the media. The attitude of those who controlled Boston during the 1950s was "out with the old, in with the new."[4]

It is almost ironic that Boston is considered one of the most historic cities in the United States. It had lost many of its historic buildings to the past, especially during that period when the city spread first outward and then upward. During the nineteenth century, most city and state governments did not consider protecting historic Boston buildings as essential, especially when such structures stood in the "way of progress" (new streets, new landfilling, new developments). "While the durability of institutions was loosely expected to ensure the permanence of the buildings they occupied, it did not necessarily follow that protecting the buildings was a particularly high priority."[5]

After the property devastation caused by the Civil War in southern American cities, small groups of civic-minded people began to privately preserve buildings historically linked to the past rather than erect a monument in their place. In Boston, in the late 1800s, this attitude gained wide attention when, in 1863, the home of the American hero John Hancock, situated atop Beacon Hill, was sold and torn down. The loss of Hancock House, as it came to be called, created such controversy that it became "a pivotal event in the history of American preservation."[6] Bostonians were now aware of the importance of preserving such landmarks, especially in a city filled with reminders of its past.

In 1869 administrators of the congregation of the Old South Meeting House on Washington Street decided they could no longer maintain their 140-year-old church. They thought it easier to sell it for demolition and relocate to the Back Bay. The Old South Meeting House dated back to Puritan times: patriots had donned their Indian guises there before turning Boston Harbor into a giant teapot and, when the town's selectmen found their Faneuil Hall space too crowded in the late 1700s, they had sometimes chosen to meet at the Old South. When the church's administrators' decision was made public, members of the Boston community stepped forward and gallantly fought to preserve the building. They were led by educational reformer and philanthropist Mary Hemenway, who anonymously offered $100,000 toward overcoming legal obstacles and financial encumbrances, and to charter restrictions of its preservation. Clearly, "Bostonians had gone beyond regretting the loss of urban landmarks to try saving one."[7]

Before the 1870s were over, the group had purchased the church and converted it into a museum. "The success of the private effort to save the Old South, coming after the failure of both state and city governments to save the Hancock House, set a precedent of privatism that defined the New England preservation movement for generations."[8]

Also facing the threat of extinction by the 1870s was the nearby Old State House, which was then touted as an obstruction to street widening. This building (originally the Town House) stood near the scene of the Boston Massacre, at State and Court Streets. From the time city government had moved out of Faneuil Hall in late 1830, the Old State House housed city government for nearly a decade.[9] Later, in 1840, the building was entirely leased by the city without property restrictions to commercial tenants, who, predictably, defaced its outside walls with crass business signs and wore down its interior through lack of care. In the 1870s investors from Illinois attempted to buy the building so they could disassemble it brick by brick and reassemble it as a tourist attraction in Chicago.

But preservation efforts at the Old South Meeting House had set a precedent. In 1879 members from Boston's community came together and formed the Boston Antiquarian Club, which later was reorganized into the Bostonian Society. After bitter debates at city hall and scathing newspaper editorials against saving the aged building, the Bostonian Society overcame overwhelming odds to gain control of its management. By 1882 they had restored the landmark and the Society was given custody of the upper memorial halls; the city occupied the lower levels. Through this successful effort, preservation gained more public recognition in the minds of Bostonians. The concept of preserving historically valuable buildings labeled "no longer useful" was growing.

The Faneuil Hall Market buildings did not seem likely ever to be placed in this category. By 1956 the Boston City Planning Board (BCPB) claimed the markets were beyond any feasible use.[10] "The city planning board gave up all hope of renovation and designated the area for wholesale clearance to make way for new buildings."[11] Before this was initiated, however, Mayor John B. Hynes issued a directive for the BCPB to resurvey the area. The Cambridge-based consulting firm of Adams, Howard and Greeley had spoken of the historical significance of the area. They had pointed out that the nearby Blackstone Street block, which still held eighteenth-century pre–American Revolution buildings, and Faneuil Hall gave a colonial atmosphere to the market district, as did the last remnants of the markets themselves. In response, Mayor Hynes proposed that redevelopment be considered.

In conjunction with the Greater Boston Chamber of Commerce, the BCPB then recommended a reclamation plan for the entire area that would cost between $9 million and $13 million. No funds were ever budgeted by the city, but Walter Muir Whitehill furthered the cause to save and preserve the markets by speaking with local historians, preservationists, and the media. He commented, "In spite of recent efforts to popularize American history, the past to many Americans still means only a shadowy period beyond their own memories when people wore funny clothes and men sported whiskers and wigs. Thus many visitors to Boston, and some residents of the city who should know better, fail to understand the historical significance of the market stalls on the ground floor of Faneuil Hall and in the adjacent granite market house built by Mayor Josiah Quincy in 1826."[12]

On a national level, the 1950s brought a growing interest in the urban renewal of American cities with aid from the federal government. As early as 1949, the National Housing Act tried to help address the failure—of both private enterprise and local governments—to reverse the deterioration of many of the nation's inner cities. Recognizing the limited financial resources most of these cities had, the federal government began to underwrite two-thirds of the cost of replacing such areas through its Department of Housing and Urban Development (HUD). And in 1954 the program was expanded to include rehabilitation, in response to criticism that federally funded clearance and rebuilding programs were creating new slums faster than old slums were being eliminated. Later, program amendments gradually loosened requirements that properties receiving grants be predominantly residential. Increasing assistance was given to commercial concerns.

When John F. Collins succeeded John Hynes as Boston's mayor in 1960, he was determined to make urban renewal the centerpiece of his administration. He immediately launched into realizing his ambitious "New Boston" campaign promise by hiring as his chief consultant the development administrator of New Haven, Edward J. Logue, who had overseen that city's urban renewal efforts since 1954. Logue was to become the key in realizing Collins's vision.

Collins also began working on the other part of his campaign promise: to reorganize the Boston Redevelopment Authority (BRA), which had been established in 1957 to oversee Boston's urban renewal programs. He quickly discovered that, of the sixteen BRA employees, not one was a development planner, architect, engineer, or social worker.

Despite this lack of expertise (or maybe because of it), the BRA had focused on strengthening ties between the city and its suburbs. Mayor Collins and Logue would soon dramatically reverse this approach by attempting to capitalize on some of the city's natural assets—its ancient street patterns, its abundance of historic sites, and its compactness. Although a total of ten urban renewal projects were being made part of Collins's "New Boston," the greatest emphasis was placed on three downtown locations: the proposed new Government Center, the central business district, and the waterfront district.

Mayor Collins asked Logue to accept the directorship of the BRA. In 1961 he did so on one condition: that he be given a much broader set of powers than all of the previous directors. In particular, he demanded complete autonomy in all urban renewal decisions and broad powers to reorganize the BRA. Despite such extreme demands, Edward Logue was appointed the BRA's first development director with the endorsement of the business community, the trade unions, and Boston's three major newspapers. Logue, a sometimes controversial but always energetic reorganizer, abolished the Boston City Planning Board and absorbed its duties, powers, and staff into the BRA. He then created four new divisions within the Authority: Planning, Project Development, Land, and Operations. He also cultivated federal support by developing a close relationship with the regional HUD office for New England.[13]

In terms of BRA funding priorities, the marketplace ranked well behind the sprawling new Government Center and the expansive restoration of the waterfront itself. The markets, however, had something in their favor: They were located between these two projects, so not addressing their redevelopment could jeopardize the success of the other two. As Mayor Collins commented, "Introduction of new general businesses, institutional, office and residential uses which serve to upgrade the area and create an active pedestrian link, maximizing pedestrian protection under unfavorable weather conditions, between the Government Center and the Waterfront are to be encouraged."[14]

By the end of 1963 the BRA had completed its first study of the marketplace. It addressed all the issues that plagued the buildings and then recommended they not be redeveloped. The expense to acquire all the North and South Market stores, relocate the food merchants still using them, and completely restore all three buildings was so costly, it said, that it would have to charge rents too high for new merchants. The report called for a radical change: Clear the area for modern, sanitary buildings. The report did include a glowing description of the buildings' architecture

Photo of the South Market store units in deteriorating conditions.
COURTESY OF FREDERICK "TAD" STAHL.

and history, however, and this intrigued Ed Logue enough to reject the study's recommendation. Its analysis of the specific short-term economic benefits of demolishing the buildings and building a high-rise between Government Center and the
waterfront district was inconclusive, he thought, so he asked the BRA to sponsor a
second study to examine more closely the options for preserving the buildings.

As a result of the second study, a brief hearing was conducted before the
Boston City Council on May 16, 1964, in which BRA representatives recommended the retention all three buildings, but without any food dealers.[15] The report
contained no advisories or ideas about how to use the market buildings once they
were vacated, nor did it suggest improvement to the markets, but it did save the
buildings from being razed.

The next month the City Council legally authorized the BRA to seek federal
assistance from HUD for the acquisition and reconstruction of the North and South
Market stores. This change in attitude was a result of Walter Muir Whitehill's address-

ing the Council, with BRA officials present, about the importance of preserving the area. Whitehill appraised the market complex as "one of the principal ornaments of Boston, and perhaps the finest architectural composition of the period surviving in the United States. Those who care for the historic associations of Faneuil Hall could not do better than to insure the restoration and permanent preservation of the noble setting that Mayor Quincy provided for it."[16]

The entity that legally allowed the BRA to seek federal assistance for the marketplace was the Downtown-Waterfront Urban Renewal District, which was already on the list of federally approval sites.[17] In conjunction with the City Council initiative to seek federal funding, Ed Logue approached leaders from Boston's business, legal, real estate, and preservation communities to form the Faneuil Hall Markets Advisory Council. The council's mission was to do another study and then develop a real estate and marketing strategy for the grossly underutilized and rapidly deteriorating markets. Under the direction of the BRA's waterfront project director Robert Litke and city planner–designer Robert Loverud, this study would focus upon preliminary costs to restore and convert the market house into a general retail sales facility. The study would also consider whether the North and South Market buildings could feasibly be converted into commercial or office space, or residential apartments, or as a last resort, simply be torn down. The study would be used in the proposal to HUD for federal funding.

While this study was being prepared, two concerned Bostonians simultaneously approached the BRA, each unaware that the other intended to privately explore the possibility of rescuing the markets and also unaware that Walter Muir Whitehill had already started a preservation initiative. Architect Frederick "Tad" Stahl and developer Roger S. Webb first met independently with Litke and Loverud at the BRA, and both showed interest in exploring how the nineteenth-century architecture could be adapted to twentieth-century uses. Stahl already had extensive building experience in Boston. Besides being director of the Beacon Hill Civic Association, through his business, Stahl Associates, he had designed and initiated the thirty-four-story State Street Bank and Trust Building, financed by a Boston-British joint venture that virtually started the downtown office building boom. Roger Webb had redeveloped Old City Hall under a long-term lease with the city, and his architect, Samuel Mintz, was well respected for his work for the city at the waterfront district.

The two men were introduced and they formed a team. They were both con-

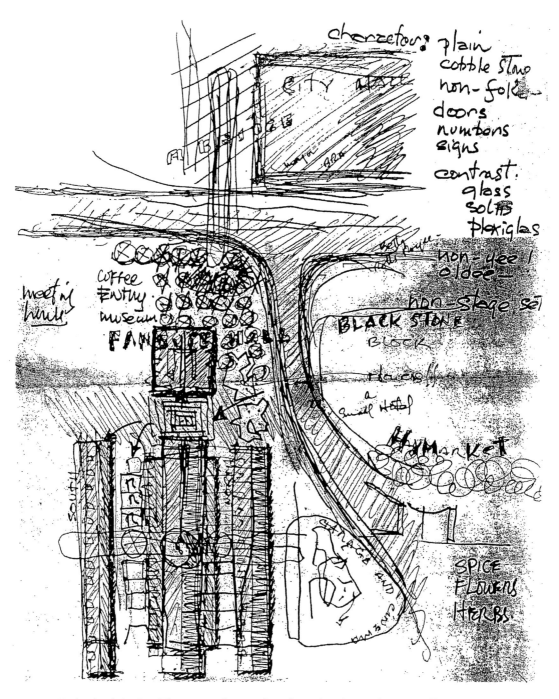

Early sketch by Ben Thompson of Faneuil Hall Marketplace and City Hall site, c. 1964.
COURTESY OF JANE THOMPSON.

vinced that, in order for the area to become usable again, a complete preservation program would be needed. They both thought it essential that the architectural beauty of this valuable survivor of Boston's early commercial life be recaptured. Once they offered to do a study independent of the Faneuil Hall Markets Advisory Council's, the BRA halted the advisory council's study. Instead, BRA staff would work with Stahl-Webb.

At about the same time, a redevelopment proposal was made to the BRA by architect Benjamin Thompson and his wife and business partner, Jane Thompson. According to Jane Thompson, her husband had developed a deep interest in seeing the buildings find a new life. "Ben walked down, explored the deserted streets, and saw the desolate physical condition of a once beautiful, vibrant place. He was saddened by the neglected condition, but as a devotee of street markets in Europe and Scandinavia, he immediately saw future possibilities of revitalization. He was hooked."[18]

His proposal suggested a mixed-use revitalization plan that would incorporate the markets as they physically existed at that time. As Ben Thompson later noted, "I presented Logue with a site plan, a space analysis, and a series of plans and designs showing how the buildings could be organized for a mixture of commercial, office, and—as we then hoped—residential use, around the traffic-free pedestrian streets."[19]

Director Logue was hesitant to move too quickly. The offer of Stahl and Webb to do their study seemed worth waiting for. But Thompson's proposal looked good too. Logue decided to engage the Arthur D. Little Company to review Thompson's proposal. Unfortunately for Thompson, they concluded that the "small-tenant, mixed-use concept would never fly."[20] Therefore, Logue sanctioned the gesture from the Stahl-Webb team to initiate a feasibility study focusing upon the area bounded by Chatham, Clinton, and Commercial Streets and Merchants Row. This action allowed the BRA to postpone a final decision and stave off frequent public arguments advocating that the site be cleared and devoted to high-rise office towers or some alternative low-rise use.

The Stahl-Webb feasibility study was done under the auspices of two nonprofit groups: the Society for the Preservation of New England Antiquities and the Architectural Heritage Foundation (Webb's not-for-profit group, whose board members by this time included noted historians and preservationists such as Walter Muir Whitehill). For the next six months, Stahl and Webb met with BRA officials, White-

Proposal sketches of rebuilt Faneuil Hall Markets area, 1968. Drawings by John Hagan for F. A. Stahl and Associates. COURTESY OF FREDERICK "TAD" STAHL.

Proposal sketch of Faneuil Hall and the market house, 1968. The previously demolished Hammond and Faxon buildings as proposed are included. They were not restored in the final renovation project. COURTESY OF FREDERICK "TAD" STAHL.

hill, leaders of the Boston business community, and allied professionals to conduct the study that they hoped would end in a recommendation for a comprehensive redevelopment plan.

Both Stahl and Webb firmly believed that a casual rehabilitation effort was unacceptable and that a long-term restoration program was the only solution. A key element of their vision was to restore the original roof lines and granite facades of the North and South Market buildings to their 1826 appearance, thereby maintaining their historic validity and that of the market house. They felt that Alexander Parris and Josiah Quincy would have approved of such an extensive rescue. Tad Stahl believed that a restored marketplace could provide a downtown area for pedestrian activity centered on a viable community of retail stores, offices, and apartments. He wanted the area to inspire the same civic pride Americans had in their great public monuments. He had seen this occur with public squares in other American cities and throughout Europe. He hoped that the redevelopment would include closing all the surrounding streets to traffic and converting the entire marketplace into its own historic district, which he termed a "restored civic monument."

Between 1966 and 1968, Stahl and Webb proceeded with their research by examining the details of the deplorable conditions at the markets. They quickly discovered that some North and South Market owners had cut away supporting timbers to relocate floors, destroyed much of the granite facades to install multilevel refrigeration units, and allowed their mechanical and utility systems to become grossly deficient. Vandalism was rampant and damage resulting from years of neglect was worse than anticipated. For example, the foundation walls had not been re-waterproofed since 1824 or so, and when the tide rose, some basements filled to a depth of five feet. Floating in the water they found not only debris but dead rats.

Walter Muir Whitehill contributed to their study. By now he had the attention of city officials and the media and was being affectionately called "Mr. Boston." In a personal letter to BRA director Logue encouraging the revitalization of the markets, he said, "As this group of buildings constructed by Mayor Quincy was one of the great efforts of city planning and rehabilitation of the early 19th century, it seems to me an ideal spot to begin a piece of work under the Demonstration Cities Program. If it could be carried out, it would be as likely as anything to gain national recognition. Certainly the result of such a project in furnishing a setting for the new Government Center would be incalculable."[21]

By 1968 the first edition of the five-volume Stahl-Webb feasibility study was completed under its abbreviated name, *Faneuil Hall Markets Report*.[22] The *Markets Report* documented the historical significance of the entire marketplace and presented redesigns and planning proposals for the buildings based on detailed drawings Tad Stahl had made after figuring what the original design had most likely been. The study cited examples of successful urban renewal projects in other cities that had preserved major historic landmarks instead of employing the wrecking ball. In

San Francisco, there was the $10 million rehabilitation of Ghirardelli Square and the Cannery—a prototype for similar mercantile projects around the country. In the view of Roger Webb, Ghirardelli Square in San Francisco was a good model for the preservation of Faneuil Hall Markets.[23]

It also included an outline of leasehold guidelines, which utilized the concept of a master ground lease encircling this district. The concept here was that the BRA, which was already funded for urban renewal projects, would buy all the properties to be included in the district and then hold a master ground lease for the district from the city (the market house and nearby streets). Under this master lease, one developer would be designated to hold a sublease with the BRA to all of the grounds of the marketplace in order to redevelop and maintain control of the complex in its entirety. Both the developer and redevelopment plans would have to be approved by the BRA, and the ground lease would be written in accordance with those approved redevelopment plans. Once completed, the designated developer would be responsible for marketplace management, and would have the right to sublease space to individual tenants within the complex. Income from the potential rentals of the retailers, offices, and other forms of tenancy would be used to make payments on the ground lease to the BRA. "Given the times, cities that wanted a shopping center downtown had to put together big assistance packages to make developments attractive."[24]

After agreeing with the study's analysis, the BRA adopted most of its recommendations and decided to seek a Historical Preservation Grant from HUD aimed at publicly assisting a private developer. Instead of selling portions of the property or renting sections of the buildings to the designated developer, the BRA decided it would buy properties that were held privately, whose owners would agree to sell, and initiate a master lease on the property held by the city, so it (the BRA) could offer a long-term ground sublease to the developer, who would also act as the managing company. Ground rent would be paid by the developer to the BRA in lieu of standard real estate taxes. "Instead of following the typical urban renewal assistance formula and selling the site at a below-market price, leasing offered the city an additional benefit: payments would not have to be returned to Washington as would proceeds from a sale disposition."[25] Creating the lease would depend upon the approved redevelopment plans and would take quite some time, however, as the legalities were complex.

Photos showing the deteriorated conditions at the second floor of the market house, 1970.
COURTESY OF THE ROUSE COMPANY.

Photos showing the deteriorated conditions at the second floor of the market house, 1970.
COURTESY OF THE ROUSE COMPANY.

As Roger Webb explained, "The feasibility study commissioned by the BRA concluded that the markets required a subsidy of $2 million to $4 million dollars of exterior renovation and site work to make the project potentially profitable enough for developers. I was aware there was up to $90,000 per building facade funding available from the Federal government under Title I, but was initially discouraged in assuming the three market buildings would only generate $90,000 per building, or $270,000 of funding. Later, realizing the North and South Markets actually comprised approximately 50 common wall units, I realized perhaps up to $4.5 million of Title I facade funds might be secured to make the project feasible to for-profit developers."[26]

When John Collins declined to seek a third term as mayor he was succeeded in 1968 by Boston's forty-fifth mayor, Kevin H. White. Kevin White saw Boston through younger eyes and vowed to complete Boston's urban renewal programs, beginning with Faneuil Hall Markets. "Perhaps of most immediate concern to the mayor was the unsightly Faneuil Hall market area, its narrow streets congested with delivery trucks, broken-down pushcarts, and piles of debris, which lay in all its embarrassing ugliness directly beneath the windows of his shiny office in the new City Hall. 'It was an eyesore, right in front of me,' said White. 'If you can visualize the expanse of window in my office as a mural, it was a mural of despair.' "[27]

This was an instance of nearly repeated history. A scene of decaying wharves and of blighted areas around Market Square and the Town Dock had similarly greeted the newly elected Mayor Josiah Quincy in 1823 from *his* upper-floor office window—at Faneuil Hall. Kevin White later said of this comparison, "My view was obviously more sweeping than Mayor Quincy's. I had an incredible window that gave me a view of the whole market area in one sweeping glance. . . . At the time it was the only view of the markets that you could get at a complete glance."[28]

In the fall of 1968 the Webb-Stahl *Markets Report* was presented to Mayor White after the BRA established a fund of $600,000 for infrastructure improvements supported by a grant from the state. On November 25, 1968, Mayor White went to Washington with the report's plan to reintegrate the markets into the community and save the buildings from extinction. He personally lobbied HUD for federal funds. If approved by HUD, the marketplace project would be the largest single city, state, and federally assisted preservation effort to date in the country. "My presence in Washington was to make clear that it had a highest priority to the mayor of Boston. The highest priority,"[29] White later said of the trip.

Photos showing the deteriorated conditions around the market house and South Market building, 1970. COURTESY OF THE ROUSE COMPANY.

In January 1969 HUD appropriated $2.1 million toward the Historical Restoration Grant during the last four days of Lyndon Johnson's administration. The funds were obtained by using the *Markets Report* and with the assistance of several people: HUD Assistant Secretary for Metropolitan Development Charles Haar, Senator Edward M. Kennedy, House Speaker John McCormack, and House Majority Leader Thomas P. "Tip" O'Neil. The $2.1 million grant was restricted, however, to stabilizing the buildings and to restoring the exteriors of the North and South Market buildings to their 1826 appearance. The funds did not apply to the market house. This federal funding was only a portion of the then-estimated $10.6 million it would cost to entirely restore all three buildings.

On July 1, 1969, the BRA and the Public Facilities Department (PFD) of the City of Boston, whose director at the time was Robert T. Kenney, contracted with Stahl-Bennett Architects (a business Stahl and Bennett formed in 1967) and Architectural Heritage (Webb's for-profit development business) as a joint venture to conduct architectural, engineering, and consulting services at the North and South Market buildings. Throughout the remainder of 1969, the Stahl-Webb team initiated exploratory surveys, drafted plans, and proposed detailed renditions for preserving the buildings. Their examinations came up with several surprises. First, the superstructures of both buildings were remarkably sound despite the deplorable conditions. Second, the load-bearing capacity of the upper floors in most of the North and South Market stores could sustain an incredible 300 pounds per square foot.[30] This meant that it could possibly cost more to tear the buildings down than to restore them. Tearing the structures down would take so much labor and equipment that a wrecking company would have difficulty making a profit from the salvage. The biggest surprise was the discovery that the pyramid-like design of the foundations resting upon a layer of Boston blue clay had apparently succeeded: The buildings had hardly settled at all on this filled-in waterfront location.

There were small signs that a pulse was still beating in the marketplace. The Boston Flea Market set up temporary stalls and exhibitions along South Market Street on Sunday afternoons. Mondo's Restaurant, a unique all-night truck stop located on South Market Street, was still serving hefty portions at moderate prices. The fabled Durgin Park restaurant was still providing old-fashioned New England Yankee cuisine with a side order of local legend. And adjacent Blackstone Street and Haymarket Square hosted the traditional pushcart vendors as Boston's last open-air market.

In January 1970 the Stahl-Webb joint venture presented its surveys and final plans to the BRA. The BRA, however, was becoming more involved with complex problems in contiguous projects and any decisions regarding the marketplace project were put on hold. In particular, it was working on how to remove the nearby access ramp to the Central Artery in order to provide better access to the Commercial Street end of the site and to expand a nearby parking lot. (Later a parking garage would be built upon this lot.)

The public's lack of understanding for the delay in moving ahead with the redevelopment created problems for the BRA. Many Bostonians, members of media, and visitors to the city complained that the marketplace project seemed plagued by inertia. Perhaps they thought it would always look like a ghost town. In response to this criticism, in May 1970 Mayor White announced a $14 million restoration program to convert the markets into a unique six-acre historic district. In the announcement, the mayor said to the media, "Without question, this is the most single historical site in the city."[31] The project would be started in the fall, he continued, and the construction would take two years. He made sure that the *Boston Globe,* the *Boston Herald,* and the *Christian Science Monitor* carried headlines about his announcement. Later he explained some of the nontechnical reasons for the delay in the project: "It wasn't until 1970 that my presence as mayor was taken seriously . . .

Existing conditions around the market house, 1970.
COURTESY OF FREDERICK "TAD" STAHL.

and the market [could become] one of my priorities. But at the same time the uncertainty and disruptions in the public sector were without question creating competition that made it more difficult to get the project moving. We had had protests and demonstrations against the war in Vietnam that ripped Boston apart, so there was this sort of destructive emotional force in the city. It was an atmosphere where if I said I want to do something about Quincy Market right now, the response was, are you crazy? There's a riot going on at Boston Common."[32]

On September 22, 1970, the BRA put out a developer's kit that outlined how it wanted bids (which were officially referred to as requests for proposals, or RFPs) made on restoring the markets. Specifications included that the redevelopment program be completed in time for the city's 1975–1976 bicentennial celebration. Bids would be due by the end of 1970.

In January 1971 Robert "Bob" T. Kenney, who had directed Boston's Public Facilities Department, was named BRA director after Logue and several other interim directors had come and gone. The markets were still a major issue, as they had been since the USDA had issued its advisory to abandon the market house in 1950. Fortunately, there was no time limit on the two-year-old HUD grant. Although an extensive amount of paperwork had been completed, there was still no visible sign of progress toward reopening the markets.

Feeling the pressure of rising costs, diminishing federal funds, and constant reminders from the mayor's office to be ready for the bicentennial celebration, Director Kenney made restoration of the markets an urgent priority. "To the outside world," he later explained, "it appeared that the BRA was not progressing with the project. In truth, it was a complicated situation that never seemed to move along as fast as it should. The project was so extensive that one must consider the Authority addressing the continuing problems of acquisitions, merchant relocation, demolition, utility reconstruction, legalities, feasibility studies, and further engineering, architectural, and survey studies. There was also the obstacle of removing a ramp to the elevated state-owned Central Artery as part of the overall process. Not a single day went by that work was not being conducted on the project by the Authority."[33]

By the time the BRA was ready to accept RFPs, the Authority had, during the ten years, acquired forty-two of the forty-seven original stores that constituted the North and South Market buildings. The three stores in the North Market building that were still owned by Durgin Park restaurant remained exempt under a previous agreement with the BRA; two others (the merged Hammond and Faxon building) had been razed in 1933 to widen North Street (to make room for the Sumner Tunnel) and would no longer be part of the development.[34] This was progress, but the BRA's ownership of the North and South Market buildings was not enough. The city owned the market house and surrounding streets, and the BRA needed some kind of total control to make the final redevelopment possible.[35]

Before making the developer's kits available, the BRA had decided that redevelopment would proceed in strict accordance with the 1968 five-volume *Markets Report*, which had included both Tad Stahl's architectural drawings of what Parris's buildings had most probably looked like and a recommendation that the BRA execute a ground lease with a developer, who would then subcontract and manage the redevelopment privately. Various city agencies and their lawyers were working on the contract, as it seemed the only way to meet the project's goals. "First, the city wanted to keep the historic buildings under public ownership and retain control over the project's design. Second, the city offered the deteriorated markets in 'as-is' condition and the high cost of interior rehabilitation in addition to the expense of the downtown land had to be borne. Third, a historic landmark preservation mandate imposed design constraints on any private developer's attempt to adapt the structures to the conventions of 20th century retailing."[36]

On July 1, 1971, the BRA took a major step toward rebuilding the markets by designating the development team of Van Arkle and Moss, which planned to use R. M. Bradley and Company as the management company, George B. H. Macomber Construction Company to build, and Benjamin Thompson and Associates as architects for the entire restoration project now estimated at $16 million.[37] Their submitted proposal kit on how they would rebuild and manage the marketplace was accepted by the BRA on the condition that if the BRA's strict deadlines were not met, the BRA would revoke their designation. Terms and deadlines included a firm commitment for financing within one month, execution of initial construction within two months, and 25 percent of the space leased within three months.[38]

Seven months later the BRA's designation of Van Arkle and Moss as developers was rescinded. The developer had failed to comply with the agreed-upon timetable despite an additional grace period of four months. Van Arkle and Moss claimed that its failure was a result of difficulty in obtaining financing from Fidelity Mutual Company of Philadelphia, and that this difficulty was caused by the BRA's

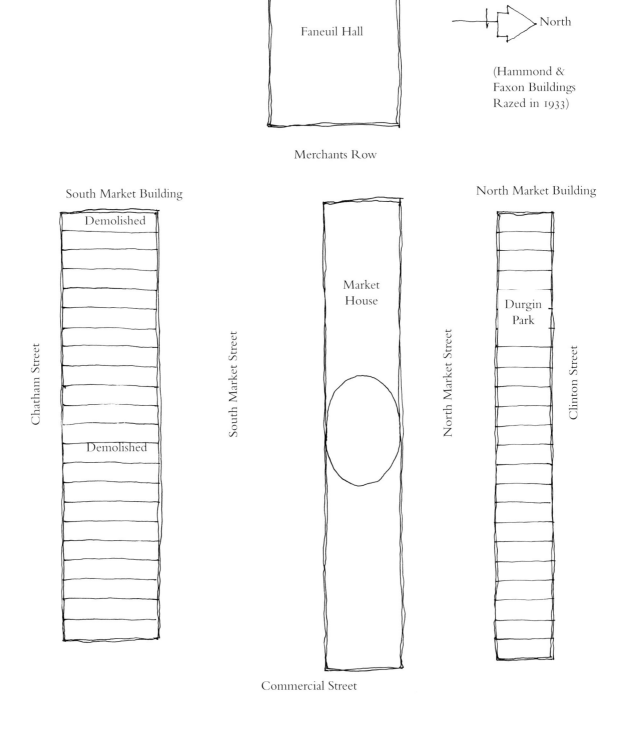

Faneuil Hall

Merchants Row

North

(Hammond &
Faxon Buildings
Razed in 1933)

South Market Building

North Market Building

Demolished

Market
House

Durgin
Park

Demolished

Chatham Street

South Market Street

North Market Street

Clinton Street

Commercial Street

not having provided the final terms of their consolidated ground lease with the city.

Director Bob Kenney later disputed their claim and pointed out that the city had already begun creating a master lease prior to the issue of the developer's kit. "Remember, at the time there was already more than $12 million of public money spent on the project and I dispute any claim that there was no effort on the city's part to provide the general terms of a master lease. The lease was already being drafted before the requests for proposals (RFP's) were issued. Van Arkle and Moss had not formed a legal entity with which the city could negotiate and there was no written communication from Fidelity included within the timetable of their submission, or by the end of the year. Some say that Van Arkle and Moss were treated unfairly at the time due to the short time frame. I disagree. They simply did not perform within the context of their submission and could not even obtain a conditional financing commitment."[39]

Charles J. Speleotis, chief general counsel for the BRA, later concurred that the BRA was not to blame: "The BRA was not in the business of rescinding designations. Extensions were always legitimately given to developers on an as-needed basis. We could have produced a basic conditional ground lease very quickly but that was not the issue. The issue was money. Van Arkle and Moss couldn't come up with a feasible economic plan to make the project work, which meant they couldn't produce a conditional financing commitment. By January 1972 it was obvious to us and it was probably obvious to Fidelity that Van Arkle couldn't make the project work."[40]

In order to keep the project going forward, Bob Kenney moved ahead without the Van Arkle and Moss development team. He did so by breaking the project into two phases. Phase I would entail restoring the exterior shells—the roofs and granite facades—of the North and South Market buildings to their original appearance. It would also include repairing the buildings so they would be structurally sound. This phase would use the plans from Stahl-Bennett and would be paid for with the $2.1 million from HUD. Phase II would convert all three buildings and adjacent streets into a commercial complex, the specifics of which would be proposed by the (yet-to-be) designated developer. This second phase would entail completion of the rebuilding of the market house, rebuilding the interiors of the North and South

Facing page: Remaining individual units as of 1972.
DRAWING BY GARY M. IRISH, ASAI, 2002.

Market buildings, and landscaping the closed-off streets as concourses in preparation for full tenancy. Phase II would be paid for by private money along with some public monies provided by the city and the state. In April 1972 the BRA put phase I out for public bid.

At the appropriate time Roger Webb's for-profit company, Architectural Heritage, was appointed developer. He would use Falzarano Construction Company for construction and LeMessurier Associates to engineer the plans Stahl had drawn. Stahl had started with what could be seen, both by looking at the building and at old photographs; Rowson's plans; and Parris's written description of the markets, which he had submitted to the city in 1826. He then took into account 1972 building codes and recreated, unit by unit, store by store, what the buildings should look like when reconstructed. Because Tad Stahl had already done most of the architectural drawings needed, he was given a separate architect's contract for phase I by the BRA.

Ben Thompson, whose mixed-use proposal to the BRA had been rejected in 1965 because of the Arthur D. Little recommendation, had later been approved as part of the Van Arkle and Moss development team in 1971. By this time, Thompson had extensive retail experience through his seven Design Research stores, which sold retail lifestyle-oriented goods across the States, and he was determined to influence at least one major developer who might be designated for phase II with an urban extension of his retail experience. During the next year he approached many major real estate developers in the United States and Canada and discussed his project concepts to one after another without success. "Almost none had experience in retail or mixed-use development, and each, despite lack of expertise for its execution, expressed enthusiasm for the possibility of impacting central Boston's business climate."[41] Finally, at the suggestion of a client, Thompson wrote to James W. Rouse, chairman of the Rouse Company, developers and builders located in Columbia, Maryland. In the early 1960s the Rouse Company had assembled and developed twelve thousand acres of farmland between Baltimore and Washington and turned it into Columbia, an ethnically and culturally diverse city that grew to 76,000. Rouse had been developing shopping centers and malls in suburban and rural areas across the United States and Canada for many years, and he was said to believe that the future held great opportunities for downtown city centers.

Rouse came to Boston to look at the possibilities. His "business success was firmly rooted in non-urban countryside malls dependent on auto access with abundant parking. He was inexperienced in developing within an existing urban fabric or historical context, but Ben [Thompson] approached him on the basis of his responsibility to the future of the cities of America—and the opportunity therein. Rouse was a fast learner with strong ideas of social responsibility who became convinced on his first visit with [Ben Thompson and Associates] that the market site in downtown Boston was a strong place to start the next movement in national urban retailing."[42]

On this first visit, Rouse saw wharf buildings on three of Boston's venerable old piers being rehabilitated into housing, shops, and restaurants. Atlantic Avenue was being rerouted around a new $3.5 million public park (Christopher Columbus Park). The New England Aquarium at the end of Central Wharf was ready to open; the Mercantile Building on Commercial Street was being extensively refurbished; and the old North End neighborhood was still active, contributing a sense of prosperity.

By May 1972, after studying Ben Thompson's redevelopment concept (which had been accepted by the BRA through the Van Arkle and Moss submission), Rouse began his own effort to persuade the BRA to designate the Rouse Company as developer. He presented a study that included statistics of tourist volume, conventioneers, office workers, local residents, and students. Represented by the Boston law firm of Fine and Ambrogne, Rouse's team also introduced Mayor White to the firm's reputation for experience, financial success, and development vision.[43] The newspapers, of course were still reporting progress, or the lack of it, on the market redevelopment project. A sense of guarded optimism was expressed by the *Boston Sunday Globe* in a front-page article in May 1972 entitled FANEUIL HALL AREA MAY SPARKLE FOR "BOSTON 200" AFTER ALL. The article detailed the extensive efforts to restore the facility to date but noted, "The BRA has met one set-back after another in the past ten years to get the historically significant enclave developed."[44]

The Rouse Company and Ben Thompson reworked their plans to include residential use of the upper floors of the North and South Market buildings. This would promote evening retail business, they said to the BRA in August. But the BRA replied that any residential components were to be restricted to the waterfront district. The markets should now be devoted to commercial uses only.

Despite this blow, Rouse and Thompson reworked their plans in accordance with the dictum and re-presented them in the hope of winning the BRA's selection of the Rouse Company as developer of the new marketplace. Ben Thompson's extensive experience in retailing prepared him for the ground-floor vending aspects of the new marketplace. Instead of merely preparing architectural drafts for his client the Rouse Company, he personally collaborated with James Rouse with the goal of building a model for the best-possible customer-merchant interrelationships. "Ben was already making that model work within his own store called Design Research at Ghirardelli Square in San Francisco. And that's why his judgment and experience were sufficient and parallel to Jim Rouse's, allowing them to collaborate and understand the problem mutually."[45]

When phase I work (to restore the North and South Market building exteriors) was ready to begin, a group of Boston area residents and architects (which indirectly included Thompson) voiced a desire to leave some traces of the changes the warehouse/stores buildings had seen through the years. Specifically, they argued for not fully restoring the slate-covered roof line of the warehouse/stores and not totally recreating their original granite facades. Many of the architects, including Ben Thompson, asserted that architecture was like a being that evolved over time, leaving a visible record of changing styles, techniques, uses, and ownership as a living history. They wanted to define preservation of these buildings to include retaining evidence of the North and South Market buildings' 150-year evolution. Rather than obliterate all past alterations, this group wanted to retain some of the expanded building fronts, the larger windows, and the raised roof lines as part of the markets' continuing story.[46]

On the other hand, historic preservationists such as Walter Muir Whitehill, Roger Webb, Tad Stahl, BRA director Bob Kenney, and most of the BRA staff wanted to restore the marketplace architecture to what it had been in 1826, to make it the largest surviving example of early nineteenth-century urban planning in the country. To them, this meant removing most of the badly mauled complex and recreating its original architecture. Besides, they argued, the $2.1 million HUD grant was contingent upon restoring the North and South Market buildings to their 1826 appearance. The BRA also argued that no one had been interested in restoring the deteriorated marketplace before the BRA began the preservation project; the BRA point of view was partly why the project existed. Mindful of past criticism for delays in the project, Kenney moved forward.[47]

The consortium of architects brought an injunction against the BRA. To

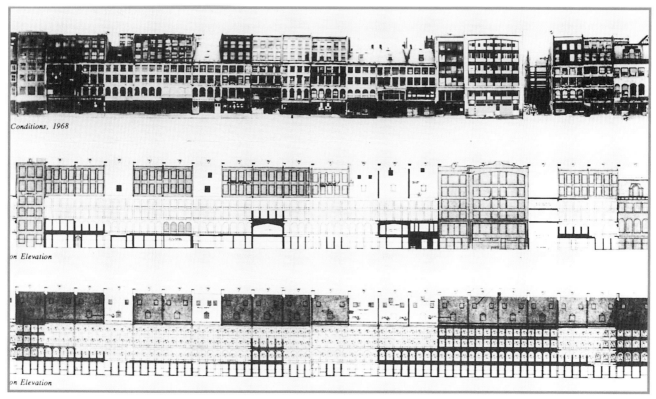

Architect's proposal for renovation of South Market building, 1968:
Existing Conditions, Demolition Elevation, and Restoration Elevation.
Courtesy of Frederick "Tad" Stahl.

defend its decision before the Massachusetts Superior Court, the BRA argued that the master plan funded by HUD was based on restoring the warehouse/stores to their original appearance. The *Markets Report* was used in the defense, as were written comments by Walter Muir Whitehill, whose work to have the marketplace restored using Alexander Parris's design had been the basis of the city's plan.[48] As a result, the injunction was lifted. "In the end, the practical need for continuous horizontal tenant spaces won out to improve economic feasibility. So that [court] decision was as much economically as philosophically [driven]."[49]

In October 1972 the masonry contractors Falzarano Construction Company began phase I exterior renovation of the South Market building; they soon moved on to

Photo of the 1972 reconstruction efforts of the North Market building (above) *and South Market building* (below). COURTESY OF THE ROUSE COMPANY.

Photos of the 1972 reconstruction efforts of the South Market building.
Courtesy of the Rouse Company.

Photo of the 1972 reconstruction efforts of the South Market building.
COURTESY OF FREDERICK "TAD" STAHL.

the North Market building. The work to demolish newer and unstable sections adhered to the plans prepared by Stahl-Bennett Architects, which the city had approved. Structural engineering was provided by LeMessurier Associates. Two of the store units in the South Market building that had been torn down after fires were reconstructed within their side and end walls and upon the original foundations.[50] Two mansard roof pavilions and various Victorian expansions were removed, as were twelve other additions built onto the roofs, in order to realign the roof profiles as they had originally been built. On seven stores, fronts that had been put up were taken down. Numerous structural wooden beams were replaced or reinforced. The facades that had had their granite removed were reconstructed or refaced; this part of the process took more than four hundred pieces of granite. In order to replicate the original granite, these pieces were cut by hand. When completed, the roofs were covered in sturdy slate in a mixture of similar, muted colors. This was the only essential change made; the original slate had been black. In conjunction with this reconstruction, the city began installing new underground utility lines, using an interconnecting tunnel system that could service all three buildings.

Every effort within reason and within the limits of available contemporary materials and craftsmanship was made to restore the North and South Market roofs and facades to their unique repetitive pattern. Fortunately, the Chelmsford, Massachusetts, quarries that supplied the granite for the original development had been expanded and were still operating as the Fletcher Granite Company, which was able to provide stone of exactly the same white granite.

This basic work of demolishing and replacing elements was essential to the restoration, Tad Stahl remarked later. "[Bob Kenney] was so critical in making the entire project real. . . . We didn't know what was going on behind the scenes. But we did know that not a single developer would touch the area without the basic work having been accomplished."[51]

Bob Kenney may not have known if the project would ever be completed, but he was determined to do whatever it took to give it its best chance. "Those that say cities are rebuilt by having a great vision," he said later, "are naive. Cities are rebuilt with stubborn hard work and a sense of public entrepreneurship. At the time it was a colossal risk because we weren't sure if we'd find a developer capable of bringing the entire project to fruition with private funds. The city had already spent $12.4 million on the streets and other things like purchasing the individual stores and mer-

Photos of the 1972 reconstruction efforts of the South Market building.
COURTESY OF FREDERICK "TAD" STAHL.

The Chelmsford, Massachusetts, quarries that supplied white granite for the market buildings in 1824–1826. During the 1972 reconstruction, then operated by the Fletcher Granite Company, they provided replacement pieces of the same white granite.
COURTESY OF FREDERICK "TAD" STAHL.

chant relocation. The last thing we wanted was to end up bailing out the developer. Also, if most of the initial structural risks were removed, then obtaining private financing would be easier. But we went ahead with the idea that spending enough money through public entrepreneurship would assist the right developer in securing the proper financing."[52]

As work proceeded on the North and South Market buildings, the BRA began drafting the master ground lease with the city, which would later be used to create the sublease with the designated developer. Lawyers, including Charles Speleotis and Edward J. Lonergan, and the executive assistant to the BRA director, Paul L. McCann, represented the BRA. The City of Boston prepared the necessary documentation to legally allow the nearby streets to be closed to traffic. By the end of 1975 the city-owned market house and streets were officially incorporated with the two BRA-owned buildings into one leasable six-and-a-half-acre site. (The original seven-and-a-half-acre site was reduced by an acre because Chatham and Clinton Streets, parts of Commercial Street, land adjacent to Faneuil Hall, and the triangular lot situated between Clinton and North Streets were not included in the ground lease.)

Paul McCann later stated, "The lease drafting was just another milestone in the revitalization of the markets. Over the ten-year period preceding the lease, we accomplished the approval and funding of the Downtown Waterfront–Faneuil Hall Plan, we acquired each building, and we relocated all of those tenants. Even the completion of the mundane utility work was an important milestone of progress. Every accomplishment, every step forward was a struggle since few outside the city and the BRA believed in the project. Under the [Downtown-Waterfront] Urban Renewal Plan, all of the individual forty-two building owners were given the option of retaining their buildings and rehabilitating according to our specifications. [Unlike the private owners-to-be who lined up at auction to buy lots and erect their own buildings in 1824 and 1825,] not one of the forty-two owners of property [in the early 1970s] had sufficient faith in the markets' success to remain and invest in the future."[53]

Rebuilding the Markets

By the beginning of 1973 the phase I (exterior) reconstruction work of the North and South Market buildings was continuing and the streets by the markets had been closed off to most traffic. The BRA had a draft of a master lease for the new district in accordance with the advisories of the Stahl-Webb 1968 *Markets Report*. This master lease draft defined the district to include the market house and the North and South Market buildings, together with North and South Market Streets, a portion of Commercial Street, and a portion of Merchants Row.[1]

The Rouse Company lobbied the BRA to be appointed developer of phase II of the redevelopment project. It intended to use the plans Ben Thompson had submitted (which had been approved in 1971 as part of the Van Arkle and Moss team) for the reconstruction of the market house, the landscaping of the concourses, and finishing the interior of all three buildings. The Rouse Company's proposal was fully documented with retail and office uses and Rouse was ready to seek financing to begin putting his building plan into action. Behind the scenes, though, the Rouse Company directors were looking unfavorably upon the likelihood of long-term success if Thompson's concepts were employed, and word that they were uneasy spread to the BRA.

Also seeking to be named developer of phase II was Roger Webb's for-profit development company, Architectural Heritage. Webb was backed by the preservationist groups and city politicians. His proposal to the BRA, however, met with mixed reaction. His company proposed to act as a limited-dividend corporation (which meant it would pay the BRA a portion of profits only if there were any profits from potential rental income). His redevelopment proposal did not specify long-term tenancy, and it followed a schedule whereby he would rebuild only portions of the marketplace over several years in multiple phases (waiting until each phase proved successful before moving on to the next). To BRA officials, Webb's submission seemed too conservative and it relied too much upon trial and error.[2] Although the BRA had accepted the Stahl–Webb *Markets Report* conceptions of rebuilding the marketplace into a civic monument with pedestrian concourses as initial ideas on saving the marketplace, and although these conceptions had helped secure federal funding, the area of the Stahl–Webb proposal that addressed the long-term reuse of all three buildings was vague and it did not give a full description of tenant occupancy.

At this time there were grave doubts about fully tenanting all three buildings because not a single real estate expert could guarantee the financial success of the marketplace as retail, office, or hotel space, residential apartments, or even light industrial[3] use with any certainty. And the doubters included the experts whom Webb had engaged. "[His] proposal did not suggest the kind of [dynamic] retail center envisioned by Rouse and Thompson, but called for office space, specialty stores, and apartment units in the north and south buildings."[4] The BRA was also convinced that any limited-dividend or for-profit company (which Webb's development company was) acting as a nonprofit corporation (which Webb's research company was) would find it more difficult to attract the necessary private financing.

Yet Webb remained optimistic. He had redeveloped the Old City Hall landmark as a limited-dividend corporation under a long-term lease with the city, he had allies in Boston, and the architect he had engaged for phase II of redevelopment, Samuel Mintz, had a good reputation with the city for his earlier work on the waterfront project. Webb's enthusiasm over breathing life back into the markets was undeniable, and many felt certain he would be the designated developer of phase II.

Mayor White and Director Kenney hesitated to make a choice. There was a national recession and the economy was weak. Would that make it more difficult for one or the other to obtain financing? And which team could better handle a project of this complexity?

The Rouse Company was a well-known commercial real estate firm in the States and in Canada. But because Rouse was principally a shopping mall developer, Mayor White thought he might be better suited for a project like Downtown Crossing, a project in the Washington Street shopping district. Norman B. Leventhal, CEO of a respected construction firm and organizer of a key group of business leaders and community activists called the Neighbors of Government Center, disagreed. He carefully reviewed the Rouse proposal and then suggested that it had not been properly evaluated by the BRA.[5] He later said of that time, "Ben Thompson came to me and said that the BRA was ready to appoint Roger Webb as the designated developer. I knew Webb had redeveloped Old City Hall and done a remarkable job preserving the building. But I didn't know if his proposal was appropriate for the Quincy Market site. I did know that Jim Rouse's experience spoke of his competency, especially with regard to his Columbia, Maryland, project."[6] Leventhal also personally assured the mayor that the Rouse-Thompson concepts were better suited for the markets than the submission from Architectural Heritage.

BRA director Bob Kenney was grateful for the advice. "We [the BRA] weren't sure if Webb's idea would succeed. We weren't sure if Rouse could succeed, either, because some of his top people were trying to talk him out of going ahead with the project. Before we started construction on the North and South Market buildings, Jim Rouse wanted the $2 million of HUD money, and other project funds that had been budgeted by the city and state, turned over to his company. We weren't about to do that for anyone. My view at the time was that if the Quincy Market project failed, the city would ultimately be left with three refurbished buildings."[7]

In February 1973 the Boston City Council's Committee on Urban Renewal rubber-stamped the concept of uniting the city-owned market house and adjacent streets with the BRA-owned North and South Market buildings into one leasable district. Although the committee held two public hearings to evaluate the competing proposals, they left the issue unresolved. A month later, BRA director Robert Kenney recommended the Rouse Company as the designated developer. Their proposed lease payments and their solid track record made them the better choice. The BRA's board concurred and the matter was sent back to the City Council.

After Norman Leventhal testified that the city would profit more substantially from the Rouse proposal, the City Council unanimously endorsed the BRA's designation of Rouse. In less than a year the Columbia, Maryland, firm had won over Boston's political decision makers. Robert Beal of the Beal Companies (a prestigious Boston commercial real estate firm) later said of the process, "You have to remember how important this project was to the city. Faneuil Hall and Quincy Market

Model of the Faneuil Hall Markets redevelopment proposal, 1975.
Pictured from left to right: *Architect Ben Thompson, BRA director Bob Kenney, developer James Rouse, and Mayor Kevin White.* Courtesy of the Francis Loeb Library, Graduate School of Design, Harvard University.

defined old Boston. I stood in Mayor White's office with Norman Leventhal and gazed down at Faneuil Hall and saw how the whole complexion of the city could be changed at the markets. The new Government Center was behind us and the waterfront district was spread out in front of us. Sitting right there between the two, in stark contrast, was the sprawling market district just waiting to connect the[m]. But it had to be done by a firm with the capacity of seeing it through without the city coming to the rescue."[8]

On March 15, 1973, Mayor White's public endorsement of Rouse was published in the *Boston Globe.* "[James] Rouse has agreed to guarantee the city $600,000 annually after the project has begun or 20 percent of the gross income, whichever is greater. He will also contribute $500,000 for promotion of the bicentennial, over a two-year period."[9]

The final development team included the Rouse Company as developers and management company, Benjamin Thompson and Associates as architects and planners, and George B. H. Macomber Company as builders.[10] They were formally designated on March 22, 1973.

Kevin White later explained some of his reasoning on the decision. "Jim Rouse had a great presence about him but . . . I didn't think [he] was up to it. He was unfamiliar with the history of the extensive problems at the markets. Being a politician, I was a bit skeptical. But [as] I listened to him . . . his personality gave me a confidence, a maturity of balance that I instantaneously took to. If I was going to be responsible for doing something with this gem, Rouse's personality gave me a confidence [in him] as a person."[11]

Between the spring of 1973 and 1974, the BRA and the Rouse Company negotiated the terms of the ninety-nine-year sublease that would be part of the provisions in the master lease signed between the BRA and the city. The national recession was

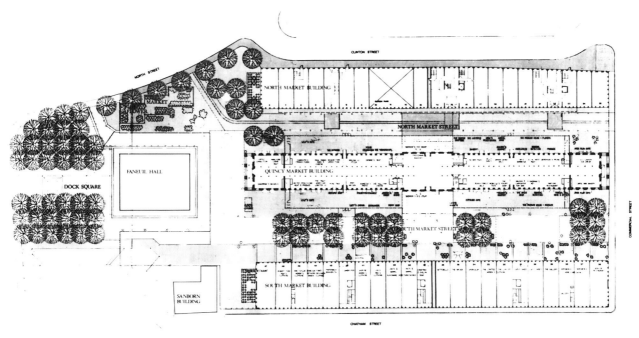

*The Faneuil Hall Marketplace District as drawn by
Benjamin Thompson and Associates, 1975.* COURTESY OF THE FRANCIS LOEB LIBRARY,
GRADUATE SCHOOL OF DESIGN, HARVARD UNIVERSITY.

worsening and a fuel shortage crisis erupted that raised the price of construction products made of plastic.[12] "As a result, lease negotiations took place in an atmosphere of economic stagnation and financial maneuvering as both sides worked to line up the necessary commitments."[13]

The Rouse team stressed all of the major economic risks that their company was taking as the recession worsened. "They bargained hard for economic concessions that would reduce their risk and enhance the ability to recoup their investment. They also pushed for total control over the design and related matters, believing the project would proceed more quickly if the entire job was placed in private sector hands. The city team did eventually give in on some of the economic terms of the deal because it wanted the developer to have sufficient incentive, but it did not compromise on design matters."[14]

On April 22, 1974, the city granted the BRA its ninety-nine-year master lease for the market house and its adjacent public streets for $1.00 per year. This made it possible for the BRA to finalize the promised ninety-nine-year sublease with its developer. The following month, the BRA signed a ninety-nine-year sublease with Rouse's subsidiary, Faneuil Hall Marketplace—the entity responsible for the financing, construction, maintenance, tenancy, and custody of all three buildings and closed-off streets. The markets and their nearby public streets were finally incorporated into one privately controlled district, which was henceforth called "Faneuil Hall Marketplace™."

The final terms of the ninety-nine-year sublease included a two-tier payment formula. The first tier required (a) that the initial minimum base rent payment would be due as each building was completed: It would be $200,000 annually after the market house was done, changing to $400,000 annually after the South Market building was finished, and then to $600,000 annually after the North Market building was rebuilt; and (b) once all three buildings were reopened, the city would receive from the Rouse Company $600,000 each year thereafter as the minimum base rent.[15] The second tier required that the city be paid 25 percent of the absolute gross rental income (defined as collected rents plus collected common area maintenance fees once all three buildings were built and occupied), plus a percentage of the net rent (rent after operating expenses not covered in the common area maintenance fees) over certain amounts. (The formula for those amounts was: (a) 20 percent of net annual rental income in excess of $3 million plus (b) 10 percent of net annual rental income in excess of $4 million plus (c) 11 percent of net annual rental income in excess of $5 million.)[16]

Even given the economic environment in which the sublease was negotiated, not everyone in the BRA thought the sublease a wise one. Chief general counsel for the BRA Charles Speleotis, for example, was against it. "I was against the ninety-nine-year term from the beginning. Forty or fifty years was more reasonable. It was in accordance with depreciation schedules and loan amortization rates. But the banks insisted that if the city was going to stand behind the project, they wanted us to execute the ninety-nine-year long-term lease."[17]

As the BRA sublease was being signed, public attention temporarily turned to a few events in the neighborhood of the market district. The famed grasshopper weathervane atop Faneuil Hall was reported stolen. After an intensive citywide weeklong search, amid speculation that a helicopter was used in the heist, the gilded grasshopper was discovered under a pile of flags in the attic space of the building. Painters working on the cupola had simply misplaced it.[18]

Also, the parking area around the Sam Adams statue at Adams Square was converted into a pedestrian plaza. This granite, brick, and cobblestone park was actually classified as sidewalk construction included in the ongoing reconstruction of Congress Street. The idea of planting trees there, however, forced the relocation of numerous underground utilities. Once the planting holes were dug, they filled with seawater at high tide. Ultimately, a solution was found to correct this problem and Adams Square was incorporated into the new Dock Square Park.[19]

By June 1974 the continuing phase I reconstruction of the roofs and the granite facades of the North and South Market buildings had exceeded their estimate of $2.1 million (received in the HUD grant). The BRA needed an additional $300,000 to complete the work. In a repeat of history, the city (through the BRA) called in the masonry contractor's bondsman to cover the cost overrun, as Mayor Josiah Quincy had done with Gridley Bryant and his associates on two occasions between 1825 and 1826.

Also by June 1974 it had been discovered that both buildings had sustained more damage over the years than the Stahl–Webb inspectors had estimated. Decades of leakage from unrepaired roofs, from faultily replaced facades, and even from leaking old iceboxes had completely rotted many of the heavy wooden interior timbers. The media following the project's progress weren't always supportive. "As Falzarano [Company] crews dig deeper into the buildings they discover, claim city officials, more defects and construction problems than they bargained for. The result has been several hundred thousand [dollars'] worth of additional costs that [have] exhausted the original $2.5 million [*sic*] in Federal funds for the exterior restoration."[20]

By the summer of 1974 the total public funds contributed toward the stabilization of the market area since 1950—by HUD, the Commonwealth of Massachusetts, and the City of Boston—had climbed to nearly $12.5 million. In addition to the public contribution, the estimated cost to complete the entire redevelopment had risen to $21 million, of which $7.5 million was needed to rebuild just the market house.[21] (This made a total cost estimate of $33.5 million.) In July, the Rouse Company received a $21 million permanent financing commitment from Teachers Insurance and Annuity Association of America. Two months later, Chase Manhattan Bank of New York agreed to provide 50 percent of the total reconstruction financing[22] for all three buildings ($10.5 million). An estimated $3.75 million of this loan would be spent on the market house. The construction loan commitment from Chase Manhattan Bank, however, came with the stipulation that Boston area lenders finance the other $3.75 million to rebuild the market house. The source of the other $6.75 million dollars was still not finalized at this time.

After watching the city's nearly twenty-year struggle over the markets' revitalization, not a single Boston lender in 1974 would even consider lending money for the risky redevelopment. They all doubted there would be sufficient retail tenancy and they were unconvinced that customers would come back to shop in that part of the city. In addition, the expense of remodeling very old buildings was difficult to accurately gauge; unforeseen problems had already escalated construction costs on the North and South Market buildings.

For seven months the Rouse Company tried to persuade Boston lenders of the project's validity, but neither Rouse nor Thompson could interest a single bank to act as co-lender with Chase Manhattan. As a result, at the end of 1974 BRA officials extended the construction deadline until the end of 1975, making it doubtful that the market house would partake in its scheduled activities for the city's upcoming bicentennial celebration. The plan had called for preparing the market house's second-floor east wing for an exhibit by February 15, 1975, and work to be finished on the rest of the building by April 15.

Arguments over whether the partially redeveloped area was worth the investment risk went back and forth. The *Boston Globe* reported, "For some three months [*sic*] now Rouse, who has been pumping his own money into the project and successfully lining up tenants, has been negotiating with the First [First National Bank of Boston], as well as presenting plans to State Street [State Street Bank and Trust Company], Merchants [New England Merchants National Bank], and local savings institutions, but thus to no avail. The criticism that Boston banks have shown little faith in their own city is historically true. Furthermore, if Boston banks turn down a Boston project it puts a sort of kiss of death on efforts to raise money elsewhere."[23]

Mayor Kevin White later gave his side of the story: "The fact that the Rouse Company secured $21 million in permanent financing during the summer of 1974—that in itself was no small task, that in itself would impress anyone. I was mayor of the city. . . . I represented the public sector and I had to find someone in the private sector of equal power who could deliver."[24]

But Mayor White had many other issues to handle at the time. "Between 1974 and 1975 the city was also torn apart by school desegregation and federal court-ordered busing of the Boston public schools. We went from the Vietnam demonstrations right into the busing issue. Racial protests and . . . busing had a great impact upon the city at the time. Even so, Faneuil Hall Market remained one of my top priorities."[25] His administration tried to persuade Boston lenders to help out.

No one seemed in agreement over how well potential vendors and customers would do if the marketplace opened. Although an unprecedented amount of urban renewal completed throughout Boston by the early 1970s had improved the city's overall image, it was still failing to entice residents to live downtown or office workers to remain after work. Apartment rents remained so low throughout Boston and vacancy was at its highest level since the Great Depression. During weekdays, most downtown retail stores closed by late afternoon and, for the most part, restaurants stopped serving early in the evening or shut their doors after lunch hours. But outside the city there were new apartment complexes, shopping malls, movie theaters, fast-food restaurants, and places that featured nightly dining with entertainment—all conveniently located within driving distance of suburban neighborhoods.

The idea that people would flock back to the city's now defunct market dis-

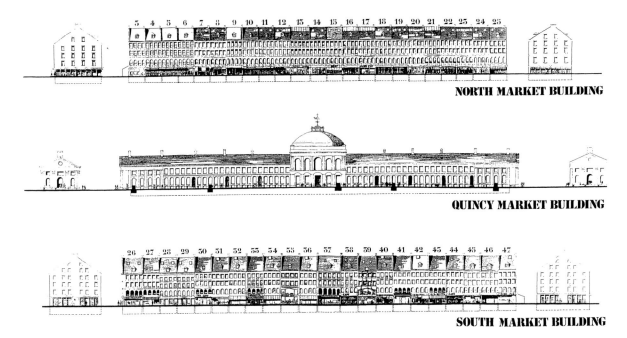

5 4 5 6 7 8 9 10 11 12 13 14 15 16 17 18 19 20 21 22 23 24 25

NORTH MARKET BUILDING

QUINCY MARKET BUILDING

26 27 28 29 30 31 32 33 34 35 36 37 38 39 40 41 42 43 44 45 46 47

SOUTH MARKET BUILDING

Early rendition of the redeveloped buildings, 1974, by Benjamin Thompson and Associates.
Courtesy of Jane Thompson.

trict to shop, eat, and be entertained day and night was beyond the comprehension of most Boston lenders. Not only was the location seen as too inconvenient to customers, but the food merchandising at this market area had steadily declined since the end of World War II. Adding to the proposed project's uncertainty as a shopping center was the lack of the two conventional shopping-center standards: There would be no national chain of retail stores acting as anchors to stabilize the project, and there would be no exclusive parking areas. Instead, the concept relied on a variety of small start-up businesses, local merchants, and specialty food vendors placed in close quarters. Parking was available only at a few nearby parking garages, parking lots, or downtown streets with metered spaces.

Despite the lack of precedent, Rouse and Thompson continued to theorize that a series of small concessions situated along both sides of the market house colonnade would draw shoppers to a lively bazaar setting, which would offer fresh produce, meats, fish, cheese, ready foods, and bakery goods. As Ben Thompson commented at the time, "Good markets and fairs thrive on movement and action. They don't necessarily occur in architectural masterpieces, but in lively open spaces that mix people with functions."[26] Thompson envisioned the market house as a magnet that would draw throngs to the refurbished area, with its new pedestrian sidewalk arcades, its food courts, and its many places for night entertainment. Pushcarts outside the market house and along traffic-free streets, vending individual crafts, books, novelties, or other handmade accessories, would also lure a diverse group of shoppers. As Ben Thompson reflected, "Small space with low overhead, benefiting from steady foot traffic, will build opportunities for young entrepreneurs to start up businesses, test their markets, discover their customers, adjust their production levels, and keep on growing."[27] Although Rouse and Thompson didn't even have a name for their concept, they were convinced that the marketplace redevelopment would trigger revival in downtown Boston and reverse the trend of "white flight" into suburbia.

But to Boston lenders, so many small, independent merchants meant a danger of increased tenant turnover and greater credit risks than the more traditional blue-chip-rated shopping center counterparts. Part of the problem for them was the lack of a model to measure the feasibility of Thompson's imaginative new ideas. The concept of a food court located in a center for butchers and other such market men, enhanced or not by outside pushcart peddlers, seemed improbable and highly risky. They kept coming back to the stance that, since people weren't making Boston's market district a shopping destination, there would be no customers and therefore no food courts. They were also disturbed by the lack of tenant mix in Thompson and Rouse's proposal, which left a question as to which vendors exactly would attract this diverse group of shoppers.

But Thompson and Rouse insisted that the strength of the concept was Boston's highly dissimilar customer base—it had office and blue-collar workers, tourists, college students, neighbors on Beacon Hill and mostly Italian-American neighbors still living in the North End. All would shop there. Thompson argued, "Historic marketplaces, sprung up at intersections of navigation and trade routes, were traditionally the seed and heart of great cities. Physically, people need the variety and abundance that markets bring. Socially, they need the communal security of mutual exchange and personal contact. Psychologically, they hunger for the festive activity that markets add to a central city."[28]

Finally, after months of pressure exerted by the White administration, a consortium of Boston lenders—led by senior vice president Ephron Catlin Jr. and president William Brown, both of the First National Bank of Boston—agreed to pool resources and spread the risk of loan failure. White did not succeed alone. "By my second term as mayor I had established good ties with the business community. Richard Hill was the preeminent power in Boston's business community. He was very bright and he became a constructive element of the lending pool. . . . When push came to shove, Dick Hill was the one who made the shove productive. He was the man who organized the lending agenda through 'the Vault.' He was without question as powerful as any factor in the city."[29]

With First National Bank committing the largest share—$2.5 million—additional local lenders agreed to make up the difference of $1.25 million—more as a civic duty than as a prudent investment. "The banks, headed by the First National Bank of Boston, are in the process of pooling a $10 million [*sic*] construction loan for the Rouse Co. of Columbia, MD., before the mandatory deadline is imposed on the firm by the Boston Redevelopment Authority. The project was helped in recent weeks when Mayor Kevin H. White and [BRA director Robert] Kenney met with representatives of Boston banks and officials of the Rouse firm, including chairman James W. Rouse."[30]

The BRA's chief general counsel, Charles Speleotis, later commented that even managing the promised local loans did not go smoothly at first. "What made it worse," he said, "was that all of these banks—ten or eleven of them—wanted to lend money individually on their own terms, using stipulations voted by their own boards of directors and executed with their own loan officers and lawyers. There was no way that I was going to allow that to happen, so they agreed to pool the money through the First National Bank. Immediately the BRA was sent this long detailed checklist of conditions regarding how the funds would be dispersed. I remember there was a list of forty stipulations that we negotiated down to seven."[31]

One stipulation was that 10,000 square feet on the second-floor west wing of the market house be pre-leased to the Magic Pan restaurant franchise. Another was that the marketplace reconstruction occur in stages over a three-year period, with one building being finished each year in accordance with the sublease rent schedule.[32] The three phases were: the Market House (1975–1976); the South Market building (1976–1977); and the North Market building (1977–1978).

"Ten Boston financial institutions finally came up with the other half [only] after Rouse had broken the project up into three phases, the first, Quincy Market, to cost $7.5 million."[33] And Mayor White pointed out that when the project was completed, it would represent "an investment of between $25 million and $30 million, in addition to [public] funds used for the purchase of the buildings, the exterior work and the relocation of merchants who wanted to move."[34]

In October 1975 Rouse signed construction loan agreements for redevelopment of the market house with Chase Manhattan Bank for $3.75 million and a consortium of Boston financial institutions for another $3.75 million.[35] The Boston area lender consortium included the First National Bank of Boston, the New England Merchants National Bank, the Commonwealth Bank and Trust Company, the National Shawmut Bank, the Charlestown Savings Bank, the Union Warren Savings Bank, the New England Mutual Life Insurance Company, the John Hancock Mutual Life Insurance Company, and the Massachusetts Business Development Corporation.[36] The Boston construction loan money was pooled and distributed by the First National Bank of Boston.

In November 1975 reconstruction began along the west end of the market house colonnade. One of the biggest obstacles that needed to be overcome was relocating those very last merchants who still remained in business. Most vendors had been assisted in their moves.[37] Twenty stubborn market men had refused to move to Chelsea, South Bay, South Boston, or any of the other places others had moved to. The BRA arranged for these market men to remain under special terms, shifting them to the east end of the market house as work advanced on the west end, then back when work was completed.[38]

Once these agreements were made, work could proceed. Since the market house had been granted federal landmark status through the efforts of Walter Muir Whitehill in 1966, any modifications to the building required approval from the Department of the Interior's National Park Service. This approval was in addition to the BRA's enforcement of the 1968 *Markets Report* guidelines, which recommended returning the building to its original 1826 appearance. Both groups had preservationists go over plans.

Ben Thompson, the architect working with the Rouse Company, made some suggestions that differed from some of the *Markets Report*'s recommendations. He felt that resurfacing the market house's inside walls with plaster and wood, in accor-

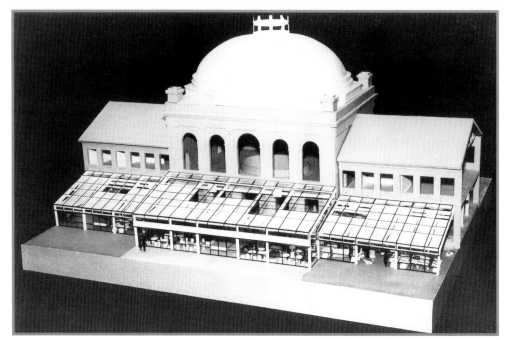

Model of Ben Thompson's makeover for the pavilion section of the market house, 1976, by Benjamin Thompson and Associates. Unadorned windows and glass arcades extending from the exterior walls of the building were unheard of until that time.
COURTESY OF THE FRANCIS LOEB LIBRARY, GRADUATE SCHOOL OF DESIGN, HARVARD UNIVERSITY; AND JANE THOMPSON.

dance with original 1826 construction, was unnecessary. In many places, the walls could simply be stripped down to the masonry materials, exposing most of the original rough-faced granite and brick. This would adequately give the feel of the time of the market house, he proposed. Though the preservationists in the BRA and in the Department of the Interior's National Park Service initially resisted Thompson's suggestions, they eventually agreed to these new ideas.

The mid-nineteenth-century practice of expanding the market's retail space under canvas and metal awnings along the outside walls of the market house was also adapted by Thompson with the agencies' permission. Single-story greenhouselike glass canopies, referred to as arcades, projected from both the north and south lengths of the market house, starting at the center and extending about 75 percent of the building's length. Forty-four multiple-hinged panels in the sloping glass roofs provided seasonal ventilation. The temperature inside the arcades could be easily adjusted by raising or lowering the "swing-up" hatch doors, which allowed for ventilation in the summer and heat retention during the winter months.[39]

In 1826 access to the basements had been only from the outside, by way of a series of half-doorways accessed by steep sets of steps. Thompson wanted the basement to be used for shopping in a similar way to the first floor, and access therefore had to be both from outside the main structure and from the inside. He added railings around each set of stairs, and patrons of a business that rented both an arcade space and its connecting basement space (in a duplex arrangement) could easily use both levels. Other sets of stairs were used to move from floor to floor as well. Thompson also wanted to convert some of the first-floor windows into doorways to provide access to the raised first floor and also to provide access to the second floor. The preservationists were initially upset with these proposed changes. But the difference of opinion was settled by modern building codes, which required such doorways, as they did handicap-access ramps, which Thompson neatly placed along the outside walls.

Thompson suggested dramatically changing the multipaned first-floor and second-floor windows into clear-glass openings. Preservationists initially objected to not recreating nineteenth-century windows with wooden sashes. So Thompson had a sample wooden-sashed window installed. To the 1826 eye, the original windows designed by Alexander Parris had created a refined appearance that softened the then-unadorned outside granite walls. But in 1976 it was clearly evident how unappealing multipane windows were to the twentieth-century eye. Thompson was allowed to substitute clear-glass pivot windows. Where the glass canopies provided protection from the elements, Thompson left the original granite-encased window and door frames open. This not only established a visual exchange between the interior and the outside but also allowed for natural ventilation and maintained the spirit of an open-air market.

Another issue that came under review was how to pave the streets and how to landscape. Once the underground utilities were completed by the city, which included the removal of original wooden drain pipes,[40] negotiations between the BRA and the National Park Service preservationists resulted in resurfacing the streets with a mix of mellow red bricks, rough-cut granite slabs, Belgium blocks, cobblestones, and split-faced granite paving, which together recreated the original

Trees being planted around the restored marketplace at nighttime, 1976.
COURTESY OF JANE THOMPSON.

appearance but provided smooth, walkable zones. Park benches, planters, solid granite seating disks, and protective bollards with chains added to the landscaping and also separated walking areas from emergency and delivery lanes. A drastic contemporary addition to the historic landscape was the planting of honey locust trees along the North and South Market concourses, to provide shade for visitors.[41] This was the first time in the long history of the marketplace that the buildings of "Quincy's Market" were shaded by trees. All the other changes were made after approval was obtained from the majority of those responsible for the authenticity of the renovation, but the issue of planting so many large trees had not been finally resolved by the time Thompson was ready to plant them. So under the cover of night, construction crews planted the trees, and when the sun rose the next day and everyone returned to the site, the preservationists agreed that Thompson was right after all.

The greatest alteration from the original design came about when Thompson recommended that the ceiling of the first-floor market hall be dramatically opened up, so visitors would see all the way to the inside elliptical dome. Thompson envisioned a rounded opening through the second floor that would create a portal to view the inner dome from the first-floor colonnade. He made the point that the rotunda was no longer used as an exhibition hall or as offices, which had needed to be sealed off from the once noisy market hall below. It could now become the central visual highlight of the market house. It took quite a lot of negotiation, but the BRA and National Park Service preservationists finally concurred. The rotunda was opened down to the first floor, entirely transforming the inside of the pavilion into the central focus of the market house. A broad wooden railing atop a clear-glass-paneled balustrade was mounted on the second floor, encircling the floor's balcony-like opening. (At this time, the space between the molding below the balustrade was unadorned.)

The dome itself was reinforced with steel I-beams inserted between new inner and outer dome shells that aided the original contoured-truss support system. Two metal tie-rods spanned the inner dome and held the steel secure. No work was done, however, to restore the dome's copper sheathing. "When dome restoration was completed in late October, it was a true construction feat."[42] A new bull weather-vane was positioned atop the dome's cupola.

The challenge of placing the master mechanical regulating panels and meters for most of the common areas of the market house also required a practical solution.

Interior construction along the colonnade, 1976, showing ventilation ducts.
COURTESY OF JANE THOMPSON.

They were conveniently hidden in the second floor and in portions of the base-ments. Electric- and natural gas–powered ventilation—fans and hot-air blowers—controlled the interior climate. Although some of the restaurants had their own individual air-conditioning, there was no central air-conditioning for the market house. In summer months the fans and the glass doors along the canopies provided the only means of cooling. It would be another twenty-five years before the market house's common areas would become air-conditioned.

Unlike the market house, both the North and South Market buildings would have their own heating and cooling exchange plants for all portions of the buildings. Thompson concealed these climate-control systems within upper floors of the buildings, where roof louvers in the attic space allowed steam to escape. The BRA would not allow an off-site utility plant to service all three buildings, but it did allow for an off-site storage and trash-compacting facility, situated about fifty feet away, on a parcel across from the now closed-off portion of Commercial Street.

Twentieth-century elements such as the clear-glass pivot windows, the honey locust trees along the concourses, and the greenhouselike arcades were consciously introduced contrasts to the original hardy granite structure. Thompson viewed every choice as a harmonious balance between old and new, between functional preservation and visual appeal. He persuaded the overseeing preservationists that his goal was not a "costumed" preservation but the conversion of an obsolete landmark into an effective, functioning building. Thompson was not prettifying the building for tourist enjoyment but offering forthright and definitive points of view that demonstrated the need to alter parts of the building with natural solutions. In nearly every instance, the preservationists eventually agreed with his novel ideas.

One major battle that Thompson lost, however, was his suggestion that stairways be installed within the rotunda to access the second-floor eating space. Preservationists could not bring themselves to approve of this change, so, for the first few years after the opening, patrons who wanted to get to the second floor had to take the original stairs inside the building. Later, two sets of wider permanent stairways provided better access to the second-floor eating area; these were redesigned and rebuilt in 1989.[43]

In the spring of 1976 workers found the market house to be in worse condition than expected. Construction costs had soared unexpectedly by an additional $1 million and the Rouse Company appealed to the BRA to renegotiate its lease. "To compensate the company for this unanticipated burden, which the BRA could not afford to absorb under the terms of its federal renovation grant, and [to] avoid the problems of verifying costs, the city reduced Rouse's guaranteed payments over the three-year phase-in period to $50,000 per year, for a total abatement of $1.05 million."[44] Some thought this too big a change, Charles Speleotis said later. "This concession was too high. The BRA staff considered that a one-third reduction was sufficient. But we compromised in order to keep the reconstruction schedule on track."[45]

Before the market was reopened, the overall private cost of reconstruction was about 10 percent higher than new construction for suburban shopping centers. After adjusting for inflation and the loss of real estate taxes, the process of adapting to historic design restraints[46] "brought the total public development cost up to $15.5 million."[47] Yet, without the participation of the city, state, and federal government, the redevelopment would have never happened.[48]

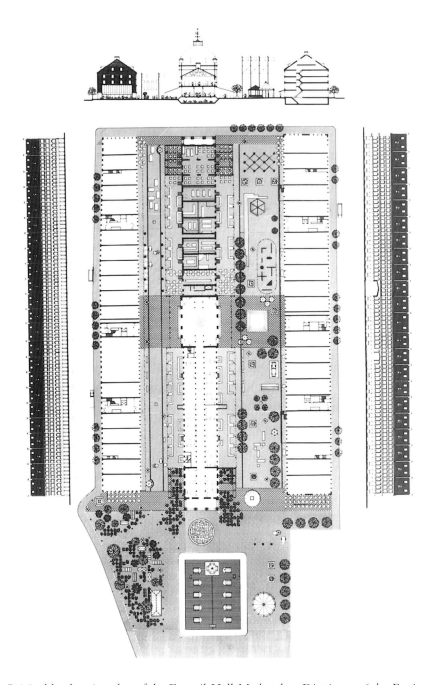

Original landscaping plan of the Faneuil Hall Marketplace District, 1976, by Benjamin Thompson and Associates. COURTESY OF THE FRANCIS LOEB LIBRARY, GRADUATE SCHOOL OF DESIGN, HARVARD UNIVERSITY.

By June 1976 swarms of construction workers were completing reconstruction of the market house by concentrating on finishing three levels: the basements, the colonnade, and the pavilion. On the second floor, in the west wing, the Magic Pan and the Proud Popover eateries were being finished; the east wing contained a gallery, which did present the bicentennial exhibit "Boston 200: The Revolution—Where It All Began."

Outside, the steel-framed glass canopies that flanked the market house were completed and landscaping was finished. The pedestrian footpaths were illuminated with cluster-globe light poles, which added a processional feel for nighttime activity. The originally planned reproductions of colonial-era antique lanterns were not used throughout the complex.[49]

While the finishing touches were being applied to "Quincy Market," major leases with restaurants and shops were signed and many new merchants for the colonnade concessions were secured. Some of these new merchants would offer a wide variety of foodstuffs cooked and prepared for consumers. Other tenants were former market house merchants such as Doe Sullivan and Company, M. Berenson, Lorden Flowers, Paul W. Marks Company, Crystal Meat Company, J. L. Dembro Meats, Produce House, Lipinski Flowers, United Provision Company, and E. N. West Meats Company.

With the renovated market house ready to open, the Rouse Company began looking for someone to oversee daily management. They found few of their own staff members interested in the position. One man who shared Jim Rouse's vision was James "Jim" B. McLean Jr., who wanted to return to his native New England and face a new challenge. In May 1976 he became the first general manager of Faneuil Hall Marketplace, a position not unlike the 150-year-old tradition of the Clerk of the Markets in the old Faneuil Hall market.[50] McLean brought to the position an unmatched level of energy superseded only by his fanatic insistence on cleanliness. Because of the market's historical significance, McLean worked in conjunction with Thompson and the BRA to exercise careful controls over merchant selection, signage, displays, and interior and exterior treatments. Under his management, the Rouse Company was able to commemorate the market house's heritage by displaying a number of salvaged nineteenth-century merchant signs in the rotunda. Other rotunda details that were resurrected were four sculpture niches, situated on either side of each of the two wing arches. These had been covered over with wooden planks.

The triumphant conclusion of reconstruction was announced to the public on August 19, 1976, when the *Boston Herald American* reported, "For three years he [Rouse] has pursued his brilliant plan to turn the old market buildings into an exciting modern marketplace. There have been setbacks, disappointments and soaring costs, but Rouse moves forward. On Aug. 26 at 11:30 a.m., Quincy Market, the first of three buildings, will open and it should be a showcase for Boston. Two mayors, four redevelopment authority directors, two architectural firms, and one real estate developer have battled for 12 years to restore the old market area. Their success will demonstrate forcibly what can be done when Boston has the opportunity and the will."[51]

As the reopening date drew near, the market house—tenanted with small shops of all varieties, restaurants and small eateries, concession merchants, and a new breed of pushcarts—was promoted as a "Festival Marketplace." Every construction worker,

The night before the grand reopening of the market house, August 25, 1976. Left to right: BRA director Bob Kenney, Mayor Kevin White, developer James Rouse, and architect Ben Thompson.
COURTESY OF JANE THOMPSON.

city worker, private contractor, Rouse Company employee, and retail merchant scrambled to be ready for business at the appointed hour. Before the scheduled reopening, however, nearly 20 percent of the space was still unleased, so the Rouse Company filled some of the vacant areas by providing pushcarts for artisans and craftspeople who had never before sold their works directly to the public.[52] Also invited to the empty spaces were throwback produce pushcart peddlers, who usually hawked their goods from nearby Haymarket Square and the Blackstone Street block. The eclectic variety of offerings was scattered inside and outside the market house. To avoid a shift in the balance of this arrangement, the pushcarts were not permitted to move from their designated spaces.

The night before the opening, Jim Rouse hosted a party at Lily's Café, the only market house restaurant prepared to serve meals. Mayor White toasted Rouse by saying, "Jim, this has been a wonderful effort but you realize Boston is a very conservative town. People don't take to new things quickly. I hope you will be prepared for little disappointments, but in the long haul the market will certainly make the grade."[53]

On the day of the opening, the *Lewiston (Maine) Journal* said of the market, "Cleansed of 150 years of shabbiness, Boston's Municipal Market Building reopens today, the center piece of the city's $140 million rediscovery of its waterfront."[54]

Early on the morning of August 26, 1976—opening day—Mayor White dedicated a bronze plaque that honored historian Walter Muir Whitehill, the first preservationist to bring attention to the importance of the markets during the 1950s. Director Bob Kenney arranged for the BRA to provide the plaque and have it mounted on the granite below the statue of Sam Adams at Dock Square Park.

The market was triumphantly rededicated 150 years to the day after its doors had first swung open. The day was hot and clear. A modest number of people gathered around the west-end portico to attend the late-morning dedication. Besides Mayor White, other notables included BRA director Robert Kenney and the staff of the BRA; developer James W. Rouse and staff members of the Rouse Company; architect Benjamin Thompson with his wife and partner, Jane, and members of their business, Benjamin Thompson and Associates; historian Walter Muir Whitehill; developer Roger S. Webb; architect Frederick "Tad" A. Stahl and his staff; and public television's French Chef, Julia Child, and her husband, Paul Child. The red-kilted Stuart Highland Regimental Group played bagpipes and drums, and an all-girl color

Jane and the late Ben Thompson, 1976.
COURTESY OF JANE THOMPSON.

guard brass band from Sudbury High School performed the national anthem as the blue-uniformed Ancient and Honorable Artillery Company stood at attention. A round granite marker, seven feet in diameter, created by Frankie Bunyard, an architect-artist turned sculptor, was unveiled. Placed flat in the ground outside the west end of the market house, it bore the inscription:

Honorable Josiah Quincy, Mayor

26 August 1826

Faneuil Hall Marketplace

26 August 1976

Honorable Kevin H. White, Mayor[55]

This was the first time in the 150-year history of Faneuil Hall Market that Josiah Quincy's name had been inscribed anywhere near the building.[56]

"Mayor White then addressed the audience, praised the imaginative work of those who had brought the old market district back to life, and called the occasion 'truly an historic event, a rebirth.' When the speeches were over, a man in colonial costume, complete with tricorn hat, swung a large handbell declaring the market officially open."[57]

Following the ribbon-cutting ceremony, the market doors were opened at the west-end portico across from Faneuil Hall, and those in attendance entered the building and followed the bagpipers the length of the colonnade, cutting green ribbons at each concession. Under the inner dome of the newly remodeled rotunda, there was a champagne reception highlighted by a two-thousand-pound cake, which replicated the original market house. The cake, which nearly filled the length of the rotunda, had been prepared by Montilio's Bakery, of Quincy, Massachusetts. The ceremony was covered locally and nationally by the news media, and the *Boston Globe* headlined the occasion HISTORIC MARKET REOPENS.

A century and a half earlier, one of the only events that was noted about the August 26, 1826, opening of the market house was the scramble among its merchants to have the first sale and that Paul Wild from Quincy, Massachusetts, had sold the first waiting customer a leg of lamb. When the market house was reopened in 1976, the *Boston Globe* reported, "One of the first customers was 64-year-old Leo Sullivan of Hingham. He purchased a rib eye roast of beef from John Ciano, 42, owner of the Magliore Carne Butcher Shop."[58]

Both architects—Tad Stahl and Ben Thompson—must have felt immense pride that day. The redesigned market house and its immediate boundary had finally realized most of their visions. The market house had been effectively restored and the nearby traffic-congested streets were converted into open pedestrian concourses. All three levels of the market house (the basement and the first and second floors) had a full range of eating places, shops, cafés, and nightclubs. The glass canopies outside invited entry from all points into the arcade as well as to the cellar space and to the raised first floor of the granite building. They also sheltered restaurants, cafés, produce and flower vendors, and pushcarts.

Yet, as remarkable as the morning's ceremony proved to be, a more remarkable incident transpired at noon—one that no one had anticipated. "The ceremonies concluded just about lunchtime, and at that moment a huge wave of people came pouring out of the banks in the financial district, the big department stores in the shopping district, and the various legal offices around Government Center and made their way down into the market district. And they did not stop."[59] Within one hour the crowd had swelled from a modest few to fifty thousand eager and hungry Bostonians.[60]

The BRA's senior designer for the Downtown-Waterfront Urban Renewal

Plan, John Dobie, later described the event: "It was the crowning apex of Boston's rebirth. Everything that was dead in the city came alive on that day. I could feel the magic. The bicentennial events, the visit of Queen Elizabeth II and the Duke of Edinburgh to Boston a month earlier, the water parade of the Tall Ships—all were eclipsed by the reopening of the market house. Quincy Market made it all seem more grand to me than anything else that had happened before. Another day later and the moment would have been an afterthought."[61] The *Boston Globe* said of the marketplace, "The skeptics will be converted. The optimists will be rewarded. And those who have not followed the sometimes doubtful and tenuous progress of the Faneuil Hall Marketplace resurrection will wonder why such a splendid idea was so long in coming."[62] Ben Thompson later wrote of the opening, "It was a marvelous day, perhaps the biggest, most unexpected street fair Boston has ever enjoyed. It was the day the urban renaissance began."[63]

By evening, the curious were still arriving and, for the first time as long as most Bostonians could remember, the market district was ablaze with vibrant nightlife, which lasted well into the early hours of the next day.

Kevin White later said, "It was a great reward seeing the daily improvement from my office. Watching the vitality of Faneuil Hall Market and the waterfront evolve was a big quiet boost in my life, and if someone said I was a lousy mayor, my first rebuttal would be, 'Come look out my office window and let me show you Faneuil Hall Marketplace and the waterfront.' A little presumptuous on my part, but it was my pride and joy."[64]

Although former mayor John Collins and former BRA director Ed Logue were the acknowledged rebuilders of downtown Boston, Mayor White unquestionably made the city more livable. Near the end of his final term as mayor, Kevin White was asked about some of his greatest accomplishments while in office. In a *Boston Globe* interview he stated, "The Prudential Center is Johnny Hynes," referring to former mayor John B. Hynes. "Center Plaza and City Hall belong to [Mayor] John Collins. But Faneuil Hall?" he said, leaning forward and pointing his thumb to his chest. "Faneuil Hall is mine."[65]

9

Faneuil Hall Marketplace: Sustaining the Results

Following the historic reopening of the market house, extensive news reports gave details of the gala event. Newspapers carried feature stories, and television and radio stations aired coverage of the streams of curious Bostonians filing into the market house through the afternoon and evening after the lunchtime crowd had returned to work. By the end of that first day, the media estimated, more than a hundred thousand people had visited the newly restored market house. "A 150-year-old granite Greek Revival marketplace reopened amid jovial crowds, bagpipers and jugglers as the latest in this city's remarkable downtown renaissance—selling meat and produce," the *New York Times* wrote on Friday, August 27, 1976. "The area, called Dock Square, was the city's marketplace from its beginning, where the ships unloaded their cargo and the farmers brought their produce. Bagpipers wailed, stage bands played on, and actors dressed as vegetables."[1]

All through the following day, people from around the city converged upon the market house, determined to discover for themselves what was causing such local and national media attention. Those who simply expected to see a refurbished old building were amazed to find that an architectural, historical, and triumphal example of urban renewal had finally been accomplished. They may or may not have been aware of the similarities between the birth of the marketplace and its rebirth. "Once again, the reopening of the market house became the paradigm of public and private partnership, a watershed event for real estate development activity. By 1976, Boston's attractiveness as an urban center became manifest."[2] Aware or not, they had heard that, the day before, after many downtown offices had closed for the summer weekend, the market house had been crowded with late-night activity. The cafés, pubs, taverns, restaurants, and eateries were filled to capacity and many had waiting lines stretching past midnight.

During that late-August weekend families from around greater Boston came into the city to experience for themselves the "Festival Marketplace." "If history runs in cycles," one newspaper later said succinctly, "then Boston's waterfront has come full turn. The same area that once spawned a revolution in urban renewal has returned to its former glory. The people are reveling."[3] There was spontaneous entertainment along the pedestrian concourses that featured street shows, promotional activities, jugglers, magicians, and musical performances. The marketplace displayed a world of lively banners, balloons, streamers, brightly colored kiosks, and American flags waving to pay tribute to the bicentennial. Also saluting America's independence was the gallery in the market house's east wing presenting the bicentennial exhibit "Boston 200: The Revolution—Where It All Began."

Although there was an unexpected variety of eating and shopping, the most surprising innovation was the reintroduction of the pushcarts—especially in the section under the glass canopies, now called the Bull Market section. Once an outside fixture at the old market house, the pushcarts of forty-three independent merchants acted as a welcome to the arcades of the new "Festival Marketplace." Another twenty-five stood just outside. Unlike bygone-era pushcart peddlers who hawked only foodstuffs, the new pushcarts sold merchandise like jewelry, sweatshirts, novelty items, leather goods, sweaters, stationery, books, scarves and gloves, and souvenirs. Dozens of young artisans and craftsmen also used the pushcarts as a springboard to launch unique and untried arts and crafts. "Originally, many of the specialty shops incubated items off these pushcarts to embellish their own inventory because the things being sold were so remarkable. People just couldn't get enough of many of these novel creations."[4]

The long colonnade resembled an indoor street with more than seventy concessions selling fish, meats, fruits, farm products, cheeses, wines, flowers, and specialty foods that had both regional and international flavors. There were merchants selling a variety of prepared foods mixed in with the meat vendors who sold beef, pork, veal, sausages, poultry—plain, barbecued, smoked, and cured. Other edibles being offered were candies, ice cream, fried foods, salads, and baked goods. As one newspaper commented, "Quincy Market, the monster calorie center, is done up with Greek revival style, with 108 [*sic*] white columns standing at attention along the hall. Some of them are from Mayor Quincy's day. If this is the cradle of liberty, the hand that isn't rocking the cradle is surely shoveling in the groceries."[5] The food was displayed in a world of sights, sounds, and aromas. Many of these products weren't mass-produced and none of the produce was wrapped in paper or plastic. Jane Thompson said it well: "The natural pageantry of foods—of meat, fish and crops from the fields—the things made and the things grown, all to be tasted, smelled, seen and touched, are the prime source of sensations, experience and amusement in the daily lives of whole populations—were and still are, in most nations."[6]

Although the market house still functioned in a way that was similar to its early days, when food products were the only items sold, the modern version was also transformed into a retail gallery. From behind other colonnade countertops, vendors displayed and sold a variety of merchandise or food-related items such as gourmet pots and pans, baskets, cutlery, and wares related to preparing, cooking, serving, and eating food. Many of these products consisted of unconventional merchandise or exotic spices and preserves intended to create an atmosphere that Ben Thompson called "instructive, historic, amusing and restful."[7]

The terrace restaurants under the glass canopies were as entertaining as they were functional. Patrons sitting in these restaurants could look out at the North and South Market buildings across the pedestrian concourses, where they could see passersby and the variety of ground-level shops that would soon be opened. The outside concourses also allowed space for several restaurants to provide alfresco dining, their territory marked by granite bollards with chains.[8]

Outdoor space adjacent to Faneuil Hall was integrated into the overall plan with greenhouse kiosks that became the focal point of the outer sidewalk scene. Faneuil Hall Flower Market, started in 1936 by Henry McCue with a single pushcart selling flowers, operated twenty-four hours a day and was designed to allow blossoms to be viewed year-round.

The magnificent rotunda, now the focal point of the pavilion, became the primary gathering place inside the market house; people ate at benches, tables, and counters both at the colonnade level and around the second-floor balcony. The restored decor of Alexander Parris's rosette-embellished dome rising three and a half stories, from the colonnade floor to the skylight, contributed to the rotunda's wondrousness.[9]

The restored Faneuil Hall Marketplace, 1978.
COURTESY OF JANE THOMPSON.

As the year 1976 came to an end and the bicentennial celebrations concluded, the "Boston 200" exhibition in the market house's second-floor east wing was replaced with the Alexander Parris Room, a banquet hall business operated by Ben and Jane Thompson. By that time, the market house was fully occupied with permanent merchants and vendors drawing crowds seven days a week. Some of the market house merchants doing business included Aris' Barbecue, Aegean Fare

Restaurant, Brown Derby Kosher Deli, Britton Trading Company, Freedman Bakery, The Kitchen, Faneuil Hall Wine and Spirits, Herbert's Candy, Lily's Restaurant, General Nutrition Center, Ming Tree Restaurant, Marion's Restaurant, Coffee Connection, Lawson's Ice Cream, Black Forest Delicatessen, Lily's Café and Lily's Bar, City Side Café, Tobacconist Limited, Walrus and the Carpenter Raw Bar, Ames Plow Tavern, Yogurt Cup, and Miles of Faneuil Hall Marketplace.

By early 1977 the newly reopened market house had become an established eating and shopping destination for many city workers, city residents, and suburban visitors. By the following summer, even while the North and South Market buildings were still being rebuilt, the "Festival Marketplace" had also become a popular attraction that strengthened the tourist industry in Massachusetts. The construction workers found themselves faced with a new dilemma: how to do their jobs around the increasing crowds that were drawn to the market house each day.

The South Market building was reopened a year after the market house—on August 26, 1977. Once again, there was a gala champagne reception—this time highlighted by a 2,500-pound cake, which replicated the original South Market building and which was devoured by more than five thousand spectators. The interior of South Market was redesigned to accommodate 80,000 square feet of retail space constructed in the basement, street level, and second floor.[10] Because of the success of the "Festival Marketplace" concept, fashionable clothing, accessory, jewelry, and gift shops were instantly drawn to space at South Market. Some of these retailers included Louis's Berkeley Shop, which offered quality men's and women's apparel, and Crate and Barrel, which provided trendy home furnishings. Other shops sold sporting goods, crafts, and imports, or had studios with art galleries. Four additional five-star restaurants served distinctive food in relatively small spaces—Café Cybèle, La Strada Restaurant, Cricket's, and Seaside Restaurant and Bar. Since the restaurants were positioned at the east and west ends of this building, the curiosity of the customers walking past the ground-floor shops was naturally aroused.

The remaining 80,000 square feet on the upper levels were divided into office suites with a historic ambience that had once been almost lost. The suites were provided with every modern convenience but retained the original granite-encased window frames, the cumbersome wooden beamed ceilings, and the exposed brick walls. A number of established downtown Boston firms relocated to offices at South

Market; one of the first to move from a modern high-rise tower at One Boston Place was Bay Colony Properties, the former Land-Trust division of the international real estate firm Cabot, Cabot and Forbes.

At the North Market reopening on August 26, 1978, the markets' earlier failing reputation was completely exonerated. The popular conductor Arthur Fiedler enthralled a nationwide television audience by leading the Boston Pops Orchestra in an inspiring repertoire. Once again, there was a champagne reception highlighted by a 2,500-pound replica cake of the original North Market building. North Market was smaller than South Market by 40,000 square feet. When finished, North Market was leased to retailers in much the same way as South Market (with the exception of Durgin Park, which, as an original tenant, owned its units). Shops situated between the basement and second-floor levels included boutiques, home furnishings and accessories, personal services, fast-food eateries, taverns, and more quality restaurants. The Landmark Inn (owned by Ben and Jane Thompson), the largest multilevel restaurant in the Marketplace, opened at the west end of North Market. It had an eatery situated on each level: the Flower Garden Café, Thompson's Chowder House, the Wild Goose Rotisserie, and Bunch of Grapes Tavern.

Inside both the North and South Market buildings were corridors that linked the upper-floor shops both horizontally and vertically and that allowed strollers to be sheltered from the elements when walking from one shop to another. No longer following the tradition of the past's individual stores, renovators had broken through the brick party walls that had separated the units. This not only accommodated the inside passageways to access upper-floor retail space but also allowed larger office suites on the upper floors to expand between one original store and the next. One consequence of this renovation was that all the remaining fireplace openings were bricked up and sealed off for good.

Like the South Market building, the remaining upper levels of North Market were remodeled into office suites. Each warehouse/store building had a greenhouse-like extension protruding from its west end, which allowed for glassed-in dining: South Market's glass shed was built upon part of the former Merchants Row; North Market's over a portion of the once-notorious Roe Buck Passage.[11] And in both buildings double sets of skylights were added to every section of the gable roofs.

Durgin Park, once nearly the sole occupant of the North Market building, continued serving Poor Man's Roast Beef, New England Clam Chowder, Boston Baked Beans, and a "Bale of Hay" at the same location it had occupied for 150 years. Together with its newest addition, a separate downstairs restaurant named Oyster Park, this enduring landmark business that had never made any claims about its unique style of seating customers at long tables, elbow-to-elbow, now served a new generation of customers in the same timeless fashion. At Durgin Park, with its stolid, unpretentious menu and its quirky, brusque wait staff, a side order of corn bread was readily served alongside its folklore. The only thing missing was the sawdust that once covered the floors.[12]

Collectively, the three refurbished buildings provided about 430,000 square feet of space that consisted of 290,000 for retail and 140,000 for offices—enough room for two hundred tenants.[13] The 1975 construction loan from Boston lenders, which mandated that the redevelopment proceed in three stages (despite Jim Rouse's reluctance), became one of the most beneficial aspects of the project. By working on one building each year, the Rouse Company was able to refocus its marketing and merchandising strategies. The immediate success of the market house allowed the Rouse Company to seek higher rents at South and North Market and thereby upgrade the tenant quality. When all three buildings had been reopened, some of the merchants included Carol Ann Bake Shop, Rebecca's, Pizzeria Regina II, Malben's Gourmet, Fisherman's Net, Pasta Plaza, the Prime Shop, Boston Tea Company, Belgian Fudge, Monogram's, Eagerman's Bakery, Baby Watson Cheesecake, Cardoos Spices, Boston Chipyard Cookies, Au Bon Pain Bakery, the Juicerie, the Jelly Shack of Cape Cod, Anna's Fried Dough, Nutcracker, Salty Dog Seafood, Candlewick, Left Hand Compliments, Lucy's Canvas, Bookbinder, the Poppy Shop, Wood Products, Concord Shop, Heidi's Natural Poultry Company, Jennetta's, Charcutrix, Karmelkorn Shop, the Great American Lobster Company, and Swensen's Ice Cream.

Once construction was completed, Faneuil Hall Marketplace unified all the closed-off streets into a single pedestrian mall. Street fairs were regularly featured there, as were parades, puppet shows, jugglers, magicians, promotions, concerts, and dances. The concourses also provided easy access for daytime shoppers to patronize the many stores and nighttime revelers to move around between its restaurants, cabarets, clubs, and taverns.

The Marketplace was incorporated into Boston's Freedom Trail (a published, self-guided tour of historic sites). Besides directing people to nearby Faneuil Hall, this listing now brought people to the Marketplace as well, where sightseeing and fashions were just a few feet away from fresh flowers, fried dough, or filet mignon. Downtown office workers continued to contribute greatly to the Marketplace's success by adding to the lunchtime crowds and after-hour entertainment. As Ben Thompson commented, "I'm satisfied that we achieved what we set out to achieve. The great challenge now is to maintain the quality and spirit of what we have."[14]

To do this, when the late-night establishments had closed and the evening crowds were gone, the Marketplace was thoroughly cleaned by a fifty-person maintenance crew. Under the watchful eye of the Rouse Company's general manager, Jim McLean, the brick, granite, and cobblestone concourses were vacuumed and steam-cleaned. Inside the market house, the colonnade was cleared of the debris it had accumulated that day, and the oak floors were scrubbed, waxed, and buffed. "With so many people crowding the Marketplace daily," Jim McLean said later, "security, maintenance, and sanitation were my major concerns. Cleanliness is what people notice. All that debris that's left behind—like pizza crusts, chewing gum, discarded litter—I'd make sure there was no trace of it by the next day. People began calling me 'Mac the Vac.'"[15]

Each season, new arrangements of flowers and plants were added to the concourse planters under the honey locust trees. One of the most difficult maintenance problems was keeping the exterior brick, cobblestone, and granite-block grounds cleared of snow during the winter months.[16]

McLean managed a staff of 110 that included four supervisors, two assistant managers, a comptroller, and an office manager. Legal, engineering, architectural, accounting, market research, and leasing services were provided at the Rouse Company's headquarters in Columbia, Maryland. "At the time, we had fifty-page leases that required that the larger tenants provide the names of their attorney, accountant, architect, and contractor. There were strict lease restrictions that limited the variety of the agreed-upon goods they sold, their signs, window displays, how their interiors were built out, and that they remain open seven days a week."[17]

Management also kept tight control over outside entertainment by scheduling performers at designated areas and appointed times along the concourses. This restricted merchant activity. Noticeably, there was no constant music played over loudspeakers, nor were there any supermarket-style shopping carts. Trash was continually removed to the nearby facility at the rate of twelve to fifteen tons every day.

The Rouse Company also staffed its own permanent security force, which employed at least one Boston special police officer. Boston Police maintained a presence by means of patrol vehicles, mounted policemen, and officers riding motorcycles around the nearby streets. The sight of so many security personnel and Boston police officers acted as a deterrent to potential crime.

The negative predictions by critics who had once insisted it would be impossible to lure people back into Boston from suburban shopping malls were proven wrong. When completed, Faneuil Hall Marketplace generated three times the retail revenues that were originally forecast. It attracted an incredible number of students, primary destination and secondary market shoppers, local residents, visitors, tourists, and conventioneers, "up to twelve million [visitors] in 1978 when the entire complex was finally open."[18] By 1978 Faneuil Hall Marketplace was viewed as one of the great economic success stories in America, a textbook example of twentieth-century urban renewal. Nationally, there were a number of urban redevelopment projects that preceded Faneuil Hall Marketplace. The Marketplace, however, was the first such spectacular revitalization of old commercial space into such a heavily food-oriented space, with retail and offices included. Faneuil Hall Marketplace had more restaurants, taverns, and eateries, more prepared food, produce, and other food-related merchants than the others. And at the time, the Marketplace was more successful than the others in terms of paying dividends to its investors and to the city where it was located.

The enabling mix of public money and private participation marked a shift in public opinion that established a watershed for preservation not only in Boston but in other cities as well. Like the original 1826 development, the Marketplace rapidly became the acknowledged national example of how an old city could incorporate the best of its heritage into the future. "The restoration is one of the stellar features of Boston's exemplary downtown renewal, a remarkably sensitive synthesis of new and old, from Faneuil to City Hall."[19]

It was also popular. Within its first five years of operation, the Rouse Company "estimated that [6.5-acre] Faneuil Hall Marketplace attracted more than 14 million visitors annually."[20] This represented a greater volume of patrons per acre than Disney World in Orlando, Florida, with its more expansive grounds. And the Marketplace had surpassed Disney World without a corporate structure. As Ben Thompson later put it, "The difference between Disney World and Faneuil Hall Marketplace [was] the multiple independent merchants who succeeded in making the redevelopment work. Whereas Disney is a corporation, the Marketplace is mainly tenanted by merchants who strive all year at making their businesses succeed."[21]

Now the envy of many American cities seeking to enliven downtown merchandising, its contribution was also recognized as a vehicle to restore confidence in declining urban areas of other cities such as New York, Baltimore, Miami, Los Angeles, Tokyo, and Glasgow. As Ben Thompson noted, "Quincy Market could well point the way for other cities in their replanning not only of major market centers, but of the lively subcenters and exciting streets that future cities need by the hundreds. The market concept is a matter of total attitude and works to sell apples and oranges, pots and pans, or sides of beef. The long-term program does not belong to public agencies but belongs inescapably to the people as a joint public-private constituency that affected the nearly deadly limbo that previously existed."[22]

Immediately after Faneuil Hall Marketplace opened, the downward economic trends that had plagued Boston for nearly thirty years began to turn around. The flight from Boston into the suburbs began to stop; it was no longer a mark of success to retreat from the city and live in the country. Architect Tad Stahl later related this change to the "success of the Marketplace idea [which] can only be measured by an unmeasurable event. At a certain moment, people in suburbia adjusted their behavior to include downtown. Years later, observers would credit Faneuil Hall Marketplace and its progeny with permanently shifting the balance between those lifestyles."[23]

There is no doubt that the Marketplace contributed to Boston's retail recovery. After the 1976 bicentennial celebrations ended, visitors kept returning to Boston and the economic demand for further commercial space created business opportunities where they had never before existed, especially at the waterfront district. "As the latest in a series of renewal projects started in the early 1960s by Boston Redevelopment director Edward Logue, the full opening of the waterfront in recent months has instilled a new pride and rejuvenation in this city's downtown, one of the most livable major downtowns in the United States."[24]

Some would argue that the reopening of the market house merely coincided with the area's economic recovery. Tourists had already made reservations to partake in the 1975–1976 bicentennial celebrations, for example. There were, however, many direct economic benefits. Mayor Kevin White put it well when he said there was "no question that . . . Quincy Market brought life back to the waterfront between North Station and South Station."[25]

Between 1974 and 1979, the Stahl idea of including residential space in the Marketplace began to be realized in some of its neighboring buildings. This was most noticeably seen beyond Faneuil Hall Marketplace at the waterfront district, where many old, empty buildings were converted into condominiums with commercial units on the street floors. Faneuil Hall Marketplace acted as a catalyst for other nearby areas: the Fulton Street shopping district, located within walking distance en route to the North End, was created; old buildings along Atlantic Avenue, which runs along today's harborfront, were reconstructed, including the former Prince Spaghetti building; and Boston's venerable North End was positively affected. Even the decisions to develop the nearby Marriott and Bostonian Hotels, on Long Wharf and in the Blackstone Street block, were influenced by the success of the Marketplace.

The MBTA (Massachusetts Bay Transit Authority) saw increased revenues attributable to passengers traveling to stations and bus stops near the Marketplace. Revenues from area parking meters, municipal parking lots, and private parking concessions showed a marked increase. It is estimated that, during the first five years of operation, about half the Marketplace visitors arrived by car and the other half by public transit.[26] And once the multilevel Dock Square parking garage was opened in 1980, the Marketplace finally had a permanent nearby parking facility for its patrons.

Within five years of the reopening, many of the creative products sold from Marketplace pushcarts grew into either a regional or a national business. Marketplace exposure probably contributed to that growth. According to Ben Thompson, the Rouse Company could have easily leased to merchants who sold low-end trinkets or inexpensive tourist-oriented goods—as many tourist areas did at the time—or even leased only to national franchises for eateries. Instead, they solicited high-end tenants with unique inventory and marketing know-how. Some of these merchants were Crabtree and Evelyn, Produce House, Pacos Tacos, The Original Freedman's Bakery, Geppetto's, Lord Bunbury, J. J. Donovan's Tavern, Sweet Stuff, Boxes, Boston Scrimshanders, Celtic Weavers, Kreeger and Sons, Pavo Real Gallery, Pillow Talk, Bear Necessities, Fiorucci, and Butterfly Garden.[27]

The private cost to develop Faneuil Hall Marketplace after three years was about $32 million, or approximately 35 percent more than anticipated in 1975. Public participation had reached $17 million, making the final public subsidy more than half of the private cost. This brought the total cost to about $49 to $50 million. The BRA claimed that the public cost of retaining the historic buildings in order to attract a competent developer was more than justified because private developers were compelled to work under strict restraints. During the first decade following the Marketplace's opening, lease payments to the city continued to increase: "By the end of 1987, after nine years of full payments, receipts totaled $17.9 million. After accounting for the property taxes the city would have collected if the buildings had remained privately owned and unimproved, net lease revenues totaled $15.5 million, under base-case model assumptions about property tax assessments."[28]

In terms of profitability, it was unquestionable not only that the BRA secured the best deal for the city but that its staff gained invaluable experience that was instrumental in executing subsequent tax-lease arrangements in other Boston developments.[29] The city put in about 17 percent of the $17 million of public money used to develop the market area.[30] During development "the city took comfort in their financial advisor's estimate that the project would generate annual revenues of $1.5 million by the mid-1980s. This was almost seven times what the old dilapidated markets yielded before renovation. In addition, the city faced no additional public expense because, under the terms of the lease, the Rouse Company was responsible for maintaining the streets and providing security for the marketplace."[31] Twenty years later, analysts agreed that the ground sublease with the Rouse Company was financially favorable to the city. Over the first twenty years the Rouse Company also "paid $41.5 million in city real estate taxes . . . or just over $2 million annually." And the "2,500 jobs generated by the Marketplace has meant $16.2 million in payroll taxes since 1976, plus $27.8 million paid by employees in personal income taxes. And on sales of $1.5 billion since it opened, the Marketplace has paid $62 million in retail sales taxes, or typically between $3 million and $3.5 million annually."[32] Although it is difficult to pull out of these numbers what part would not have existed if the Marketplace had not been restored as it was, it is clear that Rouse Company statistics show the creation of new money and new jobs for the city. Jim McLean later recalled that, during the first five years of operation, the Marketplace's office space employed 750 to 800 people.

❧

After its five-year honeymoon period, problems began to be acknowledged and solutions were sought.

The original merchant leases included a basic rent payment schedule plus a provision that tenants contribute a portion of real estate operating expenses, usually referred to as CAM (common area maintenance) fees. These fees were prorated by the area of leased space in proportion to the size of the Marketplace. Operating expenses included in the CAM fees were the maintenance costs, utilities expense, and real estate taxes. By 1982 CAM fees increased dramatically. The Rouse Company claimed that the costs to operate the Marketplace had continued to increase with the growth in the Marketplace's popularity. The newly formed 150-member Faneuil Hall Merchants Association (FHMA) disagreed and charged that the Rouse Company was increasing CAM fees unfairly. Claiming they were being overcharged, FHMA initiated a lawsuit against the Rouse Company to recover what the merchants saw as unsubstantiated CAM fees. Three years later, a $3 million settlement was paid to FHMA.

In 1989 the BRA and the Rouse Company took part in the Faneuil Hall Marketplace Revitalization Program. Unlike the efforts made in the 1800s to keep up with growth and change, the late-twentieth-century improvements were made with at least some oversight by groups to keep up with the wear and tear caused by the volumes of people flocking to the marketplace during its first ten years.

Contractors A. Bonfatti and Company, together with architects Robert Wood Associates, completed a $5 million revitalization campaign, which focused on improving the concourses, making building repairs, erecting an information pavilion along the South Market concourse, and providing better outside lighting around the Marketplace. Additionally, the market house's oak flooring was replaced with glazed tiles, suggestive of bricks and granite, that spanned the width and length of the colonnade. Several original wooden doors, complete with antique hardware, were restored and placed at principal entrances. The broad wooden railing atop the glass balustrade encircling the second-floor opening of the rotunda was replaced with metal. And in a decision to go with functionality over history and aesthetics, two newly designed curved metal stairways were installed inside the rotunda, so that visitors could access that space by means of permanent, wider sets of stairs. Also, around the ceiling opening of market hall, on the space below the glass balustrade, gold-leaf lettering was inscribed that said: THIS BUILDING HAS SERVED THE PEOPLE OF BOSTON AS THE CENTRAL MARKET OF THE CITY SINCE ITS DEDICATION IN AUGUST, 1826. That same year, a gilded QUINCY MARKET sign was suspended across each portico of the market house and gilded NORTH MARKET and SOUTH MARKET signs were affixed to the end walls of those buildings. This was the first time in the 163-year history of Faneuil Hall Market that the name Quincy Market appeared on the market house.

It is difficult to maintain cutting-edge thinking in business, and Quincy Marketplace was no exception to the rule. Between 1980 and 1990, there was a gradual change in ambience at Quincy Market. The "Festival Marketplace" was taking on a more corporate feel. Some of the original meat, produce, and flower vendors were replaced with larger restaurants. The Disney Store moved in and displaced eleven smaller shops in the North Market building. The Nature Company, Waterstone's Booksellers, and Warner Brothers stores soon followed, forcing many smaller family-owned businesses from their locations. By 1995 the Warner Brothers store, in particular, became a symbol of all that seemed to be going wrong. Architect Ben Thompson said in an interview at the time, "There's been a shift from local business to national chains and tourist shops. We warned in the beginning tourism would corrode, and it's come true. Tourism changes what merchants sell, and that affects the environment. Also, it's now run by a mall developer applying mall principles to what he once agreed would be a more delicate local environment. Bringing in Disney is trendy, but its out of context and makes Faneuil Hall like every mall in America."[33]

By this time Jim Rouse had died, and the initial enthusiasm the Rouse Company had shown for quality seemed to be waning. Thompson went on to voice what many were feeling. "Most of the news I get about Faneuil Hall is not good. Architectural friends say the controls are not effective. Disney's there, which is too bad, because it's strictly tourist, and that's not what we had in mind. What would I have done differently? Well, I might have planted more trees."[34]

Thompson's concern was also shared by preservationist Walter Muir Whitehill and BRA director Bob Kenney. In 1979, his last year as director, Bob Kenney made every effort to establish for the Marketplace a BRA committee, which he wanted to call the Market Oversight Panel and Design Control Committee. Such a committee had been one of the stipulations of the Rouse Company's sublease, but it had never been created. If it had been, it would have been there over the years to approve or reject changes in the types of merchants represented at the Marketplace (along with any other proposed changes). Regulations governing physical changes to the buildings and streets, which had remained city-owned, had been mostly enforced. Bob Kenney later commented dryly of the Marketplace at the time, "Walter Muir Whitehill would be rolling over in his grave at the thought of Disney and Warner Brothers stores occupying space at the historic markets."[35]

The reasons for this change were more complex than a total lack of oversight. The severe national recession during the early 1990s caused a downward trend in consumer spending. Many Bostonians stopped coming to the Marketplace and merchants had to begin to rely more heavily on tourists. This led to changes in the ambience of the Marketplace. "The problem is that tourists have more interest in trinkets and souvenirs. As these items proliferate, the character of the market changes. Locals regard tourists as obstacles. Already the effects are apparent. Butchers slide into fast food items, fruit cups and sandwiches. A florist sells soda pop, the produce man devotes more energy to takeout salads, and everywhere in America, the proliferation of T-shirts threatens to build the image of an underwear factory. We predict it will be as hard to maintain the Marketplace as a delightful 'place' to go as it was to create it."[36]

Although the number of tourists remained constant in Boston during this period, their spending waned and Marketplace retail sales flattened. Many shops at the Marketplace faced serious competition from sleeker suburban shopping malls built during the boom years of the 1980s. This worsening of retail sales and suburban competition caused vacancies at the Marketplace to increase.

The *Boston Sunday Herald* wrote, "And the quirky, enchanting character of the place—a delightful Boston blend of eccentric goods and unique services—has been flattened. Quincy Market is turning into Anywhere-There's-A-Warner-Brothers-Store-USA. It was once the jewel of urban redevelopment when Rouse restored the granite marketplace during the Kevin White glory days. The posh, grand opening of Quincy Market became a national event carried on network television. Now the place that once epitomized prosperous pride and optimism has become a ratty tourist trap of bad restaurants, cookie-cutter mall stores and crime after dark."[37]

Between 1993 and 1995 the Rouse Company began to increase CAM fees without explanation and without justifying the increase. When these fees became too costly for the smaller merchants, some were forced to leave and their space was rented to the regional and national chain stores typically seen in suburban malls and neighborhood shopping centers.

An intense acrimony again surfaced between the merchants and the Rouse Company. The Faneuil Hall Merchants Association claimed that the Maryland company had purposely forced out many small retail operators by ignoring the standards established by its now deceased founder, James Rouse.

The Rouse Company contended that shopping centers were always reinventing themselves and, by attracting the best and most unique tenants, the Marketplace could not sustain its expensive operating costs. The company claimed it was doing business with the best merchants, which included national chains, and "dismissed claims that smaller merchants were being systematically removed from the Marketplace, noting that 80 percent of the shops [were still] smaller businesses and locally owned."[38] The company also noted that "there [had] been 25 small shops added over the past three years, all with local owners who maintain[ed] only a Faneuil Marketplace store," and that "statistics also reveal that 81 percent of the stores would fall into the category 'small' while just 19 percent are run by large, national operations. On a square footage basis, 54 percent of the space is occupied by the small stores, while 46 percent is run by the national behemoths."[39]

By 1996 the Boston mayor's office found itself in the middle of this finger-pointing between the merchants and the Rouse Company. As a result, members of the FHMA met with Mayor Thomas Menino, who in turn met with representatives of the Rouse Company. "For his [Menino's] part, he would say only that he is concerned about the impact of large stores at the marketplace."[40] After meeting with the mayor, Rouse Company officials announced to the press that management would not displace any smaller merchants by renting to the larger stores. This was not enough to help the relationship between merchants and the Rouse Company.

Charges and countercharges reflected the deteriorating relationship between them. Unable to come to reasonable terms out of court, the FHMA filed a class-action lawsuit in federal district court against the Rouse Company, claiming that "the tenants accuse Rouse of systematically, secretly defrauding and gouging them by inflating fees for rent and maintenance. The lawsuit formalizes the frustration that merchants have felt for months and years."[41]

The Rouse Company immediately filed a countersuit alleging that the merchants weren't abiding by the terms of their leases. "Beyond the lawsuit itself, Faneuil Hall Marketplace has also been under fire of late for supposedly detracting away from its original concept of small, specialty stores and for catering more to a tourist audience than the local Bostonian. The advent of large conglomerates such as Warner Brothers Studio store and Victoria's Secret has, critics claim, given Faneuil Hall Marketplace more of a mall atmosphere than the unique operation for which it is famous."[42]

A year and a half passed before the Rouse Company named Joseph "Skip" Coppola to the position of vice president and general manager of Faneuil Hall Marketplace in May 1997. He was the third person to hold that title. By hiring Coppola, the Rouse Company took its first step in bettering relations with the Faneuil Hall Merchants Association and in improving the company's corporate image within the city of Boston. Skip Coppola later said of this step on the part of the Rouse Company: "I was brought in with the primary objective of resolving a major lawsuit between certain tenants and the Rouse Company, which had been lingering since 1996. By 1999 the lawsuit was resolved and part of the resolution was that the Rouse Company would renovate Faneuil Hall Market in accordance with a scope of work which the city, the tenants, and the Rouse Company had mutually agreed upon. This renovation would end up costing close to $20 million. An additional agreement resulting from the resolution of the lawsuit was a commitment by the Rouse Company to target local merchants to lease rental space as it became available. This challenge was met with some success in the immediate aftermath of this agreement."[43]

Before the lawsuit was settled, as a gesture of goodwill, in 1999 the Rouse Company began major renovations in a three-year building improvement campaign. After twenty years of demands put upon the market house, the need to modernize parts of the building was apparent. The wear and tear on the copper-clad dome, repairs required for the glass canopies, and the need to provide better handicap access in accordance with the 1990 Americans with Disabilities Act[44] were just a few of the all-too-obvious issues that needed to be addressed. Elevators were rebuilt, handicap accesses to restrooms were improved, and the colonnade became fully temperature-controlled for the first time in its 174-year history. Under architects D'Agostino Izzo Quirk, the building improvements entailed the restoration of the market house's granite facades (once again, the same Chelmsford quarries at Fletcher Granite Company provided the requisite white granite); the installation of new outside lighting and new outside planters, furniture, benches, and granite seating; a new signage and identity program; the use of new specialty pushcarts; the restoration of the colonnade's market hall;[45] and a complete restoration of the copper-topped dome. In addition, four new major restaurants were planned for a 2001 opening, including Cheers, the Boston establishment made famous by a popular 1980s television series of the same name.

"At that moment in time, the Marketplace was positioned to implement a program which was intended to accomplish specific objectives agreed to by both merchants and the Rouse Company. The resolution of the longstanding lawsuit with certain tenants and a recent agreement with the tenants and the city on the much-needed renovation were the springboards from which we moved forward. The physical renovation in conjunction with the re-merchandising of the Marketplace, which had as its primary objective the upgrading of the restaurants in an effort to attract 'the locals,' progressed on schedule. Upon completion of this program, Faneuil Hall Marketplace was positioned to reconnect with the community at large while maintaining its position as the number-one tourist attraction in Boston."[46]

By the end of 1999 the copper sheathing of the market house dome was fully restored to its original appearance for the first time in its long history. The old copper sheathing was entirely stripped and the dome was clad with new copper provided by Paul Revere Copper, a company that dated back to its American patriot namesake. According to Peter "Pete" Leyden, project supervisor for Walsh Brothers Construction Company, which was overseeing the dome restoration, laser-guided levels were required to align the copper sheathing to its original contoured wooden planking. The exterior planking was still tight to the weather. And it was noted that the supposition about where the laminated supporting ribs for the dome had been assembled in 1825–1826 was correct: They had clearly been assembled on the ground, probably by shipbuilders of that era, and then hoisted into place. Other historical evidence was also noted: traces of smoke damage from the 1925 fire; wooden-beam reinforcement from the 1935 repairs; and the steel I-beams that had been inserted during the 1976 renovation.

Pete Leyden pointed out that, over the years since 1826, the weight of the elliptical dome had pushed out the pavilion's exterior granite support walls by an aver-

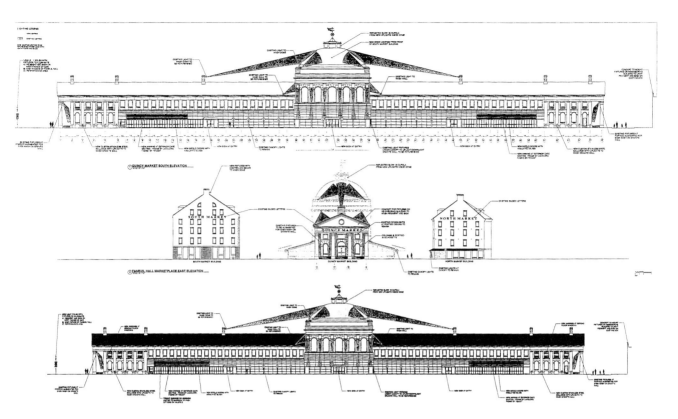

Quincy Market enters the new millennium.
COURTESY OF D'AGOSTINO IZZO QUIRK ARCHITECTS.

age of four inches. The 1976 steel I-beam insertions, however, had compensated for this by fortifying the octagonal base with steel.

The space between the inner and outer domes was in remarkably good condition—there was no graffiti, no debris, no evidence of vandalism, despite all the years it had been left derelict. Work on the dome also revealed some historical data: the name J. EMERY was neatly carved into the side of one of the laminated beams but it was undated. This same name was found listed in the ledger kept by the Committee on the Extension of Faneuil Hall between 1824 and 1826, with the indication that he had been paid $107.00 for his "bill of freight of lumber," on September 14, 1825.[47]

After being reopened to the public for twenty-five years, the market house was designated an individual Boston landmark by the Boston Landmarks Commission.

Although Faneuil Hall Market was already listed on the National Historic Register, the city landmark status gave the market house additional protection by the city against future redevelopment that would alter its exterior. Any future redevelopment proposals would first have to be approved by the Boston Landmark Commission. Never again would "Quincy's Market" be threatened with extinction.

In January 2001 Michael Kelleher replaced Joseph "Skip" Coppola as the fourth vice president and general manager of Faneuil Hall Marketplace. Kelleher's immediate goal was to restore the Marketplace to the Boston Mecca it had been in the late 1970s. His retail-leasing strategy was to accommodate those local merchants who offered their own unique inventory. Additionally, he increased the seating capacity around the Marketplace by 125 percent and the lighting by 75 percent, and installed signage throughout the complex that would both enhance the complex and assist visitors. "The Marketplace had . . . lost some share of the downtown Boston office market during the recession," Kelleher later explained, "and I was determined to recapture that share as another means of enhancing the local atmosphere around the complex."[48]

By spring of 2001 visible changes were evident. The new copper dome, the extensive landscaping and exterior seating, and the introduction of signage identifying parts of the complex were finally completed. New retail tenants and restaurants began opening, such as Rustic Kitchen, McCormick and Schmick's Seafood Restaurant, Ned Devine's Irish Pub, Local Charm, Head Games, Pinang, Jazz Café, Zoinks!, and the Bostonian Society's Historical Museum Store. Kelleher later said of these results of his initial efforts, "It was good to see that the Marketplace was finally evolving back to what the Rouse Company had intended in 1976, but there is still much more to do in the near future. When the Central Artery is finally removed I plan to make sure that the Marketplace effectively interacts with the new recreational parks and other new waterfront attractions. My challenge will be to return Faneuil Hall Marketplace back to where it was [socially] located once before, back to the Boston waterfront where history, excitement, and enjoyment interact within this great area, in this great city of Boston."[49]

By the time Faneuil Hall Marketplace celebrated its twenty-fifth anniversary during the summer of 2001, Warner Brothers, Waterstone's Booksellers, the Disney Store, and other large retailers were gone or were scheduled to close. As part of its commitment to the Boston community, the Rouse Company pledged to restore the caliber of merchants that had existed when the Faneuil Hall Marketplace was first reopened. Positive changes around the Marketplace were evidence that, 175 years after "Quincy's Market" first opened its doors, Faneuil Hall Marketplace was ready to serve as yet another marketplace for another Boston.

Conclusion

History has been repeated again and again around Quincy's Market. Growing out of Faneuil Hall in the area considered to be the birthplace of Boston, Quincy's Market was a large part of the city's rebirth in the early nineteenth century, and again, as Faneuil Hall Marketplace, during the latter part of the twentieth century. During periods of decline, like Boston itself, the marketplace has always found a way to improve without losing its essential character. It has been blessed with the right guiding spirit in each moment of its need.

The memory of my father's words from that snowy afternoon in 1963 still resonates, linked with the pleasing scent of Christmas trees being sold just outside the old market house and the sight of what looked like the last remaining pushcart peddler. "Your great-grandfather used to say to my father, when he took him as a boy to these markets during the late 1800s, 'Let's see what they're cooking up today down at Old Grampy Jo's Place.' "[1] "Old Grampy Jo's Place" is the traditional family term for the market house, fondly named for "our" Mayor Josiah Quincy.

Before we left the marketplace, later on that wintry December day, my father led me to Faneuil Hall and turned me around to face all three market buildings from across busy Merchants Row. "I don't think a single person in this city could tell you who built those buildings," he said with concern, placing his large hands on my shoulders. "People have been coming here for nearly a hundred and fifty years and I'll bet hardly a person knows why it's even called Quincy Market. I think it's unforgivable that Mayor Quincy has never been given the full credit he deserves for endowing Boston with one of its greatest landmarks. I wish somebody would write down the story behind the markets and give Old Grampy Jo Quincy his due before there's nothing left to remember."[2]

That day I became curious about this family icon who was Josiah Quincy, and his ghost pleasantly presented himself to me the moment I touched those once-blackened white granite columns at the market house. As an adult, I began researching every available aspect pertaining to the history of the markets, while Josiah's spirit guided my search and led me to uncover rare documents that helped complete the story of Quincy's Market. In the process of my research, I was fortunate to witness the resurrection of the three market buildings during the mid- to late 1970s and to be allowed to inspect portions of the markets' original construction that were uncovered during the renovations made between 1999 and 2001. Not surprisingly, I have come to regard the 1826 development of Quincy's Market as nothing less than hallowed antiquity.

The story of the Faneuil Hall Market's founder, Josiah Quincy, is more than a Quincy family story. It is the story of a man who could be as hard as the market house granite and who could deliver such persuasive arguments that he went from having no supporters to being highly appreciated. As mayor, he worked relentlessly for the good of Boston's citizens. He did not tolerate profiteering, corruption, dishonesty, avarice, self-interest, or duplicity in any form.

In reading his words and the words of others of his day, I came to see these qualities most clearly in the meeting he called on Christmas Eve 1824. On that night Mayor Quincy called the City Council into an emergency session to resolve the Nathan Spear's Wharf issue to the city's advantage. Needless to say, the mayor, who remained temperate his entire life, knew that the members of the Council were anxious to get home and imbibe their own Christmas cheer. He used the timing to his advantage.

He did not threaten retribution against the Spear heirs, although their attempt to stall the project until they got the highest price for their property angered him. He simply found an alternative solution that allowed the city to acquire the property at the same price as other properties and also protected the city from the effort and expense of unnecessary litigation. The decision he wrested from the City Council that night—to move the market house over far enough so that it would not be on Spear property—allowed the project to go through as planned (and disallowed the Spear heirs from unfairly profiting from a city endeavor).

Josiah Quincy never let a minor excuse like inexperience keep him from doing what had to be done. Although he had never so much as built his own house, he involved himself in every aspect of the project in addition to all his other duties.

Portrait of Josiah Quincy, 1839.
COURTESY OF THE MASSACHUSETTS HISTORICAL SOCIETY.

When the project was completed, Mayor Quincy did not take the credit for himself. He attributed the markets' success to the faith placed in him by his colleagues and fellow citizens. For he knew he was fortunate to have experts as his allies.

Without Alexander Parris, the buildings would not have the technical achievements and the visual beauty they have today. He not only moved Asher Benjamin's designs to a higher level of aesthetics and unity; Parris also brought with him the best talent to skillfully implement his ideas. These builders and craftsmen helped maintain the project's quality.

Mayor Quincy closely monitored the progress of the project, as when he sent Alderman Child and others to the Chelmsford quarries and Portsmouth, New Hampshire, to refresh the supply of granite. And when more labor was needed than the city could supply, Mayor Quincy hired prisoners to help build the streets and deliver stone by ship and drag stone from the canal to the work site and complete the granite work on the market house in time for its summer 1826 opening. This labor source is probably why restorers found irregular measurements and less-than-professional workmanship in some parts of market house construction.[3]

For their extra time, only Alderman David Weld Child was possibly paid more than his normal salary. (He was budgeted $1,000 per month for his position as superintendent of the Building Committee.) There is no evidence that Asher Benjamin was ever paid anything other than his alderman's salary for his efforts at designing the new marketplace (and this may have had something to do with his subsequent bankruptcy). I believe, though I cannot prove, that even Alexander Parris was never paid more than the $2,500 he was initially offered (which was the same amount the mayor earned for a year's term of office). I expect that Mayor Quincy convinced the architect that this most notable public commission would lead to a greater reputation and therefore higher commissions—which it did.

Josiah Quincy combined his sharp mind and firm convictions and never-ending energy to better his city. He used the methods at his disposal to give Boston the marketplace it needed. This is not unlike Peter Faneuil, who with personal means gave the city the market house it needed in his day. It is appropriate that Faneuil Hall officially bears his name. Yet Quincy's Market has never been officially designated with Quincy's name.[4] Still, to this day, both Bostonians and city visitors persist in calling it "Quincy Market," as a fitting tribute to this Quincy family member I so admire. I am delighted that, in 1989, signs were put up at the market house to acknowledge him. Although he spent little time basking in the glories of his administration, Josiah Quincy was indeed "the Patriarch of all Public Men in America."[5]

Thanks to the efforts of people such as Walter Muir Whitehill and Frederick "Tad" Stahl and Roger Webb and Benjamin Thompson and James Rouse and Kevin

White and Robert Kenney and others[6] who could put together a mix of historical and financial and political and technical know-how, Faneuil Hall Markets became, and remain, Faneuil Hall Marketplace today. Although it does not pretend to be an engineering marvel like San Francisco's Golden Gate Bridge or New York City's Empire State Building or the Alaska pipeline, Faneuil Hall Marketplace has been cited as a leading example of urban renewal. It has spawned similar downtown revitalization projects around the United States and abroad.

Quincy's Market has actually had two lives: the one from its birth and the one from its rebirth. Tad Stahl describes these lives succinctly: "It took Mayor Quincy twenty-six months to solve the blighted conditions around Faneuil Hall by assembling and filling seven acres of land, upon which three distinctively colossal buildings were erected at no cost to Boston's citizens. . . . [W]hen the area was again in chaos, it took the city, state, and federal governments working with two private developers more than twenty-six years just to restore all three market buildings and nearby streets at a cost of nearly $50 million."[7]

How the project survived the morass of modern-day red tape is close to a miracle. It is an example of how Quincy-like tenacity still pays off. "The BRA was really the enabling conduit," the agency's chief general counsel, Charles Speleotis, said later. "I don't care how many architects, contractors, and developers were involved, it was the BRA that kept this project alive through funding, studies, and redevelopment initiatives from the beginning. All the credit should go directly to Bob Kenney because he would not allow the whole project to collapse in on itself once it got rolling."[8] Mayor Quincy would have approved.

Although the enormous amount of credit that has been heaped upon former BRA director Bob Kenney is well deserved, "it was [Mayor Kevin] White who made the final decision [to complete the project as] a fitting tribute to the past but also an exciting and vibrant part of a changing city's future. . . . [Like Mayor Quincy,] White deliberately flew in the face of most experts in the field [who] were absolutely certain that the concept of a downtown shopping mall was a losing proposition and bound to be a commercial disaster."[9] Reflecting on the effort it took to rebuild the markets, former mayor White grinned as he responded to my question. "What would our ancestors say if they could see the place today?" he said. "I think they would be speechless with pride."[10]

Josiah Quincy's Market, with its long, tangled history, is the comeback story of the twentieth century. Its growing pains since its 1976 opening are part of that comeback.

I hope that, as its two hundredth anniversary approaches in the year 2026, it will be remarked, as it was at its centennial celebration in 1926: "When another century has passed, may the men of 2026 be able to say of us, as we can say of Josiah Quincy and the Bostonians of his day who built Faneuil Hall Market: 'They were honest and patriotic citizens of Boston, who did well with the means at their disposal. Thank God for the record of service and good citizenship they have left as an example to us!' "[11]

A bronze statue of Josiah Quincy was erected in 1879. It can be seen in the courtyard of Old City Hall, on School Street in Boston.

Author's Note

Although there are a number of early paintings and prints of the markets, including one that doesn't even show the original North Market and South Market warehouse/stores, I could not locate anything that truly represented the concepts prepared at the time of the project, between 1823 and 1826. According to records at the Boston City Archives, there are plans in the market house cornerstone, but, of course, no one wants to destroy the building to get to them!

The earliest illustration of the market house appeared in Caleb H. Snow's *A History of Boston,* published by Abel Bowen in 1825, a year before the market house was completed. This rendition, delineated and engraved by Snow, shows the market house columns as uniformly thin instead of tapered from their broad base to the top of the shafts. The cupola (sometimes called the lantern) is not pictured. There is only one chimney, and the pavilion's walls are shown as looking like those of the east and west wings of the market house. This image was most probably reproduced from one of Alexander Parris's earliest sketches, before the columns were lathed, because they had yet to be installed (in their tapered shapes) by the time of publication. By the 1828 edition of the book, Snow had added the cupola but had not corrected any of the other previous errors.

The only evidence of the original ground plan for the development I found was in the 1852 edition of Josiah Quincy's *A Municipal History of the Town and City of Boston,* written twenty-six years after the market house opened. That plan showed the completed development with finished streets, including City Wharf, all superimposed over the original area of redevelopment. When the market house was opened in August 1826, Marginal Street had not yet been named Commercial Street and it had only been extended north from State Street across the eastern bulkhead, to the far end of the North Market warehouse/stores. The indications of Commercial Street veering off at a northeast angle, the delineation of Fulton and Blackstone Streets, and City Wharf with its warehouse/stores were not actually completed until after 1830.

Between 1966 and 1968 the authors of the BRA-sponsored *Markets Report* made every effort to find at least some of the original plans and specifications of the development, either by Alexander Parris or by any other planner on the project. But they found no such documents, sketches, plans, scale models, construction notes, builder's contracts, or architectural renditions. They concluded, however rightly or wrongly, that all must have been put to the flames sometime after Mayor Quincy left office.

The only other available evidence of the original plans and model available to date appear in the 1824 portrait of Josiah Quincy by Gilbert Stuart, where Stuart's view of Faneuil Hall Market seems to be an accurate interpretation of the building as planned at that time. Josiah Quincy's eldest daughter, Eliza Susan Quincy, wrote in her private letters that in November 1824 she accompanied her father to Stuart's house on Essex Street in Boston for the initial sitting. She indicated that the artist intended to represent the mayor seated at a window of Faneuil Hall (presumably a window of his office), commanding a view of the edifice. The rolled plans that Mayor Quincy is holding and the representation of the new building had only recently been prepared by Alexander Parris and provided to the artist by the mayor, her letters say. Although Josiah Quincy carefully maintained extensive documentation regarding the markets' development on file at Faneuil Hall, once he left office on the last day of December 1828 most of his records were never seen again. Whether they were lost or intentionally destroyed is not known.

In researching this book, I used supporting materials from some sources that have not been previously incorporated into any reports, news or media reports, books, or other descriptions of the markets. Unlike those who compiled the 1968 *Markets Report,* I uncovered materials from the original development at the Boston City Archives, documents that had not seen the light of day since 1826 or so. These included records kept by the Market Committee; a ledger kept by the city treasurer; personal letters and other correspondence to and from Mayor Quincy, the Market Committee, and members of the City Council; and the minutes of the aldermen, Common Council, City Council, and respective executive committees. One of the most crucial discoveries was the minutes of the aldermen, the Common Council, and the executive committees, which clearly indicated that city government refused the gesture to rename the market's Great Hall "Quincy Hall," not only in 1832 and 1834 but also several times later throughout the nineteenth century. Much of the detailed information I have presented about the creation of Faneuil Hall Market and the North and South Market warehouse/stores comes from the sources and materials listed in the Bibliography.

The mystery concerning the "Market Bull" weathervane still remains. The minutes of the aldermen and of the City Council from 1822 to 1954 revealed no records of the Market Bull weathervane being installed with the original development or attached to the cupola atop the dome later. Some of the earliest illustrations reveal a weathervane but do not show whether it was a Market Bull. Other illustrations show flagpoles with banners not only protruding from the cupola atop the dome but also at both the east and west ends of the roof ridge.

Notes

Introduction

1. Christopher P. Monkhouse, Faneuil *Hall Market: An Account of Its Many Likenesses* (Boston: Bostonian Society, 1969).
2. Josiah Quincy, *A Municipal History of the Town and City of Boston During Two Centuries, from September 17, 1630, to September 17, 1830* (Boston: Little, Brown, 1852), 84.
3. Edmund Quincy, *Life of Josiah Quincy of Massachusetts* (Boston: Ticknor and Fields, 1867), 46.
4. Josiah Quincy, *Municipal History,* 75.
5. Edmund Quincy, *Josiah Quincy,* 398–399.

Chapter 1

1. The words *Tramountain* and *Trimountain* both appear throughout many historical texts as the name for the hills. They are attributed to the French *trois montagnes,* meaning three hills. The name of Boston's Tremont Street is derived from the shortening of these words. *Tramountaine* (with an *e*) was the spelling used for the peninsula itself.
2. Blackstone's dwelling was located near where Beacon and Spruce Streets now face the west side of Boston Common.
3. The first spring the settlers viewed is believed to have been located near where Spring Lane is now, in downtown Boston, not far from the Old State House.
4. "A Model of Christian Charity," in *Winthrop Papers, 1629,* 5 vols. (Boston: Massachusetts Historical Society, 1929–1947), 2:282–295.
5. Susan Wilson, "How Boston Got Its Name," *Boston Sunday Globe,* 24 September 1995, City section: Night and Day: History Notebook, p. 13. Old Boston, England, had taken its name from Reverend John Cotton's St. Botolph's Church. Botolph, whose name means "boat helper," was the seventh-century patron saint of fishing. The name was appropriate, since both Bostons were linked to the ocean.
6. Justin Winsor, *The Memorial History of Boston, Including Suffolk County, Massachusetts, 1630–1880,* 4 vols. (Boston: James R. Osgood, 1881), 1:530. The first paragraph in the town records establishes the fact that in 1634 this was the chief landing place.

7. Winsor, *Memorial History of Boston,* 1:530.

8. Because of subsequent landfilling to the east of it, the Town Dock is no longer by the sea. It was near the present site of the Sam Adams statue in Adams Square, on the west side of Faneuil Hall.

9. Winsor, *Memorial History of Boston,* 1:156.

10. Winsor, *Memorial History of Boston,* 1:151.

11. Samuel G. Drake, *The History and Antiquities of Boston, from Its Settlement in 1630 to the Year 1770 A.D.* (Boston: Luther Stevens, 1856), 116.

12. Peter Benes, "Of Time and Markets," *Boston Sunday Globe,* 15 September 1968, pp. 38–45.

13. Abram English Brown, *Faneuil Hall and Faneuil Hall Market, or, Peter Faneuil and His Gift* (Boston: Lee and Shepard, 1900), 66.

14. Richard S. Dunn and Laetitia Yeandle, eds., *The Journal of John Winthrop 1630–1649,* abr. ed. (Cambridge: Harvard University Press, Belknap Press, 1996), 63.

15. Charles Carleton Coffin, *Faneuil Hall* (pamphlet) (Boston: Bostonian Society Proceedings, 1906), 3:42.

16. George E. McKay, *Faneuil Hall Market* (pamphlet) (Boston: Bostonian Society Proceedings, 11 January 1910), 34.

17. Years later the name would be changed to Superintendents of the Market.

18. Brown, *Faneuil Hall and Market,* 190.

19. Established in 1537 in England, the Ancient and Honorable Artillery Company applied for an act of incorporation in the Massachusetts colony in 1638. Governor John Winthrop initially refused the request. The rigid Puritans feared that granting such a charter could empower this militia to overthrow the colony. Nevertheless, in 1638 a charter was granted them and they were allowed to have a company captain and to make use of arms. They stored their uniforms and equipment in the Town House.

20. Reverend Edward G. Porter, *Rambles in Old Boston, New England* (Boston: Cupples, Upham, 1887), 10.

21. McKay, *Faneuil Hall Market,* 34.

22. McKay, *Faneuil Hall Market,* 35–36.

23. McKay, *Faneuil Hall Market,* 34.

24. McKay, *Faneuil Hall Market,* 36. A market cross represented the church/state relationship from which the Puritans had fled in 1630. According to *Webster's Third New International Dictionary,* it was "a cross or cross-shaped building set up where a market [was] held and often the scene of public business such as giving of notices and reading of warrants."

25. Brown, *Faneuil Hall and Market,* 68.

26. Walter Muir Whitehill, *Recycling Quincy Market* (Boston: Boston Athenaeum, 1977), 155.

27. At one time, a portion of the Town Cove was even separated from the harbor by a swinging bridge.

28. In 1748 the Town House was rebuilt into the present form of the Old State House. It housed colonial government and, after Faneuil Hall was built, state government. The

building was used by the Massachusetts Legislature until it moved to the State House atop Beacon Hill in 1798. The Town House was then rented to businesses, except for the years 1830–1839, when it was used as City Hall. In 1882 it was restored and re-dedicated to the public as a memorial hall.

29. These were possibly Boston's first leash laws.
30. Boston Town Records, Commissioners' Reports, xii:44.
31. McKay, *Faneuil Hall Market*, 36.
32. Boston Town Records, Commissioners' Reports, xii:66.
33. The name *Faneuil* was also first erroneously inscribed as "Funel" at the family burial site in the Old Granary Burial Ground before it was corrected.
34. Four died in childbirth and one, Francis, remains unaccounted for.
35. John (Jean) Faneuil seems to have either immediately returned to France or not remained in Boston for long. Little is known about this man other than that he died in La Rochelle, France, some years later.
36. Even in death Andrew Faneuil's vindictiveness for his nephew Benjamin did not abate. The first clause in Andrew Faneuil's last will and testament stipulated that his estate revert to his heirs, "excluding Benjamin Faneuil, of Boston, and the heirs of his body forever" (Brown, *Faneuil Hall and Market*, 25). The exact age of Andrew Faneuil at his death in unknown but research finds the terms "aged friend," "the old Huguenot," and "a fussy old man in his dotage" in various sources.
37. Boston Town Records, Commissioners' Reports, xii:259. Also "On the Original Building and Enlargement of Faneuil Hall," 1805 handwritten document attributed to Charles Bulfinch (Print Department, Boston Public Library).
38. Boston Town Records, Commissioners' Reports, xii:259–260.
39. Brown, *Faneuil Hall and Market*, 82. Once passed, this petition allowed for marketing either in a market building or elsewhere.
40. Selectmen's minutes, 2 September 1740, p. 252, quoted in Frederick C. Detwiller, *Historic Structure Report: Faneuil Hall* (Boston: U.S. Department of the Interior, National Park Service, North Atlantic Region, 1977), 6.
41. "On the Original Building and Enlargement of Faneuil Hall."
42. A grasshopper appeared on the family crest of Sir Thomas Gresham, who built the Royal Exchange, to which Peter Faneuil belonged, having inherited his uncle's membership.
43. During the Revolutionary War and the War of 1812 colonists alluded to the grasshopper to identify spies. Suspects were asked to describe the weathervane atop the building, and anyone who claimed to be a true Bostonian but couldn't identify the grasshopper weathervane was declared an impostor.
44. Brown, *Faneuil Hall and Market*, 137.
45. McKay, *Faneuil Hall Market*, 37.
46. Selectmen's minutes, 2 September 1740, p. 252, quoted in Detwiller, *Structure Report*, 7.
47. Brown, *Faneuil Hall and Market*, 46.
48. Boston Town Records, Commissioners' Reports, xii:306.

49. Boston Town Records, Commissioners' Reports, xii:306. Also, "On the Original Building and Enlargement of Faneuil Hall."
50. Brown, *Faneuil Hall and Market,* 85.
51. Brown, *Faneuil Hall and Market,* 101.
52. Austin Flint, M.D., *A Practical Treatise of the Diagnosis, Pathology, and Treatment of Diseases of the Heart* (Philadelphia: Blanchard and Lea, 1859), 34–229.
53. Brown, *Faneuil Hall and Market,* 108.
54. According to English law, despite Andrew Faneuil's will's stipulation against him, Benjamin and his sisters would inherit the estate by default, since Peter Faneuil had left no will.
55. Coffin, *Faneuil Hall,* 3:51.
56. McKay, *Faneuil Hall Market,* 37–38.
57. McKay, *Faneuil Hall Market,* 45.

Chapter 2

1. Brown, *Faneuil Hall and Market,* 96.
2. After Faneuil Hall was rebuilt in 1763 Abijah Adams once again resumed his duties.
3. In 1753 Boston was shaken by an earthquake. This was two years before the 1755 great earthquake in Lisbon, Portugal, that is still remembered for having taken 60,000 lives.
4. Brown, *Faneuil Hall and Market,* 137.
5. Harold and James Kirker, *Bulfinch's Boston, 1787–1817* (New York: Oxford University Press, 1964).
6. Coffin, *Faneuil Hall,* 3:53.
7. According to John Bartlett, *Familiar Quotations,* 16th ed., ed. by Justin Kaplan (Boston: Little, Brown, 1992), 327, these words, used by Patriots, were attributed to Otis, but he actually wrote in his *Rights of the Colonies* (Boston: 1764), 64, "No parts of His Majesty's dominions can be taxed without their consent."
8. Josiah Quincy, *Memoir of the Life of Josiah Quincy, Junior, of Massachusetts* (Boston: Cummings, Hillard, 1825), 10–11.
9. Edwin W. Small, "National Register of Historic Places Nomination of Faneuil Hall," Bostonian Society report, 1967.
10. Samuel G. Drake, *History and Antiquities of Boston,* 777.
11. At Harvard's seventieth reunion (in 1833) of the class of 1763, Josiah Quincy Jr. was fondly remembered as "the Patriot" in reference to his class oration regarding patriotism and his foresight of the brave fight for independence in the American Revolution.
12. Josiah Quincy, *Memoir of Josiah Quincy Jr.,* 35.
13. Josiah Quincy, *Memoir of Josiah Quincy Jr.,* 36.
14. Josiah Quincy, *Memoir of Josiah Quincy Jr.,* 38.
15. Coffin, *Faneuil Hall,* 3:54.
16. When £9,000 valuation of tea in 1773 is compared to the £2,000 needed to rebuild a large part of Faneuil Hall after its fire in 1761, its monetary value becomes more understandable.

17. Coffin, *Faneuil Hall,* 3:57.
18. Coffin, *Faneuil Hall,* 3:57–58.
19. Coffin, *Faneuil Hall,* 3:58–59.
20. Coffin, *Faneuil Hall,* 3:59.
21. Selectmen's minutes, 25 February 1789, p. 83, quoted in Detwiller, *Structure Report,* 17.
22. Coffin, *Faneuil Hall,* 3:43–44.
23. "On the Original Building and Enlargement of Faneuil Hall."
24. *Shambles* was a colloquial name for a meat market or a place to exhibit food for sale. Besides selling fish, meat, and vegetables at the Shambles by Faneuil Hall, vendors also slaughtered animals on its open tables.
25. Old butchers' meat hooks can still be seen hanging from the first-floor ceiling.
26. Susan Wilson, "Sights and Insights: Faneuil Hall," *Boston Globe,* Calendar section (vol. 13, no. 28) 31 March 1988, pp. 13–14.
27. "On the Original Building and Enlargement of Faneuil Hall."
28. Coffin, *Faneuil Hall,* 3:61.
29. "Explore the Shoreline," *Bostonian Society Newsletter* 30 (April 1995): 2.
30. Robert V. Sparks, "Abolition in Silver Slippers: A Biography of Edmund Quincy" (Master's thesis, Boston College, 1978), 9.
31. Josiah Quincy, *Municipal History,* 44. This verse is found in 1 Kings 8:57.
32. Josiah Quincy, *Municipal History,* 75.
33. Josiah Quincy, *Municipal History,* 65.
34. Josiah Quincy, *Municipal History,* 75.
35. At that time most of the cattle came from places within a fifteen-mile radius of Boston.

Chapter 3

1. Edmund Quincy, *Josiah Quincy,* 19.
2. Before he stepped outside during the winter months, Josiah was also compelled to put both feet into a pail of cold water, soaking his shoes and stockings, as a further preventative measure to sustain good health.
3. Grandfather Josiah was referring to the immigrating Edmund's grandson, Edmund Quincy (1681–1738), Harvard graduate in 1699, successful Boston and Braintree merchant, Boston selectman, justice of the peace, militia colonel, representative of the General Court and member of the governor's council, and justice of the Superior Court of Judicature. He settled the boundary dispute between Massachusetts and New Hampshire and was awarded 1,000 acres in Lenox, Massachusetts, by the General Court for public service. He died of smallpox while in England and was buried at Bunhill Fields, London.
4. Josiah Quincy, of Braintree, to Josiah Quincy, 16 March 1780 (Josiah Phillips Quincy Papers, Massachusetts Historical Society, Boston). See Robert A. McCaughey, *Josiah Quincy, 1772–1864: The Last Federalist* (Cambridge: Harvard University Press, 1974).
5. The Magna Carta (or Magna Charta or the Great Charter) was the English charter of liberties by which the English barons forced King John to give his assent to a funda-

mental guarantee of their rights and privileges. The king affixed his seal to the charter in June 1215 at Runnymede, England, thereby granting the barons more liberty.

6. Edward Elbridge Salisbury, "Pedigree of Quincy," *Family: Memorials,* 2 vols. (a series of genealogical and biographical monographs privately printed at New Haven: Tuttle, Morehouse and Taylor, 1885). The coat of arms shows seven mascles conjoined. The motto is: *Sine macula macla* (a sheild without a stain).

7. According to the first page of the town records, the members of this committee included Edmund Quincy, Samuell Wilbore, William Balston, Edward Hutinson, and Constable William Cheesbrough. Included in the valuation were the lands at Muddy River, the cows, the goats, young cattle, and a horse, less the charges for "torn and worn."

8. Josiah Quincy, "Oration," pronounced 4 July 1798 (private collection of the author), 29.

9. Josiah Quincy, *Municipal History,* 58–62.

10. Josiah Quincy, *Municipal History,* 59–62.

11. Josiah Quincy, *Municipal History,* 375–376.

12. Cows were allowed to roam there, but they had to be tagged with a license that identified their owner. The purpose of these "milky mothers" was to provide a source of milk and to graze the grass, acting as natural lawn mowers.

13. Josiah Quincy, *Municipal History,* 268–269.

14. The tonnage was ascertained by a precise accounting Mayor Quincy demanded: Every wagonload was weighed before it was deposited at the city's dump. More than seven thousand tons were collected during the ensuing years.

   At the time, the 3,000-ton pile of street debris consisted of biodegradable materials that included animal waste, human waste, street dirt, mud, and sewage. Also collected were discarded produce that had rotted, rancid meats, and spoiled fish. Excess body parts from slaughtered animals, customarily tossed into Boston Harbor, were also heaped onto the pile. This huge mound (later mounds) presented an unsightly appearance and created an intolerable odor but it was a godsend to the country farmer as manure. The area where this debris was piled was the far end of Boston Common, which came up to the marshy Back Bay, so any drainage from the pile leaked into the Back Bay's marshlands.

   Nonbiodegradable household items thrown out by residents, such as furniture, kitchenware, or clothing, were collected by town-appointed scavengers for salvage, or were thrown into the town's dump near the Back Bay.

15. Detractors included:
   - Those traditional Bostonians who didn't want to see any changes whatsoever because their lineage stretched back to the founding fathers and they descended from families who had resisted changes to the town for nearly two centuries and who had approved of changes only when absolutely necessary (this resistance to change had included resistance to converting the town to a city for nearly forty years after the end of the American Revolution);
   - American Revolution patriots, most of whom still clung to the recent past;

- The wealthy and privileged, who would have preferred to see the city's growing populace leave the new city rather than accommodate the newcomers' needs;
- The leaders of the Federalist Party, who orchestrated the execution of the city charter to closely follow the rules of old town government;
- Religious conservatives, which included former mayor John Phillips, who believed that any necessary changes within society would come from divine intervention;
- Newspapers and periodicals that supported the ideals of the Federalist Party leaders;
- And those who didn't want the city to risk bankruptcy by spending tax dollars and borrowed funds for untested changes.

    Mayor Josiah Quincy found more support from the emerging Middling Interest Party than from his own Federalist Party. The Federalists' ideals of clinging to the past no longer benefited the growing new city.

16. Josiah Quincy, *Municipal History,* 68.
17. *Boston News-Letter and City Record,* City Record: Board of Aldermen, 19 August 1826, p. 79.
18. James Walker, D. D., "Memoir of Josiah Quincy," in *Proceedings of the Massachusetts Historical Society,* 1866–1867, 83–157.
19. Walter Miller, *Cicero de Officiis* (Cambridge: Harvard University Press, 1961), 210–211.
20. Walker, "Memoir of Josiah Quincy," 83–157.
21. Josiah Quincy, *Municipal History,* 268–269.
22. Walker, "Memoir of Josiah Quincy," 83–157.
23. Josiah Quincy, *Municipal History,* 59–62.
24. During Boston's first year as a city (from May 1822 through May 1823) Mayor Phillips did almost nothing to improve Boston. Real estate and personal property tax collections went unspent. By 1823, therefore, the new city was in a good financial position to borrow up to $1 million from banks. During the course of the Quincy administration (May 1823 through December 1828; in 1825 the election time was moved from April to December and the beginning of the term of administration changed from May to January 1—Quincy ran twice that year and won both elections) money was borrowed and paid back. The only major publicly funded city project in process in 1823 was the construction of the sixty-acre House of Industry debtor's prison in nearby South Boston to replace the failing almshouse and provide adequate accommodations for debtors then being incarcerated at the Leverett Street Jail. Begun in 1821 by the then town of Boston, it required $100,000 to build and maintain, and was completed by early 1825.

    This habit of collecting taxes, in good times and bad, and spending little on urban improvements or salaries came out of the tradition-bound Bostonian way of thinking. Mayor Quincy wanted to change that habit, for the betterment of the city.
25. The waterfront area designated for expansion was the same area where Andrew, Peter, and Benjamin Faneuil had once owned wharves and warehouses.
26. Josiah Quincy, *Municipal History,* 77.
27. Josiah Quincy, *Municipal History,* 76–77.

28. According to Josiah Quincy, *Municipal History,* 81, the first proposition offered all owners the opportunity to combine their property interest and rights into one common stock, which, together, would be "appraised at their real value by commissioners mutually to be chosen, who were authorized to lay out the estates on a plan specified, and to divide the whole interest into shares, in proportions conformed to the appraisement, and to make sales for the best interests of the concern, the city to be considered as a proprietor for the amount of its estates, but streets and lanes, not to be considered in any estimate." The cost incurred for the land under the proposed vegetable market, however, would be borne by these proprietors according to their respective shares.

    The second proposition offered any proprietor the opportunity "to state his willingness to sell his land at an appraisement to be made by five or seven disinterested persons, mutually chosen; the city declaring its willingness to consent to such appraisement, upon the single condition that the result should only be obligatory in case of ultimate success of the general project."

    The third proposition offered proprietors the option "to transmit to the Mayor the terms on which he would be willing to sell his land to the city, with the assurance on the part of the city, that either they will be accepted, or a counter-proposition made on its part, limited only by the single condition expressed in the second proposition."
29. Josiah Quincy, *Municipal History,* 76.
30. Josiah Quincy, *Municipal History,* 82.
31. Josiah Quincy, *Municipal History,* 82–83.
32. Josiah Quincy, *Municipal History,* 79–80.
33. Josiah Quincy, *Municipal History,* 84.
34. Josiah Quincy, *Municipal History,* 84.
35. Josiah Quincy, *Municipal History,* 383.
36. "Meeting at Faneuil Hall," *Columbian Centinel,* Saturday morning, 17 January 1824, p. 2.
37. Quincy family anecdote from notes and letters, privately collected and owned. Within the long history of the Quincy family the fact that Faneuil Hall Market was called "Quincy Market" has always been a source of mixed pride, humor, and conjecture. When Edmund Quincy wrote his father's extensive biography in 1867, he devoted very little to the development of the marketplace. Instead, he alluded to his father's *Municipal History of Boston* and made the statement that he believed that the Great Hall had been renamed Quincy Hall. This untrue assumption was based upon misinformation. Edmund Quincy believed that the market's popular name was a derivation of Quincy Hall and that was why people called Faneuil Hall Market "Quincy Market." The name "Quincy's Folly" is derived from other sources within the genealogical spectrum. The author's father, John Quincy Sr. (1917–1983), was fond of telling his own tales of Boston, which included his recollection of hearing it called "Quincy's Nightmare" by his grandfather, among other things. See also McKay, *Faneuil Hall Market,* 40–41.

Chapter 4

1. At this writing, the Commonwealth of Massachusetts defines such value as: The highest price in terms of money which a property will bring if exposed in a normal market, allowing a reasonable time to find a purchaser who buys with the knowledge of all the uses to which it is adapted and for which it is capable of being used, with neither party under compulsion to buy or sell.

2. Today the superintendent might be called project supervisor or general contractor.

3. Josiah Quincy, Mayor of Boston, Records of the Proceedings of the Committee on the Extension of Faneuil Hall Market, March 1824–November 1826, 2 vols. (Boston City Archives), 6.

4. Eliza Susan Quincy, personal journal, 30 May, 20 June, 27 August 1821 (Quincy Family Papers, MHS).

5. Josiah Quincy, Mayor of Boston, Records of the Committee on the Extension of Faneuil Hall Market, 6.

6. Jonathan Mason, letter to Mayor Josiah Quincy regarding the purchase of Boston Pier, 24 December 1824 (Boston City Archives).

7. Mayor Josiah Quincy, draft copy of letter to the clerks of the proprietors of Long Wharf (also called Boston Pier), 28 July 1824 (Boston City Archives). This is considered to be the standard language employed when property owners used tactics to drive up their prices.

8. Davis Parker, letter to Mayor Josiah Quincy, 10 July 1826 (Boston City Archives). The city could (1) demand payment of back taxes plus interest before negotiating a purchase price for these properties; or (2) seize the property and take the rental income for back taxes plus interest while implementing its new powers of eminent domain; or (3) arrest those who denied ownership and bring them before a judge in municipal court, after which they could be put into Leverett Street Jail for debt if they were found liable for portions of back taxes.

9. Mackay, Treasurer of the City, Committee on the Extension of Faneuil Hall Market Accounting Ledger, June 1824–November 1826 (Boston City Archives). "Fair price" in many instances included the real estate, personal property and fixtures, the business value of a going concern, the residual value of a lease or leases, future potential rents from the property, etc. In other instances, if the owner was willing to agree to a longer term of the note pledged by the city, the "fair price" might also increase.

10. Initially, this conduit was left open but was covered over by 1828 as the market district's northern boundary and named Clinton Street.

11. Josiah Quincy, *Municipal History,* 126.

12. Josiah Quincy, *Municipal History,* 126.

13. Mayor Josiah Quincy, letter to the clerks of the proprietors of the Long Wharf, 1824 (City Council records, Boston City Archives).

14. It has not been discovered where the demolished structures and waste were dumped. Presumably, they were barged to outer Boston Harbor.

15. *Boston News-Letter and City Record,* II (19 August 1826), pp. 79–80.

16. Josiah Quincy, Mayor of Boston, Records of the Committee on the Extension of Faneuil Hall Market, 59.

17. Josiah Quincy, *Municipal History,* 128–129.

18. Josiah Quincy, Mayor of Boston, Records of the Committee on the Extension of Faneuil Hall Market, 59–61.

19. According to a May 4, 1818, billboard photo in the collection of the Society for the Preservation of New England Antiquities, the Old Feather Store sold such items as "Feathers: Russian, French, Sea-Fowl, Southern, Common and Live-Geese; Feather Beds of all prices, Mattresses, Bedspreads, Sacking Bottoms, Best Down, Bed ticking of all kinds, White and Coloured Counterpanes, Wool and Cotton Coverlets, Rose Blankets, Sheetings, Bindings, Carolina Moss, Curled Hair, Coarse Line, etc. Beds of any price made and filled with feathers at the shortest notice." The Old Feather Store was believed to have been built around 1680 by Henry Symonds at the edge of the Town Cove, almost touched by the tide. The colonial-style building was constructed with hand-hewn oak timbers and covered in cement plaster. Embedded in the plaster were fragments of broken glass and bottles, and the plaster surface was ornamented with diamond motifs.

20. Many alderman and Common Council members also worked outside the sphere of their city employment. It is possible that Mayor Quincy put pressure on Alderman Benjamin to continually prepare new drafts and models for the markets to the point where Benjamin was not making enough money doing private commissions. It is curious that there are no records indicating that Alderman Benjamin was paid for his time, although Alderman Child was budgeted $1,000 per month to act as the Building Committee's superintendent.

21. Alexander Parris, letter to the Committee on the Extension of Faneuil Hall Market requesting employment, 1824 (Boston City Archives).

22. Mackay, Accounting Ledger.

23. Josiah Quincy, Mayor of Boston, Records of the Committee on the Extension of Faneuil Hall Market, 63–65.

24. Josiah Quincy, Mayor of Boston, Records of the Committee on the Extension of Faneuil Hall Market, 77–78.

25. The Hammond and Faxon buildings employed the same granite facade system of the North and South Market buildings, but each building was only eight bays wide, four stories high, and had a hip roof. The North and South Market buildings would be longer, be four and a half stories high, and have gabled roofs.

26. The remaining six lots were sold within the next month at comparable prices.

27. Josiah Quincy, *Municipal History,* 127–131.

28. Josiah Quincy, Mayor of Boston, Records of the Committee on the Extension of Faneuil Hall Market.

29. *Columbian Centinel,* 2 October 1824. The line "The lots were 26 in number" is incorrect. According to the deeds filed at the Suffolk County Registry, there were 25 lots within the North Market range of stores. The cited figure $20.83 is also incorrect

according to the same source.

30. Josiah Quincy, Mayor of Boston, Records of the Committee on the Extension of Faneuil Hall Market, 85.
31. These construction terms and information were provided by Peter "Pete" C. Leyden, superintendent and project supervisor for Walsh Brothers Construction Company, responsible for renovations at the marketplace between 1999 and 2001. In excavating a new elevator core under the central market building, they were able to extract layers of material down to the blue clay. It was found that several layers of unevenly sized granite slabs (some as large as 10 feet by 6 feet by 2 feet). This stonework (called granite rubble) was stepped up with multiple layers of tree trunks in order to be kept in position. Some of the trees were left in place, between the granite rubble. These "steps" of support rose 9 feet 6 inches above the hardpan to receive the foundation walls. When sections of the "corduroy roads" were unearthed in 2001 the tree boles had not rotted, indicating that they were not exposed to oxygen over their 175-year use. The tree boles were left lying in the pit, atop the stepped granite of the granite rubble for the foundation walls and the inner perpendicular carrying walls.

    The source of information on the transport of blue granite from Quincy to the construction site is William Churchill Edwards, *Historic Quincy, Massachusetts*, 3d ed. (Quincy, Mass.: City of Quincy, 1957), 125.
32. There are no records of where Lumber Wharf was located. Presumably, since these supply ships were deepwater-hulled, it was off Long Wharf, which reached into the deepest waters of Boston Harbor. Shipments were stored along Long Wharf until needed, and then moved down State Street to the appropriate construction site (either that of the market house or of the warehouse/stores).
33. Josiah Quincy, *Municipal History*, 79.
34. Josiah Quincy, *Municipal History*, 80.
35. Josiah Quincy, *Municipal History*, 80.
36. Josiah Quincy, Mayor of Boston, Records of the Committee on the Extension of Faneuil Hall Market, 95.
37. Josiah Quincy, *Municipal History*, 131–132, 413.

Chapter 5

1. Some deed restrictions in the area of use of the properties (other than that they be built by spring 1826, in accordance with the city's plans) included the owner's not making major renovations without city approval. Signs, however, were not specifically spelled out as something that would need to be approved.
2. The September 1824 budget of $75,000 for the market house itself was doubled once Alexander Parris propelled the scope of the project to its present proportions.
3. Josiah Quincy, *Municipal History*, 135.
4. Josiah Quincy, *Municipal History*, 132–135.
5. That same year Asher Benjamin left Boston and took a job as a mill agent in New Hampshire.

6. Josiah Quincy, *Municipal History*, 136.

7. The walls of the rear of the North and South Market buildings and of the ends were brick-faced. Only the fronts were faced with white granite.

8. About 90 percent of the granite came from the town of Westford, Massachusetts. The term "Chelmsford granite" is derived from the fact that Westford was part of Chelmsford until 1792. Most of the granite was actually shipped from the Chelmsford station by way of the Middlesex Canal.

   The quarries at Westford and Chelmsford were directly accessible to Boston by means of the Middlesex Canal, a revolution in water transport that was dug with the aid of local farmers, constructed with sixteen locks of hewn granite, and first opened in 1803. By 1820, the canal stretched twenty-seven miles south from the Merrimack River in Lowell, Massachusetts, to Charlestown, where it ended, opening into the waters of the Charles River.

9. McKay, *Faneuil Hall Market*, 40. When the packet boats carrying marketplace stone arrived at the end of the Middlesex Canal in Charlestown, where the Charles River met Boston Harbor, they would be guided from a nearby causeway across the open waters of the Charles River and Boston Harbor into Boston itself (near where the Charlestown Bridge connects Boston to Charlestown today). They were then guided into a second canal that began near where North Station stands today. This canal paralleled today's Canal Street and ended in Mill Pond, not far west of Faneuil Hall. There, stone wagons and drag skids would meet the shipment and haul the stone to the construction site. As Boston's Mill Pond was filled in during marketplace development, the length of the overland haul from the Canal Street canal became longer. Finally, the packet boats were floated from the end of the Middlesex Canal in Charlestown, around the waterfront of Boston's peninsula, to wharfs at the construction site. Then the stone was dragged up ramps, which sometimes could barely support the weight of the heavy granite block.

10. This information comes from the Chelmsford Historical Society.

11. In 1825 a conflict of interest was not considered to be a legal or moral issue that concerned public officials or members of society.

12. *Columbian Centinel*, 12 April 1825.

13. The South Market building had twenty-two lots instead of the twenty-three at the North Market building. The South Market lots were wider than the North Market lots.

14. Josiah Quincy, Mayor of Boston, Records of the Committee on the Extension of Faneuil Hall Market.

15. Josiah Quincy, *Municipal History*, 415.

16. Brown, *Faneuil Hall and Market*, 177.

17. Later, Creek Street was built over part of the creek's original course, connecting the outer boundary of the development site with Ann Street.

18. There is no available account or record of the total number of laborers who worked on the development. The assumption can be made, however, that the number of individ-

uals was extensive because of the construction involved (the market house, forty-seven private stores, and the public streets); because of the short period of time in which the development was completed; because of the use of convicts from the state prison at Charlestown; and because of the use of debtor-inmates from the House of Industry, which had opened in South Boston in 1825.

19. Courtenay Guild, *Men and Market of 1826* (Boston: Bostonian Society Proceedings, 18 January 1927), 31.

20. And, unlike in modern times, smoking in public was vigorously prosecuted with arrests and fines.

21. As the development plan had become more refined under Alexander Parris, the city realized it would be best to build only the central market house and have individual owners build the flanking North and South Market buildings. The Hammond and Faxon buildings had been built early, as a model of what the North and South Market buildings could become. By mid-1825, the city saw that other land and buildings in this northern area, bought before the plans were final, were no longer needed. Hence the sale of these parcels with restrictions that were meant to ensure a sense of uniformity over buildings built in the project area.

22. The order of decision making was: (1) The Market Committee decided issues of overall planning, architecture and engineering plans, and purchase of lots; it oversaw accounting, especially the purchase or sale of properties and the payment of bills, as well as legal aspects. As it made such "soft" construction decisions, the Market Committee would instruct the Building Committee on how to implement its decisions and receive reports from them. The Market Committee then reported to the City Council. (2) The Building Committee hired the market house and streets workmen and contractors, ordered supplies, and ensured that Parris's plans were followed by the construction crews of all areas, including the privately built North and South Market buildings. It had a budget of $1,000 per month for incidental expenses (for example, for travel to the quarry to see why the pillars had not been delivered, or for miscellaneous items needed for construction). Any expenses over this budget would have to be approved by the Market Committee, but the Building Committee never exceeded its budget. (3) The City Council received reports through the Market Committee and ultimately approved everything for final decision.

23. A hogshead is about 63 U.S. gallons, typically the size of a wooden cask.

24. The need to keep certain provisions cooler than others, like fish and raw meat, was also taken into account when assigning areas to merchants.

25. Josiah Quincy, Mayor of Boston, Records of the Committee on the Extension of Faneuil Hall Market, 173.

26. Josiah Quincy, Mayor of Boston, Records of the Committee on the Extension of Faneuil Hall Market, 173.

27. Nineteenth-century custom dictated that each man working on the waterfront project receive a jigger of rum near the end of the workday, in keeping with the tradition of sailors and dockworkers.

28. Charles Bulfinch resurrected the term *trabeated* from the Latin *trabs* (beam).

29. *Boston Monthly Magazine* 1, no. 3 (August 1825): 143.

30. *The Columbian Centinel,* Wednesday, 5 October 1825, notes that the article first appeared in the *New York Daily Advertiser,* 30 September 1825.

31. Alexander Parris, October 1826 report to City Council, attached to the final report of the Market Committee to City Council, Records of the Committee on the Extension of the Faneuil Hall Market, November 1826, 34–36.

32. Reverend Edwin R. Hodgman, *History of the Town of Westford, Massachusetts* (Lowell, Mass.: Collection of the Chelmsford Historical Society, 1883).

33. Herbert E. Fletcher, "The Granite of Middlesex," a lecture delivered to the Lowell Historical Society, 8 May 1912 (private papers of the Fletcher family).

34. Hodgman, *History of Westford,* 237.

35. Other such buildings were the Massachusetts General Hospital, the new Boston Courthouse, the new Leverett Street Jail, and St. Paul's Church.

36. "Improvements in Boston," *Columbian Centinel,* 5 October 1825. The anonymous writer also praised Boston's new U.S. Bank, but labeled Bulfinch's State House "a clumsy affair."

37. Josiah Quincy, Mayor of Boston, Records of the Committee on the Extension of Faneuil Hall Market, 140–141.

38. David Weld Child, letter to Mayor Quincy and the Market Committee, 11 August 1825 (miscellaneous papers of the Faneuil Hall Market Committee for the year 1825, Boston City Archives).

39. The defect was a major crack from the outside to the center of the column, which would have caused the column, if installed in the market house, to lose a portion around the crack when subjected to the pressure of heat and cold through the years. It may even have broken completely.

    Hobie Fletcher, a former owner of the Chelmsford quarries, recalled a spoiled column resting in the nearby quarry woods, which had been rejected by the city in 1825. It remained at the quarry at least until the mid-1940s. It is presumed it was eventually broken up by quarrymen because it was an obstruction to present-day business.

40. David Weld Child, letter to Mayor Quincy, 11 August 1825.

41. Josiah Quincy, Mayor of Boston, Records of the Committee on the Extension of Faneuil Hall Market, 147.

42. Josiah Quincy, Mayor of Boston, Records of the Committee on the Extension of Faneuil Hall Market, 149. This was principally a beef market, hence the appropriateness of the bulls' heads.

43. The animals held on Boston Common were slaughtered in Brighton, then delivered to the market hall through the side doors to the pavilion, where they were cut up for sale. The floors were brick, covered with sawdust, to facilitate cleanliness.

44. The cast-iron compression posts were forged at the foundries in South Boston.

45. The copper for the dome's outer sheathing was supplied by Copper and Brass Indus-

tries, of London, England. During construction the interior under the dome was protected from the weather by sails leased from a nearby ship.

46. It is uncertain if a weathervane fashioned in the shape of a bull was attached to the top of the cupola when first built. Some of the earliest illustrations indicate a flagpole with a banner atop the cupola, as well as flagpoles with banners positioned on the east and west ends of the roof. Other illustrations indicate a small weathervane, some in and some not in the shape of a bull. Research of city records dating between 1824 and 1954 did not reveal any city order, committee discussion, or private invoice for a bull weathervane. Thus it is uncertain when the original bull weathervane was mounted atop the cupola.

47. Parris may also have referred to a European precedent for the dome design by employing Peter Nicholson's *Architectural Dictionary,* published in London in 1819. Parris sold his three-volume set to the Boston Athenaeum after completing his work on the markets. In the section labeled "Constructive Carpentry," Nicholson comments on dome construction, and in the margin of page 288 there is a broad, faded pencil mark next to this passage, possibly left by Parris.

48. The exterior grounds have been built up over time, obscuring much of the original foundation and some of the granite steps.

49. Caleb H. Snow, *A History of Boston, the Metropolis of Massachusetts, from Its Origin to the Present Period, with Some Account of the Environs* (Boston: Abel Bowen, 1825), 377–378.

50. *Boston News-Letter and City Record,* I (4 February 1826), pp. 80–81.

51. A ledge quarry is excavated down through layers of rock until the desired rock is found. This differs from a stone quarry, which excavates one large glacial boulder situated above and below ground.

52. This data was provided by Hobie Fletcher, a former owner of the Chelmsford quarries. Alexander Parris had already completed extensive stoneworks projects for the U.S. Navy. Between Parris's affiliations with naval representatives and Josiah Quincy's relationship with two former USS *Constitution* commanders, it is possible they both influenced the naval authorities to sell the Portsmouth Naval Yard granite to the City of Boston.

53. Their bondsmen were compelled to pay the entire claim against them, in this case the cost to locate, procure, retrieve, and deliver the rest of the granite to Boston.

54. The count of forty-seven stores includes the two stores of the Hammond and Faxon buildings (one each), the twenty-three of the North Market stores, and the twenty-two of the South Market stores.

55. Mackay, Accounting Ledger. History repeated itself when, in the 1970s, lenders agreed to pool money for reconstruction of the marketplace.

56. The North and South Market buildings, when turned on end, resemble the window design of turn-of-the-twentieth-century high-rise structures.

57. Walker, "Memoir of Josiah Quincy," 83–157.

Chapter 6

1. *Boston News-Letter and City Record,* City Record: Board of Aldermen, 12 August 1826, pp. 69–71.

2. Thomas H. O'Connor, *Building a New Boston: Politics and Urban Renewal, 1950–1970* (Boston: Northeastern University Press, 1993), 271.

3. There were also nearly a hundred more tenants-at-will (who rented stalls still unrented after the bid).

4. "New Faneuil Hall Market," *Boston News-Letter and City Record,* 19 August 1826, p. 79.

5. Boston India Wharf merchant named Ripley, letter to his sister, a teacher in Kingston, Massachusetts, 25 August 1826 (Boston City Archives).

6. Boston City Records, 1826, vol. 4, 314–317.

7. Boston City Records, 1826, vol. 4, 314–315.

8. Brown, *Faneuil Hall and Market,* 179.

9. "Boston, New Market," *Columbian Centinel,* Wednesday morning, 30 August 1876, p. 2.

10. John Quincy Sr., conversation with John Quincy Jr., over lunch at Durgin Park restaurant, December 1963.

11. Mackay, Accounting Ledger.

12. Josiah Quincy, Mayor of Boston, Records of the Committee on the Extension of Faneuil Hall Market, 200.

13. Josiah Quincy, *Municipal History,* 201–203.

14. Josiah Quincy, *Municipal History,* 201–203.

15. Josiah Quincy, *Municipal History,* 201–203.

16. Boston City Records, Report of the Building Committee, 13 November 1826.

17. Josiah Quincy, Mayor of Boston, Records of the Committee on the Extension of Faneuil Hall Market, 229.

18. Josiah Quincy, Mayor of Boston, Records of the Committee on the Extension of Faneuil Hall Market, 238. These improvements were paid for with funds from the auction of the lots and with funds borrowed (and paid back) by the city.

19. Josiah Quincy, *Municipal History,* 201–203. This statement can be interpreted as a precursor of the real estate tax–incentive to development financing.

20. Josiah Quincy, Mayor of Boston, Records of the Committee on the Extension of *Faneuil Hall Market,* 241.

21. The project of buying private properties in the area near the market district, of filling in to create more land, and of creating new lots and new streets continued after 1826 until about 1836.

22. Samuel Adams Drake, *Old Landmarks and Historic Personages of Boston* (Boston: James R. Osgood, 1873), 128–129.

23. McKay, *Faneuil Hall Market,* 42. Over the course of the next century, the term *draymen* for drivers of wagons was first replaced with *haulers* and then with the name *teamsters.*

24. Josiah Quincy, *Municipal History,* 257.

25. Although Harvard had been the country's premiere college for nearly two hundred years, by 1829 its demise seemed imminent. Financial insolvency, declining enrollment,

deteriorating faculty morale, rampant student misbehavior, a diminishing public reputation, and disaffected alumni all contrasted sharply with the original visions for the
school. During his sixteen years as president, Josiah Quincy expanded Harvard's curri-
culum, restructured its finances, and even expelled the entire sophomore class in one
day. These hands-on tactics displeased enough people that he became known as the
most unpopular president in Harvard's history. Even so, after he published the very first
chronicle of Harvard's history in 1840, his two-volume *History of Harvard* was credited
with galvanizing the alumni into forming Harvard's renowned Harvard Alumni Association, which kept the college from ever suffering financial reversals again.

26. Edward H. Savage, *Boston Events: A Brief Mention . . . of More Than 5,000 Events, 1630 to
    1880* (Boston: Tolman and White, 1884), 142.

27. E. C. Wines, "A Trip to Boston," *New York Daily Advertiser,* 1838, p. 213.

28. There are no known surviving architectural plans of Faneuil Hall Market produced by
    Alexander Parris. Parris did write a description of the market house and its architec-
    tural details, however. The description is attached to the final report of the Market
    Committee to City Council, Records of the Committee on the Extension of the
    Faneuil Hall Market, November 1826, 34–36. The original of the plan Rowson pre-
    sented is now in the collections of the Bostonian Society. This plan is the only surviv-
    ing nineteenth-century rendition of Faneuil Hall Market.

29. McKay, *Faneuil Hall Market,* 40.

30. "City Solicitor's Opinion on Alterations in the Market House," *Documents of the City of
    Boston* (Boston: Moore and Crosby, 16 April 1855). These full-shed dormers could span
    the width of a store's unit at the roof level and provide an additional floor with full
    head room.

31. "Improvements to the Market," *Documents of the City of Boston.*

32. "Improvements to the Market," *Documents of the City of Boston.*

33. "City Solicitor's Opinion," *Documents of the City of Boston.*

34. "Report on Faneuil Hall Market," *Documents of the City of Boston.*

35. "Report on the Joint Special Committee on Free Markets," *Documents of the City of
    Boston.*

36. William W. Wheildon, *Semi-centennial Celebration of the Opening of the Faneuil Hall
    Market,* August 26, 1876 (Boston: L. F. Lawrence, 1877).

37. In many instances, it is impossible to determine legal ownership of Boston's downtown
    streets because many of the paths they grew out of once crossed private property that
    had been awarded by Governor John Winthrop in land grants. As time passed, the paths
    became either private or public ways, and there remained the question how the town/
    city of Boston gained legal title to some of those original paths as public ways. In an
    effort to avoid a future challenge, the base of the Sam Adams statue was positioned
    within streets known to be public at that time. Its base, therefore, remains off center,
    almost askew, because of the effort not to encroach upon streets that might someday be
    contested.

38. Wheildon, *Opening of the Faneuil Hall Market.*

39. McKay, *Faneuil Hall Market,* 46.

40. Wheildon, *Opening of the Faneuil Hall Market.*

41. Brown, *Faneuil Hall and Market,* 217–218.

42. McKay, *Faneuil Hall Market,* 43.

43. *Boston Daily Globe,* Saturday, 9 May 1925, p. 1.

44. *Boston Daily Globe,* Thursday, 26 August 1926, back pages.

45. "Faneuil Hall Marketplace Begins 100th Anniversary Program," *Boston Globe,* Tuesday, 14 September 1926, p. 8. Josiah Quincy was never known to wear a hat, especially at public functions.

46. "Faneuil Hall Marketplace Begins 100th Anniversary Program," *Boston Globe,* Thursday, 16 September 1926, p. 15. On September 16, 1926, the article from September 14 (referenced in note 45 of this chapter) was reprinted and expanded.

47. O'Connor, *Building a New Boston,* 15.

48. Boston Redevelopment Authority (BRA), Survey and Planning Application, citing a 1950 USDA Study, Document No. R-102, BRA, June 1962 (Boston City Archives), 3.

Chapter 7

1. Route 128, which is four lanes in each direction, forms a wide circle around Greater Boston on the inland sides, where land was available for expansion. When it was first opened during the 1950s it was largely empty, but it soon became a busy highway as businesses moved out of the city and residents moved to towns and cities beyond the close suburbs.

2. Thomas H. O'Connor, *The Boston Irish: A Political History* (Boston: Northeastern University Press, 1995), 225.

3. Lyman H. Butterfield, ed., "Historical Continuity versus Synthetic Reconstruction," in *Walter Muir Whitehill: A Record Compiled by His Friends, 13 September 1985* (Minot, Mass.: Athenaeum Press, 1958), 22–24.

4. City officials were more concerned with bigger urban renewal projects such as the West End, Government Center, and the Boston waterfront.

5. Michael Holleran, *Boston's "Changeful Times": Origins of Preservation in America* (Baltimore: Johns Hopkins University Press, 1998), 85.

6. Holleran, *Boston's "Changeful Times,"* 94.

7. Holleran, *Boston's "Changeful Times,"* 94.

8. Holleran, *Boston's "Changeful Times,"* 109.

9. The town of Boston moved its offices from the upper floors of Faneuil Hall at the end of 1830 and occupied the Old State House, along with some preexisting businesses, until 1839. In 1840 city government relocated to the nearby county courthouse (built by Bulfinch in 1810). In 1865 city government moved to its new city hall on School Street (called Old City Hall at this writing). The city leased space in the Old State House to commercial tenants until the early 1870s.

10. Boston City Planning Board (BCPB), Government Center Study: A Preliminary Report, BCPB, Generalized Land Use Plan, Exhibit D, August 1956.

11. O'Connor, *Building a New Boston,* 271.

12. Butterfield, *Walter Muir Whitehill,* 22–24.

13. Edward J. Logue's excellent track record began showing impressive results in Boston. In the ranking of major cities according to total urban renewal grants awarded, Boston moved from seventeenth in 1959 to fourth by 1963.

14. John F. Collins, "The $90 Million Development Program for Boston," *Boston City Record,* 24 September 1960, p. 7.

15. Under Mayor George Albee Hibbard (1907–1911) the former composition of the City Council, the Board of Aldermen, and the Common Council was replaced by a nine-member City Council.

16. Walter Muir Whitehill, *Boston: A Topographical History,* 2d ed. (Cambridge: Harvard University Press, Belknap Press, 1963), 97–98.

17. Ironically, not a single lawsuit was filed against the BRA during these proceedings, either from the individual owners or from those merchants who were being relocated.

18. Jane Thompson, interviews by the author, March and May 2001.

19. Benjamin Thompson, "Making a Marketplace," *Boston Magazine* 78, no. 8 (August 1986).

20. Jane Thompson, interviews.

21. Walter Muir Whitehill, letter to Edward J. Logue, director of the Boston Redevelopment Authority, 9 February 1967 (Boston Athenaeum library).

22. The BRA-sanctioned Stahl–Webb feasibility study was initiated by two nonprofit groups: the Society for the Preservation of New England Antiquities (SPNEA) and Webb's Architectural Heritage Foundation. Tad Stahl convinced two other noted preservation consultants to become involved in the story: William Endicott, director of SPNEA, and Abbott Lowell Cummings, assistant director of SPNEA. Also attracted to the project was noted historian and author Walter Muir Whitehill, director of the Boston Athenaeum and board member of Architectural Heritage Foundation.

23. The D. Ghirardelli Company, which had been in business since 1852, had left its rambling harborfront chocolate factory abandoned for some years. It was reclaimed and fashioned into a multiuse complex with private financing. The refurbished Ghirardelli Square first opened to the public in 1964, with its 55,000 square feet of rentable space that held a diversity of shops and a number of restaurants and food services on various levels around a central plaza and fountain. Three years later, an additional 120,000 square feet was leased to retail shops and food services. When it was finally completed, the occupancy rate rose to a staggering 95 percent. The largest and most prestigious anchor store was Design Research, which had been started in Cambridge in 1953 by Ben Thompson. Ghirardelli Square's owner and developer, William Roth, was on the board of directors of Design Research.

    Webb chose Ghirardelli Square as a good model for the preservation of Faneuil Hall Markets because it had been successful where other such projects (which Webb had studied) failed. Its mix of uses had proved feasible enough to attract lenders. It had assembled many parcels into one project under the control of one developer, and this organizational structure seemed fundamental to its success.

24. Lynne B. Sagalyn, CRE, "Measuring Financial Returns When the City Acts as an Investor: Boston and Faneuil Hall Marketplace," *Appraisal Journal* (American Institute of Real Estate Appraisers, Real Estate Issues), Fall/Winter 1989, 8.

25. Sagalyn, "Measuring Financial Returns," 8.

26. Roger Webb, letter to the author, 15 May 2001. The actual number of warehouse individual units was forty-two. Durgin Park restaurant added three additional units.

27. O'Connor, *Building a New Boston,* 271.

28. Former mayor Kevin White, interview by and correspondence with the author, May 2002.

29. White interview and correspondence.

30. Frederick A. Stahl, AIA, et al., *Urban Design and Architectural Report: Structural, Mechanical and Electrical Reports,* vol. 4 of *Faneuil Hall Markets Report* (Boston: Architectural Heritage and the Society for the Preservation of New England Antiquities, October 1968), A-1.

31. Anthony J. Yudis, "Market Site to Be Restored," *Boston Globe,* 7 May 1970, p 3.

32. White interview and correspondence.

33. Former BRA director Bob Kenney, interviews by the author, August 2000, May 2001, and April 2002.

34. According to Charles J. Speleotis, former chief general counsel for the BRA, the owners of Durgin Park restaurant were informed by the BRA that the city was in a position to take their property as a landmark by eminent domain if they refused to agree to the terms of reconstruction. The restaurant owners consented to the BRA's terms. Only the roof sign on Clinton Street, the fire escapes on the restaurant's back wall, and the wood-sashed double-hung windows remain unchanged.

35. According to Charles Speleotis, the legal department of the BRA had difficulty researching ownership of land titles of the streets back to the seventeenth century. Legally, the BRA could not exactly determine how many of the nearby streets came into existence or what private ownership was relinquished for public ways. This was especially true with regard to Frog's Lane. As a result, the BRA did a confirmatory taking of the whole.

36. Sagalyn, "Measuring Financial Returns," 8.

37. Two other firms not selected were Brookline-based Fred Mahony and Company, whose architects Wurster, Bernardi, and Emmons had designed Ghirardelli Square in San Francisco; and Architectural Heritage, under a subsidiary called Faneuil Hall Landmarks Corporation, which utilized Samuel Mintz as architect. The Mahony proposal envisioned covering portions of the marketplace in the style of American inventor R. Buckminster Fuller's (1895–1983) clear-spanned geodesic domes. According to former BRA director Bob Kenney, neither firm was ever officially designated as developer.

38. Kenney, interviews. Also, Robert T. Kenney, Faneuil Hall Markets, Waterfront Project, Mass. R-77, Revocation of Tentative Designation of Developer, BRA Open Memorandum, 12 January 1972.

39. Kenney, interviews.

40. Charles J. Speleotis, former chief general counsel for the BRA, interviews by the author, June 2001.

41. Jane Thompson, interviews.

42. Jane Thompson, interviews.

43. A unique feature of the Rouse scheme was a proposal to erect a central weather-proofing glass corridor between the three buildings, as his company had done in other retail centers, to allow for climate control, but the BRA was against the idea of glass enclosures.

    According to Jane Thompson, the first time Kevin White met with James Rouse and the Thompson team, the mayor strongly suggested that Rouse's efforts would be better suited for the redevelopment of Downtown Crossing, which was the nexus of two major department stores, smaller retail facilities, and numerous restaurants.

    According to former BRA director Bob Kenney, Rouse also wanted to include the federal money in his proposals, or, in essence, he requested that the $2.1 million in federal funds and all the monies contributed by the state be turned over to his company.

44. Anthony J. Yudis, "Faneuil Hall Area May Sparkle for 'Boston 200' After All," *Boston Sunday Globe,* 26 May 1972, pp. 1, 10.

45. Jane Thompson, letter to the author, 18 June 2001. The Rouse Company's in-house architects were busy with other projects, and this was part of the reason why Ben Thompson worked as architect on the project with the Rouse Company.

46. The attitudes and approaches to demolition or reuse have subsequently changed with time. Currently, there are many examples of retained architecture incorporated with new construction around Boston. The office tower located at 101 Arch Street is a prime example of a building in which the original facade—and prior retail use—is recreated within the lower floors of a modern high-rise building.

    In the case of the markets, removal of many timeworn elements was severe and sometimes unnecessary; for example, the footworn but still useful granite door sills were replaced with clean, new materials.

47. Coincidentally, a major fire destroyed the nearby Clinton Produce and Poultry Market building in April 1971. This caused concern for the safety of the then-emptied North and South Market buildings. The wooden full-shed roof dormers, the stacked construction, and other additions implemented during the past century seemed to invite arson. The BRA was therefore eager to begin the first phase of construction over architect Ben Thompson's objections that the evolving modifications to the North and South Market buildings since the 1850s were just as historic as Alexander Parris's original designs.

48. Through Whitehill's efforts, Faneuil Hall Market had been designated a federal historic landmark in 1966. The market house was listed on the National Register of Historic Places as a contributing structure to the Faneuil Hall Market National Register District. The North and South Market buildings, however, were not so protected.

49. Frederick C. Detwiller, letter to the author, 28 June 2001.

50. These two demolished stores of the South Market building are not to be confused with the two lots of the merged Hammond and Faxon building near the North Market building that was purposely razed in 1933 to widen nearby North Street. After two separate fires, the two units in the South Market building, one near the center and one at the west end of the South Market building, were declared unsafe and taken down by order of the fire marshal.

51. Tad Stahl, letter to the author, 17 May 2001.

52. Kenney, interviews.

53. Paul L. McCann, interview and correspondence with the author, March and April 2002.

Chapter 8

1. Before the master lease was finalized, the BRA had rights to lease only the North and South Market buildings (except for Durgin Park restaurant, which, as an original occupant, had deeded rights to its space). In order to proceed with the project, the BRA had to obtain the right to lease the market house and also South and North Market Streets, Merchants Row, and Commercial Street, and all above-surface and below-surface street rights and utilities from the city. Once obtained, this new master lease that encompassed the whole project area allowed the BRA to create a sublease for the area to its developer. The sublease, which was for a ninety-nine-year term, was seen as giving the developer enough control for profit incentive. Faneuil Hall, Dock Square Park, and its surrounding land were not included in this agreement.

2. McCann, interviews.

3. The New England Telephone Company had informed the BRA that they would occupy all three buildings if the BRA rebuilt them to suit their needs, hence the reference to potential light industrial tenancy.

4. O'Connor, *Building a New Boston,* 274.

5. At the time, Norman B. Leventhal was president and CEO of Beacon Construction Company and the chairman of the Neighbors of Government Center. Beacon Construction Company would later be called the Beacon Companies. On behalf of the Neighbors of Government Center he personally delivered a written endorsement of Rouse to Mayor White.

6. Norman B. Leventhal, interviews by the author, May 2001. By the time of the Rouse Company made its proposal, it had already built at least twenty-six shopping centers in the United States and Canada.

7. Kenney, interviews.

8. Robert Beal, interviews by the author, May 2001.

9. Anthony J. Yudis, "Maryland Company Favored for Faneuil-area Project," *Boston Globe,* 16 March 1973, p. 3.

10. It is somewhat of a coincidence that George B. H. Macomber Company became the construction company for phase II. The Van Arkle and Moss subcontractors—George B. H. Macomber Company (construction) and R. M. Bradley (property management)

—were no longer necessarily part of the development team once Van Arkle and Moss lost its designation.

11. White, interview.

12. The year 1974 was known for its long lines at the gas stations. Fuel supply was low and many stations were not open because they couldn't keep their tanks full. That year, in order to help conserve fuel, President Nixon went so far as to order that the country begin Daylight Saving Time on January 6, on the assumption that more daylight during prime business hours would help cut down on the usage of fuel and electric power.

13. Sagalyn, "Measuring Financial Returns," 8.

14. Sagalyn, "Measuring Financial Returns," 9.

15. The $600,000 annual base rent was not adjusted for inflation over the ninety-nine-year period of the lease.

16. McCann, interviews. Net annual rental income was defined as 66.67 percent of the gross annual rental income, to allow for a fixed 33.33 percent expense deduction.

17. Speleotis, interviews.

18. The legendary grasshopper weathervane also became the trademark symbol of Faneuil Hall Marketplace in 1976, when it was redesigned by Ben Thompson and Associates and used on signs. (The bull weathervane remained atop the market house.)

19. The Sam Adams statue was left in place as originally erected in 1879, leaving the base of the statue noticeably askew with the rest of Dock Square Park.

20. Anthony J. Yudis, *Boston Sunday Globe,* 9 June 1974, Real Estate, section A, p. 49.

21. This figure did not include the $2.1 million in HUD funds for the North and South Market buildings' initial restoration. Any public funds contributed to the market house were derived from city and state agencies.

22. In 1974, because of the size of the loan, most conventional lenders (banks) would not lend $21 million to be paid off over many years. They would, instead, provide comparatively short-term (re)construction loans, disbursing funds and accruing interest on the balance, but only if a corporate insurance company was prepared to pay off the lenders within a year or so of the project's completion. The insurance company holding this so-called permanent financing would then receive mortgage payments from the developer over the longer term of the loan.

    With regard to the marketplace development, Chase Manhattan wouldn't have even entertained the thought of lending such a great amount of money for such a risky redevelopment project during a national recession if Rouse hadn't first got a commitment from a corporate insurance company for permanent financing by pledging his company's other assets. (If the development had failed, Rouse would have had to use income from his assets or developments to pay off the loan.) This permanent financing was most probably disbursed by Teachers Insurance Company as each building was reopened, to pay off the construction loan debt.

23. Ian Menzies, "City Banks Give Rouse Death Kiss," *Boston Globe,* 15 January 1975, City section. Exacerbating this negativity, across town, Boston's tallest and newest sixty-story office tower, the new John Hancock Building, located in the Back Bay, persisted in

shedding the glass panels that constituted its exterior facade. Some remarked that office furniture would have to be equipped with seat belts if the windows continued to blow out.

24. White, interview and correspondence.

25. White, interview and correspondence.

26. Jane Thompson, on behalf of her husband, Ben Thompson, letter to the author, spring 2001.

27. Jane Thompson, interviews.

28. Jane Thompson, on behalf of her husband, Ben Thompson, letter to the author, spring 2001.

29. White, interview and correspondence. "The Vault" was formed in 1959 by prominent business leaders who were concerned about the city's potential bankruptcy at that time. The sixteen-member committee was nicknamed "the Vault" by the media because it convened in the inner sanctum of a large walk-in vault at the Boston Safe Deposit and Trust Company. Initially, the committee was composed mostly of men from Boston's old Yankee families, who lent not only their prestige and influence but also their extensive investment experience.

30. Anthony J. Yudis, "Faneuil Hall Project Revived by Hub Banks," *Boston Globe,* 31 January 1975, p. 29.

31. Speleotis, interviews.

32. Magic Pan restaurant had already been a successful merchant in Denver's Larimer Square and San Francisco's Ghirardelli Square for five years. By 1976 this chain of restaurants had been bought by General Foods Corporation; it would be the only sizable tenant at that time.

    The Rouse Company had intended to redevelop all three buildings at the same time.

33. William Marlin, "The Case for Design Quality in Today's Marketplace," *Architectural Record* (December 1977), 127. The value of $7.5 million at a 5 percent inflation rate is approximately $26.6 million in 2001 dollars.

34. James Hammond, "Historic Market Reopens," *Boston Evening Globe,* 26 August 1976, Front Page.

35. "Rouse, Boston, BRA Sign Lease for $20M Faneuil Hall Markets Rehab—365,000 S/F," *New England Real Estate Journal* (21 March 1975), 1.

36. Although some newspaper accounts cite $20 million construction costs shared by Chase Manhattan Bank and the Boston consortium of ten lenders at this period, the actual amount of $7.5 million was shared by nine lenders for reconstruction of the city-owned market house and the immediate perimeter. As time went by, the cost to redevelop the North and South Market buildings and complete the project by the end of 1978 had risen to higher than $20 million. There were no precise total costs available at this writing. According to former BRA director Bob Kenney, the three-year timetable resulted only because of the central market house's immediate success.

    The number of Boston area lenders included in the original consortium varies from one source to another. Later participants included State Street Bank and Trust Company, the Boston Five Cents Savings Bank, and the South Boston Savings Bank. Of the aforementioned lenders, only State Street Bank and Trust Company, John Hancock Mutual Insurance Company, and the Massachusetts Business Development Corporation remain in business at this writing. There was also a $5.2 million equity financing provided by JMB Urban Investment and Development Company of Chicago, Illinois.

37. The estimated cost to move these tenants was $4.2 million. Funds were provided by HUD and the Small Business Administration. Since 1964, the BRA had been preoccupied with the relocation of approximately six hundred marketplace merchants to other places where they could continue doing business. Some, like the fruit and produce dealers, joined together and established the New England Produce Center on a thirty-acre site on the Chelsea-Everett city line. Forty meat dealers from the market's Meatpackers Row formed the New Boston Food Corporation and relocated to South Bay. By 1971, most of the remaining fish dealers had set up business at the New England Seafood Center at 145 Northern Avenue. Several flower merchants went to the Flower Exchange at 540 Albany Street, near South Bay.

38. Each operator still in business was given a favorable three-year, no-risk lease at the existing city-based rent of $3.00 per square foot—about 25 percent of the cost to new vendors coming into the market house. Some remaining long-term merchants included E. N. West, J. L. Dembro, Doe Sullivan, and M. Berenson. When construction began on the west end of the building, these merchants were moved to temporary new stalls at the east end, then moved back to their renovated space at no cost and no loss of valuable business days.

39. At this time, there was no central air-conditioning.

40. According to the BRA director's executive assistant, Paul L. McCann, the city funded all the labor and materials used to convert the surrounding and intersecting streets into the pedestrian concourses.

41. The market house did not lose its powerful presence by the addition of these contemporary but complementary elements. According to Jane Thompson, the trees were installed during the night. Some preservationists resisted these ideas but the BRA supported the concept.

42. Architect William L. McQueen, interviews by the author, May 2001.

43. Thompson recommended that circular stairs be positioned under the rotunda opening as an obvious and direct solution for accessing the second level. The Department of the Interior's National Park Service and a preservationist advisory group, however, ruled that new interior stairs would alter the design of the rotunda too much. Consequently, the public was initially compelled to get to the second level of the rotunda by means of the original stairways. A double set of interior stairs was later installed to allow patrons to ascend to the second level more easily.

44. Sagalyn, "Measuring Financial Returns," 9. Year one was reduced from $200,000 by $150,000 to $50,000; year two from $400,000 by $350,000 to $50,000; year three from $600,000 by $550,000 to $50,000, totaling $1.05 million abated, $150,000 to be paid.

45. Speleotis, interviews.
46. Additionally, the city had forfeited real estate taxes from the individual units within the North and South Market buildings for nearly a decade (at an average yearly amount of nearly $300,000) and the Commonwealth forwent sales taxes during the same period.
47. Sagalyn, "Measuring Financial Returns," 10.
48. General public "hard costs" included North and South Market unit acquisitions, tenant relocation, capital improvements of all three buildings, park construction participation, public utilities, Central Artery exit ramp removal, and the purchase and preparation of a nearby parking lot. The public "soft costs" included preliminary planning, consultants, engineering surveys, public and private studies, bid solicitation and evaluation of proposals, tax and lease agreements, and more. By 1978 these costs increased total public participation to at least $17 million (at a breakdown of 70 percent from federal funds, 13 percent from the state, and 17 percent from the City of Boston). The value of $15.5 million, using a 5 percent inflation rate, is approximately $55 million in 2001 dollars.

   The BRA had negotiated with the state highway authorities to purchase nearby parcel E-8, the site where a Central Artery exit ramp was removed in 1972, so that also became a public cost. Thus, the public participation increased to nearly 78 percent.
49. An example of colonial-era antique lanterns can be seen outside Durgin Park restaurant on the North Market concourse.
50. The position of superintendent (originally the Clerk of the Market) still exists at Faneuil Hall.
51. Dan Ahern, "What Can Be Done Forcibly Shown," *Boston Herald American,* Thursday, 19 August 1976.
52. There had been a growing movement during the 1960s and 1970s to revitalize handmade crafts as a viable business, and a growing interest in buying such goods. This interest fed the need at Quincy Market for pushcart peddlers.
53. Benjamin Thompson, "Making a Marketplace."
54. Daniel Q. Hanley, *Lewiston (Maine) Journal,* 26 August 1976.
55. Judy Buswick, "Chelmsford Granite Makes History at Quincy Market," *Boston Globe,* Thursday, 14 April 1983. Frankie Bunyard, the woman responsible for creating the seven-foot-diameter granite ground marker, was asked to chisel her initials into the stone. She refused, stating that if she discreetly added her mark, she might set a trend for attracting graffiti.
56. A time capsule was entombed below the granite slab by the Rouse Company. Its specific contents are unknown.
57. O'Connor, *Building a New Boston,* 277.
58. Ken O. Botwright, "This Is Yours—Enjoy It," *Boston Globe,* 27 August 1976, Editorial page, pp. 20, 29.
59. O'Connor, *Building a New Boston,* 277.
60. On August 26, 1976, the author walked down from the offices of Quincy and Company, which were then located at 73 Tremont Street in Boston, to witness the opening ceremonies with John Quincy Sr., his father. The elder Quincy, a man known

for not wasting time, especially during business hours, exclaimed that although he was happy to finally see the market house rescued from oblivion, the swelling crowd would make it impossible to have a quick lunch and return to work. Instead, Mr. Quincy took his son to Durgin Park restaurant as he had in December 1963. Before returning to the office that day the elder Quincy, having refused to enter the market house because of the crowds, examined the building only from the exterior and remarked, "What would Mayor Quincy think of all this? I believe he would beam with pride before shaking his head in disbelief at the cost it took to restore his market house."

61. John Dobie, interviews by the author, July and August 2000.

62. Botwright, "This Is Yours—Enjoy It."

63. Benjamin Thompson, "Making a Marketplace."

64. White, interview.

65. Jack Thomas, "That's Not My Faneuil Hall," *Boston Globe,* Thursday, 15 June 1995, Living/Arts section, pp. 69, 74–75.

Chapter 9

1. John Kifner, "A 'New' 1826 Market Joins Boston's Downtown Revival," *New York Times,* 27 August 1976, section B-1.

2. Edward J. Lonergan, general counsel to the BRA, interviews by the author, May 2001.

3. Edward Schumacher, "Boston's Waterfront Gets New Face," *Denver Post,* 27 October 1976.

4. Faneuil Hall Marketplace general manager James B. McLean Jr., interviews by the author, August 2000 and May 2001.

5. Horace Sutton, "Boston's Quincy Market Offers More Than Beans, Cod," *Chicago Tribune,* 12 February 1978.

6. Jane Thompson, on behalf of her husband, Ben Thompson, letter to the author, spring 2001.

7. Benjamin Thompson, "What Will the New Faneuil Hall Marketplace Be?" (Cambridge: Benjamin Thompson and Associates, Description of the plan, 1973), 3.

8. According to Charles J. Speleotis, former chief general counsel for the BRA, the BRA took issue with the Rouse Company's encroachment onto the now closed-off streets, which the sublease explicitly stated should remain open to the public for pedestrians' use, easements, and other forms of access.

9. It is not known what the original coloring was of Parris's plaster rosettes and coffered panels.

10. When cores were drilled for the elevator shafts, pieces of ancient gravel, blue clay, wood from some old corduroy roads, sea silt, and clam shells were unearthed.

11. At the reopening of both the South and North Market buildings the author and his father walked down to examine the completed rehabilitation from the exterior, after having lunch at Durgin Park restaurant. (Old habits die hard.)

12. Look closely and you can see many original features, both inside and outside, of the Durgin Park section of the North Market building.

13. These figures come from the Rouse Company.

14. Michael Ryan, "Boston Catches Market Fever: True Stories from the Marketplace: From the Bizarre to the Bazaar," *Boston Magazine* (April 1979), 85.

15. McLean, interviews.

16. In 1985 a bronze sculpture of Arnold "Red" Auerbach, legendary coach and president of the Boston Celtics basketball team, was positioned near the information pavilion. The statue was created by Lloyd Lillie, a professor of sculpture at Boston University, and unveiled by *Boston Globe* sports columnist Will McDonough, who was the driving force for its installment. In 1990 the bronzed running shoes of noted Boston Marathon runner Bill Rodgers and the bronzed basketball shoes of legendary Celtics star Larry Bird were also installed as public art.

17. McLean, interviews.

18. O'Connor, *Building a New Boston,* 279.

19. Ada Louise Huxtable, "Why You Always Win and Lose in Urban Renewal: Architectural View," *New York Sunday Times,* 19 September 1976, p. 34.

20. McLean, interviews.

21. Ben Thompson, televised interview by Christopher Lydon, WGBH-TV (PBS), May 1992, quoted in correspondence from Jane Thompson to the author, spring 2002.

22. Jane Thompson, on behalf of her husband, Ben Thompson, letter to the author, spring 2001.

23. Tad Stahl, interviews by the author, July and December 2000.

24. Edward Schumacher, "The People of Boston Get Waterfront Back," *International Herald Tribune,* 19 October 1976, front page.

25. White, interview.

26. McLean, interviews.

27. Ben Thompson, quoted in Jane Thompson, interviews.

28. Sagalyn, "Measuring Financial Returns," 11.

29. McLean, interviews. Kenney, interviews. The Rouse Company also invested $500,000 between 1975 and 1976 for Boston's bicentennial celebration, which it never recovered.

30. Kenney, interviews.

31. Sagalyn, "Measuring Financial Returns," 11.

32. Joe Clements, "Happy Financial Returns for Marketplace at Age 20," *Banker and Tradesman* (19 August 1996), 1, 10.

33. Thomas, "That's Not My Faneuil Hall." The words published in this volume that differ from the 1995 *Boston Globe* interview with Ben Thompson were authorized by Ben Thompson, speaking through his wife, Jane Thompson, in her June 2001 interview with the author.

34. Thomas, "That's Not My Faneuil Hall."

35. Kenney, interviews. There is still no such BRA committee at the time of this writing.

36. Thomas, "That's Not My Faneuil Hall," 69, 74–75.

37. Monica Collins, "Quincy Market Gets Mugged as Officials Look the Other Way," *Boston Sunday Herald,* 1 October 1995, Downtown Journal, p. 28.

38. Shawn Bisbee, "Merchants Worry Marketplace Could Become Faneuil 'Mall,' " *Banker and Tradesman* (21 December 1994), 1, 4.

39. Clements, "Lawsuits, Tension, Hallmark of Historic Market in '90s," *Banker and Tradesman* (12 August 1996), 1, 20.

40. Clements, "Happy Financial Returns for Marketplace at Age 20."

41. Collins, "Quincy Market Gets Mugged."

42. Clements, "Lawsuits, Tension," 1, 20.

43. Faneuil Hall Marketplace general manager Joseph "Skip" Coppola, interviews by the author, May 2001 and April 2002.

44. The 1990 Americans with Disabilities Act was not put into effect until 1992. The five-or six-panel hatch doors in the canopy roofs were replaced with more functional bifold doors. In addition, the weather stripping between some glass panels needed replacing.

45. The market hall's colonnade was repainted, new woodwork and new lighting were installed, as were new heating, ventilating, and air-conditioning systems.

46. Coppola, interviews.

47. In the *Architects and Builders Boston Directory, 1789–1846,* compiled by the Massachusetts Committee for the Preservation of Architectural Records, Joseph D. Emery was also listed as a registered housewright and carpenter residing at various locations in Boston between 1820 and 1828.

48. Faneuil Hall Marketplace general manager Michael Kelleher, interviews by the author, April 2002.

49. Kelleher, interviews.

Conclusion

1. Arthur C. Quincy, quoted by John Quincy Sr. to John Quincy Jr., December 1963.

2. John Quincy Sr. to John Quincy Jr., December 1963.

3. I could find no evidence that any convict escaped while working on the project.

4. In books, newspapers, tourist information, magazine articles, etc., there are references to the Great Hall (the second-floor rotunda of the market house) being called Quincy Hall by 1837, but there is no official documentation to support these references. Josiah Quincy's personal journals do not mention his being honored and most official records refer to the market house as Faneuil Hall Market until it was officially incorporated into Faneuil Hall Marketplace in 1976.

5. Ezra Stiles Gannett, "A Discourse Occasioned by the Death of the Honorable Josiah Quincy, July 10, 1864" *(Boston) Daily Tribune,* 20 July 1864.

6. Especially also Jane Thompson and Mayor John Collins and the former chief general counsel for the BRA, Charles Speleotis, and former BRA director Ed Logue.

7. Tad Stahl, interviews.

8. Speleotis, interviews.

9. O'Connor, *Building a New Boston,* 281.

10. White, interview and correspondence.

11. Guild, *Men and Market,* 36.

Bibliography

Published Sources

Amadon, Elizabeth Reed, et al. *The Faneuil Hall Markets: An Historical Study.* A volume of *Faneuil Hall Markets Report.* Boston: Architectural Heritage and the Society for the Preservation of New England Antiquities, 1968. (Added title page reads: *Faneuil Hall Markets Report,* prepared for the Boston Redevelopment Authority by Architectural Heritage, Incorporated, and the Society for the Preservation of New England Antiquities under the direction of Walter Muir Whitehill, William Endicott, Elizabeth Reed Amadon, Abbott Lowell Cummings, Christopher P. Monkhouse, Roger S. Webb, Frederick A. Stahl.)

Architectural Heritage and the Society for the Preservation of New England Antiquities. *Faneuil Hall Markets Report.* 5 vols. Boston: Architectural Heritage and the Society for the Preservation of New England Antiquities, 1968. (Added title page reads: *Faneuil Hall Markets Report,* prepared for the Boston Redevelopment Authority by Architectural Heritage, Incorporated, and the Society for the Preservation of New England Antiquities under the direction of Walter Muir Whitehill, William Endicott, Elizabeth Reed Amadon, Abbott Lowell Cummings, Christopher P. Monkhouse, Roger S. Webb, Frederick A. Stahl.)

Bacon, Edwin M. *Boston: A Guide Book.* Boston: Ginn and Co., 1910.

———. *King's Dictionary of Boston.* Cambridge, Mass.: Moses King, Publisher, 1883.

Bartlett, John. *Familiar Quotations.* 16th ed. Edited by Justin Kaplan. Boston: Little, Brown, 1992.

Boston, City of. *A Record of the Streets, Alleys, Places, etc., in the City of Boston.* Boston: City of Boston Printing Department, 1910.

Boston Society of Architects. Text by Joseph L. Eldredge. *Architecture, Boston.* Barre, Mass: Boston Society of Architects, 1976.

Bowen, Abel. *Bowen's Picture of Boston, or the Citizen's and Stranger's Guide to the Metropolis of Massachusetts, and Its Environs.* Boston: Otis, Broaders, 1829.

Brown, Abram English. *Faneuil Hall and Faneuil Hall Market, or, Peter Faneuil and His Gift.* Boston: Lee and Shepard, 1900.

Butterfield, Lyman H., ed. "Historical Continuity versus Synthetic Reconstruction." In *Walter Muir Whitehill: A Record Compiled by His Friends, 13 September 1985.* Minot, Mass.: Athenaeum Press, 1958.

Ching, Francis D. K. *A Visual Dictionary of Architecture.* New York: John Wiley, 1997.

Coffin, Charles Carleton. "Faneuil Hall." *Bostonian Society Proceedings,* vol. 3, 1906.

Crocker, Matthew H. *The Magic of the Many: Josiah Quincy and the Rise of Mass Politics in Boston 1800–1830.* Amherst: University of Massachusetts Press, 1999.

Curl, James Stevens. *Dictionary of Architecture.* New York: Oxford University Press, 1999.

Damrell and Moore. *Sketches and Business Directory of Boston and Its Vicinity for 1860 and 1861.* Boston: George Coolidge, and Damrell and Moore, 1861.

Detwiller, Frederick. *Historic Structure Report: Faneuil Hall.* U.S. Department of the Interior, National Park Service, North Atlantic Region, 1977.

Dearborn, Nathaniel. *Boston Notions: Being an Authentic and Concise Account of "That Village" from 1620 to 1847.* Boston: W. D. Ticknor, 1848.

Drake, Samuel Adams. *Old Landmarks and Historic Personages of Boston.* Boston: James R. Osgood, 1873.

Drake, Samuel G. The *History and Antiquities of Boston, from Its Settlement in 1630 to the Year 1770 A.D.* Boston: Luther Stevens, 1856.

Dunn, Richard S., and Laetitia Yeandle, eds. *The Journal of John Winthrop 1630–1649.* Abr. ed. Cambridge: Harvard University Press, Belknap Press, 1996.

"Explore the Shoreline." *Bostonian Society Newsletter* 30 (April 1995): 2.

Edwards, William Churchill. *Historic Quincy, Massachusetts,* 3d ed. Quincy, Mass.: City of Quincy, 1957.

Erkkila, Barbara H. *Hammers on Stone: The History of Cape Ann Granite.* Woolwich, Me.: TBW Books, 1980.

Fahey, Joseph J., ed. *Boston's 45 Mayors: from John Phillips to Kevin H. White.* Boston: City of Boston Printing Section, [1975].

Flint, Austin, M.D. *A Practical Treatise of the Diagnosis, Pathology, and Treatment of Diseases of the Heart.* Philadelphia: Blanchard and Lea, 1859.

Fogelson, Robert M. *Downtown: Its Rise and Fall, 1880–1950.* New Haven: Yale University Press, 2001.

Gilman, Arthur. *The Story of Boston: A Study of Independency.* New York and London: G. P. Putnam's Sons, 1894.

Guild, Courtenay. "Men and Market of 1826" (pamphlet). *Bostonian Society Proceedings,* 18 January 1927.

Hodgman, Reverend Edwin R. *History of the Town of Westford, Massachusetts.* Lowell, Mass.: Collection of the Chelmsford Historical Society, 1883.

Holleran, Michael. *Boston's "Changeful Times": Origins of Preservation and Planning in America*. Baltimore: Johns Hopkins University Press, 1998.

Holli, Melvin G. *The American Mayor*. University Park: Pennsylvania State University Press, 1999.

Holly, H. Hobart. *Quincy's Legacy*. Quincy, Mass.: Quincy Historical Society, 1998.

Kennedy, Lawrence W. *Planning the City Upon a Hill: Boston Since 1630*. Amherst: University of Massachusetts Press, 1992.

King, Moses. *King's Hand-book of Boston, Profusely Illustrated*. Cambridge, Mass.: Moses King, Publisher, 1878.

Kirker, Harold, and James Kirker. *Bulfinch's Boston, 1787–1817*. New York: Oxford University Press, 1964.

Krieger, Alex, and David Cobb, eds., with Amy Turner. *Mapping Boston*. Cambridge: MIT Press, 1999.

Marlin, William. "The Case for Design Quality in Today's Marketplace." *Architectural Record* (December 1977).

Massachusetts Historical Society. *A Pride of Quincys*. Boston: Massachusetts Historical Society, 1969.

McCaughey, Robert A. *Josiah Quincy, 1772–1864, The Last Federalist*. Cambridge: Harvard University Press, 1974.

McFarland, Philip. *The Brave Bostonians: Hutchinson, Quincy, Franklin, and the Coming of the American Revolution*. Boulder, Colo.: Westview Press, 1998.

McKay, George E. "Faneuil Hall Market" (pamphlet). *Bostonian Society Proceedings*, 11 January 1910.

Miller, Walter. *Cicero de Officiis*. Cambridge: Harvard University Press, 1961.

Monkhouse, Christopher P. *Faneuil Hall Market: An Account of Its Many Likenesses*. Boston: Bostonian Society, 1969.

Morison, Samuel Eliot. *Three Centuries of Harvard, 1636–1936*. Cambridge: Harvard University Press, Belknap Press, 1936.

O'Connor, Thomas H. *Bibles, Brahmins, and Bosses: A Short History of Boston*. Boston: Trustees of the Public Library of the City of Boston, 1976.

———. *The Boston Irish: A Political History*. Boston: Northeastern University Press, 1995.

———. *Building a New Boston: Politics and Urban Renewal, 1950–1970*. Boston: Northeastern University Press, 1993.

———. *The Hub: Boston Past and Present*. Boston: Northeastern University Press, 2001.

Pierce, Sally. *Whipple and Black: Commercial Photographers in Boston*. Boston: Boston Athenaeum, 1987.

Porter, Reverend Edward G. *Rambles in Old Boston, New England*. Boston: Cupples, Upham, 1887.

Quincy, Edmund. *The Life of Josiah Quincy*. Boston: Ticknor and Fields, 1868.

Quincy, Josiah. *History of Harvard University,* 2 vols. Cambridge: J. Owen, 1840.

———. *Memoir of the Life of John Quincy Adams.* Boston: Phillips, Sampson, 1858.

———. *Memoir of the Life of Josiah Quincy, Junior, of Massachusetts.* Boston: Cummings, Hillard, 1825.

———. *A Municipal History of the Town and City of Boston During Two Centuries, from September 17, 1630, to September 17, 1830.* Boston: Little, Brown, 1852.

Quincy, Josiah, Jr. *Figures of the Past from the Leaves of Old Journals.* Boston: Roberts Brothers, 1883.

Rossiter, William S., ed. *Days and Ways in Olde Boston.* Boston: R. H. Stearns, 1915.

Rutman, Darrett B. *John Winthrop's Boston: Portrait of a Puritan Town, 1630–1649.* Chapel Hill: University of North Carolina Press, 1965.

Sagalyn, Lynne B., CRE, "Measuring Financial Returns When the City Acts as an Investor: Boston and Faneuil Hall Marketplace." *Appraisal Journal* (American Institute of Real Estate Appraisers, Real Estate Issues), Fall/Winter 1989.

Salisbury, Edward Elbridge. "Pedigree of Quincy." *Family: Memorials,* 2 vols. (A series of genealogical and biographical monographs privately printed at New Haven: Tuttle, Morehouse and Taylor, 1885).

Savage, Edward H. *Boston Events: A Brief Mention and the Date of More Than 5,000 Events That Transpired in Boston from 1630 to 1880.* Boston: Tolman and White, 1884

Shand-Tucci, Douglass. *Built in Boston: City and Suburb 1800–1950.* Boston: New York Graphic Society, 1978.

Shurtleff, Nathaniel B. A *Topographical and Historical Description of Boston,* 3d ed. Boston: published by order of the City Council, 1890.

Small, Edwin W. "National Register of Historic Places Nomination of Faneuil Hall." Boston: Bostonian Society report, 1967.

Smith, Richard Norton. *The Harvard Century: The Making of a University to a Nation.* New York: Simon and Schuster, 1986.

Snow, Caleb H. *A History of Boston, the Metropolis of Massachusetts, from Its Origin to the Present Period, with Some Account of the Environs.* Boston: Abel Bowen, 1825.

Stahl, Frederick A., AIA, et al. *Urban Design and Architectural Report: Structural, Mechanical and Electrical Reports.* Vol. 4 of *Faneuil Hall Markets Report.* Boston: Architectural Heritage and the Society for the Preservation of New England Antiquities, 1968. (Added title page reads: *Faneuil Hall Markets Report,* prepared for the Boston Redevelopment Authority by Architectural Heritage, Incorporated, and the Society for the Preservation of New England Antiquities under the direction of Walter Muir Whitehill, William Endicott, Elizabeth Reed Amadon, Abbott Lowell Cummings, Christopher P. Monkhouse, Roger S. Webb, Frederick A. Stahl.)

Stanley, Raymond W. *Mr. Bulfinch's Boston.* Boston: Old Colony Trust Company, 1963.

Thompson, Benjamin. "Making a Marketplace." *Boston Magazine* 78, no. 8 (August 1986).

Thwing, Annie Haven. *The Crooked and Narrow Streets of the Town of Boston 1630–1822.* Boston: Marshall Jones, 1920.

Tsipis, Yanni. *Boston's Central Artery. Images of America.* Charleston, S.C.: Arcadia Publishing, 2000.

Walker, James, D.D. "Memoir of Josiah Quincy." *Proceedings of the Massachusetts Historical Society,* 1866–1867.

Watson, Walter Kendal. "The Site of Faneuil Hall." *Bostonian Society Proceedings.* Vol. 3, 1905.

Wheildon, William W. *Semi-Centennial Celebration of the Opening of Faneuil Hall Market, August 26, 1876.* Boston: L. F. Lawrence, 1877.

Whitehill, Walter Muir. *Boston: A Topographical History.* 2d ed. Cambridge: Harvard University Press, Belknap Press, 1963.

———. *The Metamorphoses of Scollay and Bowdoin Squares.* Boston: Bostonian Society, 1973.

———. *Recycling Quincy Market* (newsletter). Boston: Boston Athenaeum, March 1977.

Whitehill, Walter Muir, and Wendell D. Garrett. *Proceedings of the Massachusetts Historical Society,* 1979.

Wilson, Daniel Munro. *Three Hundred Years of Quincy, 1625–1925: Historical Retrospect of Mount Wollaston, Braintree and Quincy.* Quincy, Mass.: City of Quincy, 1926.

Winsor, Justin, ed. *The Memorial History of Boston, Including Suffolk County, Massachusetts, 1630–1880.* 4 vols. Boston: James R. Osgood, 1881.

Zobel, Hiller B. *The Boston Massacre.* New York: W. W. Norton, 1970.

Unpublished Sources

Adams Family Papers. Massachusetts Historical Society, Collections and Proceedings.

Boston, City of: Board of Aldermen, and City Council. Records of the executive committees, 1822–1954. Boston City Archives.

Boston Redevelopment Authority (BRA). "Historic Design Critique on the Rehabilitation of the Quincy Market Complex." Architectural-Historical Report no. 10, 1964. Boston City Archives.

Boston, Town of: Common Council records. Boston City Archives.

Cass, Gilbert. "Quincy Market." Dissertation, Harvard Graduate School of Design, 1966.

Fletcher Family Papers. Privately collected and owned.

Gordon, Jacques. "Case Study: Faneuil Hall Marketplace, Boston." Prepared as part of a series of case studies of downtown development directed by Professors Bernard J. Frieden and Lynne B. Sagalyn. Cambridge: MIT Department of Urban Studies and Planning, January 1984.

Greater Boston Chamber of Commerce. Report on the Downtown Waterfront–Faneuil Hall renewal plan, prepared at the request of Mayor John F. Collins, by the Waterfront Redevelopment Division and its consultants: Kevin Lynch, AIP, and John M. R. Myer, AIA, planning/architectural; Metcaff and Eddym engineering; John R. White, Brown, Harris, Stevens, real estate; Bruce Campbell and Associates, traffic. June 1962.

Kellerhouse, Karen S. Untitled paper prepared as a research assistant, Redevelopment of the Boston Waterfront (A), under the supervision of Valerie I. Nelson, lecturer of public policy at the Kennedy School of Government, Harvard University, prepared with the assistance and cooperation of BRA Waterfront Project architect John Dobie, 1978. Kenney Personal Papers.

Kenney, Robert T., BRA director. "Downtown Boston Revitalization: Quincy Market at Faneuil Hall and Waterfront Park—The Role of Public Administrator." 1978. Kenney Personal Papers.

———. "Faneuil Hall Markets," Waterfront Project, Mass R-77, Revocation of Tentative Designation of Developer. BRA open memorandum, 1972. Kenney Personal Papers.

Mackay, William, Treasurer of the City of Boston. "The Extension of Faneuil Hall Market Accounting Ledger, June 1824–November 1826." Boston City Archives.

Quincy Family Collection. Quincy Historical Society.

Quincy Family Papers. Massachusetts Historical Society, Collections and Proceedings.

Quincy Family Papers. Privately collected and owned.

Quincy, the Colonel Josiah, and Dorothy Quincy homesteads.

Quincy, Josiah, mayor of Boston. Records of the Proceedings of the Committee of the City Council on the Extension of Faneuil Hall Market, March 1824–November 1826, 2 vol. Boston City Archives.

———. "Remarks on Some of the Provisions of the Laws of Massachusetts Affecting Poverty, Vice, and Crime, Being the General Topics of a Charge to the Grand Jury of the County of Suffolk, in March Term, 1822." Cambridge: Printed at the University Press, 1822. (Private collection of the author.)

Sparks, Robert V. "Abolition in Silver Slippers: A Biography of Edmund Quincy." Dissertation, Boston College, 1978.

Thompson, Benjamin. "What Will the New Faneuil Hall Marketplace Be?" (description of the plan). Cambridge: Benjamin Thompson and Associates (c. 1965, 1973).

Thompson, Benjamin, and Associates (BTA). BRA (Boston Redevelopment Authority) concept plan package, 1967.

Zimmer, Edward Francis. "The Architectural Career of Alexander Parris, 1780–1852," 3 vols. Dissertation, Boston University Graduate School of Design, 1984.

Other Sources Consulted

Adams Library, Chelmsford, Massachusetts.

American Antiquarian Society, Worcester, Massachusetts.

Boston Athenaeum.

Boston City Hall, Boston City Hall Annex, Boston City Archives, Boston Inspectional Services, and the Boston Public Works Engineering Record Department.

Boston Globe library.

Boston Herald library.

Boston Public Library (main library and branches).

Bostonian Society.

Chelmsford Historical Society, Chelmsford, Massachusetts.

Crane Library, Quincy, Massachusetts.

Faneuil Hall.

Faneuil Hall Marketplace records.

Fletcher Granite Company quarries, Chelmsford, Massachusetts.

Goodspeed's Book Shop, Boston (not in business at the time of this writing).

Greater Boston Chamber of Commerce.

Harvard University: Francis Loeb Library.

Harvard University: Houghton Library.

Harvard University Archives.

Kenney (Robert) Papers.

Lowell Historical Society, Lowell, Massachusetts.

Massachusetts Historical Commission.

Massachusetts Historical Society.

Massachusetts State House Archives.

Museum of Fine Arts, Boston.

National Park Service, Boston.

New England Historic Genealogical Society, Boston.

Old State House (Massachusetts).

Paul Revere House, Boston.

Quincy Historical Society, Quincy, Massachusetts.

The Rouse Company.

Society for the Preservation of New England Antiquities, Boston.

Suffolk County Courthouse (both the old and new), Boston, Massachusetts.

Westford Historical Society, Westford, Massachusetts.

Westford Public Library, Westford, Massachusetts.

Index

Page numbers given in *italics* indicate illustrations or their captions.

A. Bonfatti and Company, 219
Adams, Abijah, 21, 242*n2*
Adams and Safford, 85
Adams, Daniel, 67
Adams, Howard and Greeley, 149
Adams, John, 24–25, 28, 42
Adams, John Quincy, 42
Adams, Samuel, 22, 24, 25, 26, 27, 129
Adams Square, 129, *140*, 187
Agricultural Warehouse and Seed Store, 118
American Builder's Companion, The (Benjamin), 54
American Magazine, 106
American Revolution, 27–28, 241*n43*
Americans with Disabilities Act, 223, 267*n44*
Ames Plow Company, 125–26, 128
Ancient and Honorable Artillery Company, 7, 18, 204, 240*n19*
Andrews, John, *113*, *114*
Arbella (ship), 2
Architectural Dictionary (Nicholson), 253*n47*
Architectural Heritage, *100*, *101*, *103*, 164, 170, 181–82, 183
Architectural Heritage Foundation, 155
Argus (ship), 32
Arthorp, Mary T., 65
Arthur D. Little Company, 155
Ashburton, Lord, 119
Atlantic Avenue, 171
Attucks, Crispus, 24
Auerbach, Arnold ("Red"), 266*n16*

Baker, W. S., 117
Baltimore, 125, 216
Baltimore Clippers, 32
Baltimore Wharf, 120
Barré, Isaac, 28
Barricado, 127
Beacon Hill, 32
Beal, Robert, 183–84
Beaver (cargo ship), 26
Bellingham mansion, 13, 29
Bell's Paste Blacking Warehouse, 118
Benjamin, Asher (Ashur): career of, 53–54; and market house design, 67–68, 73–74; and Market Square expansion, 56–57, 62, 69, *70*; Parris and, 232; payment of, 248*n20*; resigns as alderman, 82
Benjamin Thompson and Associates. *See* Thompson, Benjamin/Benjamin Thompson and Associates
Billings, Hammatt, *114*
Bird, Larry, 266*n16*
Blackstone Street, 149, 164, 203
Blackstone, William, 1–2, 41
Blanchard, Jedediah, 87
Blanchard, Joshua, 15
Bonney, John, 71
Boston: British blockade and occupation of, 26–27; building boom in, 121; centralization of municipal authority in, 44–45, 47–48; early marketplaces in, 5–12; earthquake in, 242*n3*; economic depressions in, 33–34, 43, 137–40, 185–86, 221; economic recovery in, 216–17; effect of railroads on, 130, 137–38; and eminent domain, 57, 59, 60–63, 77, 80, 127, 258*n34*; evacuation of, 29; Great Fire

of, 126, 142; highways in, 141; historical preservation in, 148–49, 151–59; immigration to, 123, 125; incorporation as city, xiii, 34–35, *36–37*, 245*n24*; naming of, 239*n5*; post-Revolution expansion of, 32–34; retained architecture in, 259*n46*; sanitation improvements in, 45–47; as seaport, 9–10, 32, 125, 130, 137–38; settlement of, 1–5; and slave trade, 10; social unrest in, 189; spatial transformation in, *134*; and stone contractors, 97–99; street pollution in, xiii, 34, 244*n14*; suburban flight in, xiv, 141, 145–47, 189–91, 216; tax collection in, 64–65, 245*n24*, 247*n8*; urban renewal in, 150–51, 256*n4*, 257*n13*; zoning laws in, 141–42. *See also* Boston City Council; Boston Redevelopment Authority (BRA)
Boston and Maine railroad station (Haymarket Square), 122
Boston and Roxbury Mill Dam Corporation, 86
Boston Antiquarian Club, 149
Boston Athenaeum, 105, 147
Boston City Archives, 235, 236–37
Boston City Council: Benjamin resigns from, 82; in Boston city charter, 34–35; and City Wharf sale, 123; decision-making process in, 251*n22*; deed restrictions eased by, 144; and development costs, 112–15; and Extension of Fanueil Hall Market, 51–54, 67–69; and "fair price,"

247*n*9; Fanueil Hall as market terminated by, 105–6; and Fanueil Hall marketplace expansion, 54–57; and granite purchases, 90, 99; and historical preservation, 123, 125; and land acquisitions, 56–57, 59, 62, 65–66, 76–80; and leases, 116; and lot auctions, 72–73; and market house budget, 81; and market house construction, 86–88; and market house management, 121; and market house opening, 108–9; and naming of Fanueil Hall Market, 109–11, 119–20; Parris and, 69, 71–72; promissory notes issued by, 65, 105; public perception of, 63–64; Quincy and, 49, 230; and Quincy's sanitation improvements, 44–47; and redevelopment proposals, 183–84; and renaming of Market Square, 125; and rental income, 121–22; reorganization of, 257*n*15; and street construction, 84–85

Boston City Planning Board (BCPB), 147, 149–50, 151

Boston Coffee Exchange Building, 54

Boston Common, 7, 9, 23; British encampments on, 26; purchase of land for, 41; and Quincy's sanitation improvements, 45–46, 244*n*12, 252*n*43

Boston Cordage Company, 76

Boston Five Cents Savings Bank, 262–63*n*36

Boston Flea Market, 164

Boston Fruit and Produce Exchange, 135

Boston Gazette, 22–23

Boston Globe, 134–35, 165, 171, 184, 189, 205, 206

Boston granite style, 89, 105

Boston Harbor, 128

Boston Herald, 165

Boston Herald American, 202

Boston Landmarks Commission, 225–26

Boston Massacre, 23–25, 149

Boston Monthly Magazine, 88

Boston News-Letter, 21

Boston News-Letter and City Record, 97

Boston Patriot, 59

Boston Pops Orchestra, 212

Boston Port Bill, 26–27

Boston Produce Exchange, 125–26, 128

Boston Redevelopment Authority: and Central Artery, 264*n*48; and construction deadlines, 188–89; and costs, 218; developers' kit issued by, 166–67, 169; development teams designated by, 167–70; and hiring of phase II developer, 170–73, 181–85; and historical preservation, 172–73, 193–94, 195–99; and HUD grants, 152–53, 159; leadership of, 233; and leasehold guidelines, 159; and market house reopening, 203–4; and marketplace management, 201–2; and marketplace oversight, 220–21; and marketplace redevelopment proposals, 153–67; marketplace studies conducted by, 151–52; and master ground lease, 179–80, 181, 260*n*1; and 99-year sublease, 185–87; and phase I redevelopment, 170; public perception of, 165–66; and redevelopment financing, 187–88, 192; reorganization of, 150–51; and Rouse Company, 199, 265*n*8

Boston School Committee, 105

Boston Soap Stone Company, 85

Boston Tea Party, 25–26, 148

Boston 200 exhibit, 201, 208

Bostonian Society, 149

Bowen, Abel, 97, *113*, 235

Bray's Wharf, 54–56, 67

Brigham, Levi, 85

Brooks, John, 34, 42

Brown, Abram English, *17*

Brown, William, 192

Brown's Band, 128

Bryant, Gridley, *74*, 75, 82, 90, 99, 112, 187

Bulfinch, Charles: Benjamin and, 53; county courthouse, 256*n*9; enlargement of Faneuil Hall, 30–32, *31*, 119; India Wharf, 51, 143; Massachusetts General Hospital, 93; Parris and, 71; State House, 32; and trabeated architectural method, 88, 252*n*28

Bunker Hill, Battle of, 27–28

Bunker Hill Monument, *74*, 75, 84

Bunker Hill Monument Association, 105, 128

Bunyard, Frankie, 204, 264*n*55

Butler, Peter, 84–85

Butler's Row, 84–85

Cape Ann quarry, 99

Carr (British colonel), 24

Castle William, 26

Catlin, Ephron, Jr., 192

Center Plaza, 206

Central Artery, 141, 165, 166

Central Wharf, 138, 171

Centre Market, 11–12, 14

Chamber of Commerce, 128

Chandlier, John, 119

Charitable Fire Society, 105

Charles I (king of England), 4

Charles Street, 33

Charlestown Savings Bank, 193

Chase Manhattan Bank (N.Y.), 188, 193, 261*n*22

Chatham Street, 115, 180

Cheers (restaurant), 224

Chelmsford quarry, 82, 97, 99, 177, *179*, 224, 232, 250*n*8

Chelsea, 145

Chickatabot (Native American chief), 5

Chickering, W. E., *70*

Child, David Weld, 62, 90, 97–99, 232, 248*n*20

Child, Julia and Paul, 203

Children of the Revolution, 33, 34

Christian Science Monitor, 165

Ciano, John, 205

Cicero, 48–49

City Bank, 62, 105

City Hall, *154*, 206

City Wharf, 115, 120, 123, 127, 235

Civil War, 126, 148

Clark, Brewer and Son, 118

Clinton Produce and Poultry Market, 259*n*47

Clinton Street, 115, 180

Cobb, Smith, 85

Codman, John, 64, 65

Codman's Wharf, 54–56, 64, 65

Cogan, John, 6

Cole, Samuel, 6

Collins, John F., 150–51, 162, 206

Columbian Centinel, 86, 112

Commercial Exchange, 128

Commercial Street, 115–16, 165, 180, 235–36

Commercial Wharf, 137–38

Committee of Correspondence, 26–27

Commonwealth Bank and Trust Company, 193

Conduit Alley, 72, 103, 136–37

Congress (ship), 32

Constitution (frigate), 32, 48

Constitution, adoption of, 33

Continental Army, 28

Continental Congress, Second, 28

Conway, Field Marshal, 28

Coolidge, Poor and Head (auctioneers), 73, 83

Copley Plaza Hotel, 136

Coppola Joseph ("Skip"), 223, 226

Cotton, John, 4, 41, 239*n*6

Cottrell's Dining Room, 136

Country Builder's Assistant, The (Benjamin), 53–54

Curley, James Michael, 134, 138

Cutler, Mary, 13, 19

D. Ghirardelli Company, 257*n*23

D'Agostino Izzo Quirk Architects, 223–24

Dana, Richard, 24

Dartmouth (cargo ship), 26

David Spear's/Greene Wharf, 54–56, 67

Dawes, William, 22, 27

debtor's prison, 43, 245*n*24

Delorme, Philibert, 94

Demonstration Cities Program, 158

Denver, 262*n*32

DeQuincey, William, 41, 42

Design Research (San Francisco), 172, 257*n*23

Disney Store, 220, 226

Disney World, Faneuil Hall Marketplace compared to, 215–16

Dobie, John, 206

Dock Square, 14, 30, *52*; parking garage at, 217

Dock Square Park, 187

dogs, early regulation of, 11

Dorchester, 145

Dove (schooner), 75

Downtown Crossing, 182–83, 259*n*43

Downtown Waterfront–Faneuil Hall Plan, 180

Downtown-Waterfront Urban Renewal District, 153, 205–6

Drowne, Shem, 16–17, *17*, 21–22

Drowne, Thomas, 21–22

Durgin, John, 118–19

Durgin Park (restaurant), xv, 264–65*n*60; antique lanterns at, 264*n*49; opening of, 118–19; and reconstruction terms, 258*n*34; and redevelopment, 166–67; survival of, 137, 147, 164, 212–13

Dyling, Henry, 90

Eastern Cold Storage Company, 130

Eastern Packet Wharf, 120

Eddy, Caleb, 82

Eleanor (cargo ship), 26

Elizabeth II (queen of Enland), 206

Emery, Joseph D., 120, 225, 267*n*47

Eustis Wharf, 65, 120

Extension of Faneuil Hall Market project: beginning of, 53–54; cost of, 112–14; financial contributors to, 105; land acquisitions for, 54–59, 60–66, 67; land reclamation for, 66–67; Quincy and, 106–7; street improvements, 115–16

Fair America (schooner), 75

Falzarano Construction Company, 170, 173–77, 188

Fancy Wireworker, 118

Fanueil, Andrew (uncle), 12–13, 18, 241*n*36

Fanueil, Benjamin and Anne (father and mother), 12–13

Fanueil, Benjamin (brother), 18–19, 29, 241*n*36

Fanueil, Benjamin, Jr. (nephew), 19

Fanueil Hall, *15*, 19, *52*, 54–55, *106*, *107*; architecture of, 15–17; banquets and celebrations held at, 28–29, 32, 119, 128; British occupation of, 27, 28; Bulfinch's enlargement of, 30–32, *31*, 123; and center line of market house, 77–78, *140*; as center of revolutionary activity, 23, 25–26, 27, 29; city government in, 116, 148, 256*n*9; congestion at, *36–37*, 38; early uses of, 17–20; establishment of, 13–17; exhibitions and fairs in, *118*; fire at, 21; grasshopper weathervane of, 16–17, *17*, 32, 187, 241*n*43; lot auctions held at, 83; management of, 121; marketplace at, xiii, 38, 105–6, 150; meat slaughter and sales at, 51; naming of, 18; post-Revolution uses of, 29–30; reopening of, 21–23; town meetings at, 57–59

Fanueil Hall Flower Market, 209

Fanueil Hall Market, *106*, *107*, *113*; access to waterfront, 126–28, *135*; appropriations for construction of, 81; architectural significance of, 105, 122; architectural style of, 88–89, *100*, *114*; budget for, 249*n2*; bull weathervane of, 237, 253*n46*, 261*n18*; centennial celebration, 135–36; changes to appearance of, 123, 125–26, *127*, 128, 133, *136*; climate control in, 197–98; completion of, *110*; congestion at, *131*, 133, *137*; construction of, 84–86, 97–99, *98*, 105–6; cornerstone of, 84; cost of, 114; deed restrictions on, 249*n1*; deterioration of, 141–43, 144, *145*, *160–61*, *163*, *165*; dome of, 89, 93–95, *94*, 138, 197, 209, 224–25, 253*n47*; earliest illustrations of, *ii, iv*, 235; electrical lighting in, 130; enlargement plans defeated, 123–25; exhibitions and fairs in, 116, *118*, *124*, 128, 208; fiftieth anniversary celebration, *127*, 128; fire at, 134–35; foundation of, 75, *76*; goods sold in, 116–17, 126, 130, 252*n43*; granite for, *74*, 82–83, 88–90, 97–99, *179*, 250*n8*; interior architecture of, 91–93, *92*; as landmark, 193, 225–26, 259*n48*; lease bids for stalls in, 109; management of, 121; materials for, 75–76; merchants in, 109, 129–30, 208, 210–11; naming of, xv, 109–11, 112, 119–20, 236–37, 246*n37*, 267*n4*; oldest blueprints for, *142*; opening of, 111–12; Parris as architect of, *70*, 73–75; Parris's lost plans for, *ii, iv*, 121, *124*; popularity of, *122*; positioning of merchants in, 87; profitability of, 121–22; pushcart vendors at, 117, *137*; reconstruction of, *94*; refrigeration at, 130; reopening and rededication of, 201–6; repositioning of, 76–80, *140*; restoration of, *190*, 193–99, *194*, *198*, 223–25, *225*, 263*n43*, 267*n44*, 267*n45*;

size and dominance of, 95–97; as tourist destination, 130–33; waterproofing of, 75. *See also* North Market building; South Market building
Fanueil Hall Marketplace™, *185*, *210*; corporatization of, 220–23; costs of, 188, 199, 218, 262–63*n36*, 264*n48*; feasibility studies for, 149–50, 151–59, *154*, *156*, *157*; financing of, 188–93, 261*n22*, 262–63*n36*; grasshopper weathervane as trademark symbol of, 261*n18*; hiring of phase II developer, 181–85, 259*n43*; landscaping of, 195–97, *196*, *200*, 263*n41*; management of, 213–15; merchants in, 213, 217, 226–27, 263*n37*, 263*n38*; and 99-year sublease, 185–87, 260*n1*; opening and dedication of, 201–6, 264*n55*, 264*n56*, 264–65*n60*; pedestrian mall at, 213; phase I reconstruction, 187–88; public art at, 266*n16*; public reception of, 207–11; re-merchandizing of, 226–27; renovation of, 223–25, *225*; residential use of, 217; restaurants at, 136–37; revitalization of, 219–20; size of, 213; success of, 215–18, time capsule at, 264*n56*
Fanueil Hall Marketplace Revitalization Program, 219–20
Fanueil Hall Markets Advisory Council, 155
Fanueil Hall Markets Report (Stahl-Webb), 158–59, 167, 173, 181, 193–94, 236
Fanueil Hall Merchants Association (FHMA), 219, 222–23
Fanueil Hall Square, 141–43. *See also* Fanueil Hall Marketplace™
Fanueil, John (brother), 12, 241*n35*
Fanueil, Mary (niece), 19
Fanueil, Mary Catherine (Andrew's wife), 13

Fanueil, Peter: death of, 18; establishes market house, 12, 13–17, 232; family background of, 12–13; and naming of Fanueil Hall Market, 111; portrait of, destroyed, 29
Fanueil, Peter (nephew), 19
Faxon building. *See* Hammond-Faxon building(s)
Faxon, Nathan, 72
Federalist Party, 42, 244–45*n15*
Fender Maker, 118
Fidelity Mutual Company (Philadelphia), 167–69
Fiedler, Arthur, 212
Fine and Ambrogne, 171
Fire and Marine Insurance Company, 105
Fired Stoves and Grates, 118
fires, 259*n47*, 260*n50*
First National Bank of Boston, 189, 192, 193
Fish, Zachariah, 67
Fletcher Granite Company, 177, *179*, 224
Fletcher, Hobie, 252*n39*, 253*n52*
Flower Exchange, 263*n37*
Fort Hill, 26, 33
France, 28
Franklin, Benjamin, 28
Franklin Hotel, 118
Freedom Trail, 213–14
fuel shortage crisis, 185–86, 261*n12*
Fuller, S. P., *117*
Fuller, Stephen T., 54, 56–57, 69
Funds of the Boston School Committee, 105

George B. H. Macomber Construction Company, 167, 185, 260–61*n10*
George II (king of England), 28
George W. Almy's Clothes Warehouse, 118
Ghirardelli Square (San Francisco), 159, 172, 257*n23*, 262*n32*
Gillett, Ozias, 118
Glasgow, 216
Gleason's Pictorial Drawing-Room Companion, 122

Gorges, Robert, 1
Government Center, 151, 158, 256*n*4
Granary Burial Ground, 18
Great Cove. *See* Town Cove
Great Depression, 136, 137–40
Great Fire of Boston, 126, 142
Greater Boston Chamber of Commerce, 138, 149–50
Greene Wharf, 54–56, 67
Gresham, Thomas, 16, 241*n*42
Grey, Joseph, 18
Griffin's Wharf, 26

Haar, Charles, 164
Hagan, John, *156*
Hale, Sarah Josepha, 116
Hale's Atlas, *52*, 54–55
Hammond, Samuel, 72, 73, 83
Hammond-Faxon building(s), *106*, *139*; architectural style of, 248*n*25; construction of, 251*n*21; demolition of, 138, *168*, 260*n*50; deterioration of, 145; and Fanueil Hall Market restoration, *157*; merging of, 136–37; occupancy of, 118
Hancock House, 148
Hancock, John, 21, 22–23, 25, 27, 28, 148
Harper's Weekly, *131*
Harris, Thomas, 90
Harvard College: establishment of, 41; Quincy as president of, 119, 254–55*n*25; Quincy as student at, 41
Hastings, Daniel, II, 85
Haymarket Square, 122, 164, 203
Hayward, Caleb, 30
Hemenway, Mary, 148
Hill, Richard, 192
Hill, Samuel, *19*
History of Boston (Snow), 97, 235
Hodgson, Anthony, 20
Hollis, Charles, 89
Hornet (ship), 32
Houchin, Jeremy, 6
House of Industry, 43, 245*n*24
Hovey and Company, 118, 141
Hovey, William, 109, 118
Huguenots, 29
Hunnewell, Jonathan, 30

Hutchinson, Thomas, 18, 23, 24
Hynes, John B., 149, 206

India Wharf, 36; demolition of, 143; as example of waterfront renewal, 51; and Great Depression, 137–38; row-house-style warehouses at, 58
"Iron Hat," 135–36

Jackson, Andrew, 119
Jackson, Thomas, 18
JMB Urban Investment and Development Company (Chicago), 262–63*n*36
John Hancock Life Insurance Company, 193, 262–63*n*36
Jones Hale (sloop), 75
Joy, Abner, 65, *74*, 75, 90, 112

Keayne, Robert, 7
Kelleher, Michael, 226
Kennedy, Edward M., 164
Kenney, Robert T., 164, *184*; and Fanueil Hall Market preservation, 232–33; and hiring of phase II developer, 182–83; leadership of, 177–79; and market house reopening, *202*, *203*; and marketplace oversight, 220–21; named BRA director, 166; as preservationist, 172; and redevelopment financing, 192; and redevelopment phases, 169–70; on Rouse Company, 259*n*43
Knox, Henry, 28

L. H. Bradford and Co., *118*
Ladies' Fair, 116
Lafayette, Marquis de, 28–29
Landmark Inn, 212
Larimer Square (Denver), 262*n*32
Lavinia (schooner), 75
Lawrence, Abbott, 73, 123
Lawrence, Amos, 73
Lawrence (Mass.), 73
Lazel-Perkins and Company, 85
LeMessurier Associates, 177
Leventhal, Norman B., 183–84, 260*n*5

Leverett Street Jail, 43, 48, 245*n*24
Lewis Wharf, 138
Leyden, Peter, 224–25, 249*n*31
Lillie, Lloyd, 266*n*16
Litke, Robert, 153
Little Market Lunch, 136
Logue, Edward J., 150–51, 152, 153, 155, 158, 166, 206, 216; and urban renewal grants, 257*n*13
Lonergan, Edward J., 179
Long Wharf, 9–10, 36, 66, 67, 108, 127, 133–34; and Great Depression, 137–38; storage of construction materials at, 249*n*32
Los Angeles, 216
Lovell, John, 18
Loverud, Robert, 153
Lowell (Mass.), 250*n*8
Lowell quarry, 99
Lumber Wharf, 249*n*32

McCann, Paul L., 179–80
McCormack, John, 164
McCue, Henry, 209
McDonough, Will, 266*n*16
McLean, James B., Jr., 201–2, 218
Magic Pan, 192, 201, 262*n*32
Magliore Carne Butcher Shop, 205
Maine and Worcester depot (Portland, Me.), 122
Maine, lumber from, 75
Manning, John H., *122*
Manufacturer's Mechanics Bank, 105
Marginal Street, 71, 79, 84, 88, 115, 235. *See also* Commercial Street
market bell, 11; at Fanueil Hall, 16
market cross, 240*n*24
market house. *See* Fanueil Hall Market
Market Square, *52*; anti-peddling ordinance at, 39, 49; congestion and pollution in, *36–37*, 36–39, *50*, 58; expansion of, 32, 49–54, 76–77; and

Quincy's sanitation improvements, 45–46; renaming of, 125; survey presentation of, *117. See also* Extension of Faneuil Hall Market; Fanueil Hall Square

markets/market system: early controversies over, 5–12; at Faneuil Hall, 17, 20, 22; and waterfront access, 52–53

Massachusetts: and eminent domain, 60–62; pauperism in, 42–43

Massachusetts Bank, 105

Massachusetts Bay Company, 2, 3–4

Massachusetts Bay Transit Authority (MBTA), 217

Massachusetts Business Development Corporation, 193, 262–63*n*36

Massachusetts Charitable Mechanic Association, 116, *118, 124*

Massachusetts, Commonwealth of, 29, 188, 247*n*1, 264*n*46

Massachusetts Convention, 26

Massachusetts Department of Public Works, 141

Massachusetts General Hospital, 93

Massachusetts House of Representatives, 42

Massachusetts Legislature, 240–41*n*28

Massachusetts State Prison, labor from, 83, 90, 99

Massachusetts State Senate, 42

Massachusetts Superior Court, 173

Mercantile Building, 171

Mercantile Wharf Corporation, 120, 127

Merchants Bank of Salem, 105

Merchants Row, 14, *54–55*, 72, 84, *137, 139*, 212

Merrimack River, 250*n*8

Miami, 216

Middlesex Canal, 82–83, 89, 250*n*8, 250*n*9

Middling Interest Party, 245*n*15

Mill Creek: Boston founded near, 2; and Market Square expansion, 68; pollution of, 36; rerouting of, 65, 85

Mill Pond Corporation, 33

Mintz, Samuel, 153, 182

Mondo's Restaurant, 164

Montilio's Bakery, 205

Mount Vernon, 33

Municipal Court, 7

Municipal History of the Town and City of Boston, A (Quincy), xvii, *114*, 235

Nathan Spear's Wharf, 54–56, 66, 76–80, 230

National Historic Register, 226, 259*n*48

National Housing Act, 150

National Park Service, 194, 195, 263*n*43

National Shawmut Bank, 193

Neighbors of Government Center, 183

"New Boston," 150–51

New Boston Food Corporation, 263*n*37

New England Aquarium, 171

New England Merchants National Bank, 189, 193

New England Mutual Life Insurance Company, 193

New England Palladium, 59

New England Produce Center, 263*n*37

New England Seafood Center, 263*n*37

New England Society for the Promotion of Manufactures and Mechanic Arts, 116

New York City, 10, 32, 125, 216

New York Daily Advertiser, 120–21

New York Times, 207

Newmarket Square, 145

Nichols, Malcolm E., 136

Nicholson, Peter, 253*n*47

North End, *135*, 171; expansion of, 32; Quincy born in, 40

North, Lord, 26

North Market, 11–12

North Market building: architectural significance of, 105; architectural style of, 99–103, *101, 113*; changes to appearance of, 120, 123; city acquisition of, 166–67; climate control in, 198; completion of, *110*; congestion in, *132*; construction of, 84–86, *98*; deterioration of, 138, 141–43, 144–45, 158, *168*; dissatisfaction with, 81–82; goods sold in, 117–18, 129; granite for, 82–83; lot auctions for, 71–73, *104*; and market house dominance, 96–97; and master ground lease, 260*n*1; opening and occupancy of, 97, 102, 108–9; Parris as architect of, *70*; real estate taxes on, 264*n*46; redevelopment costs of, 262–63*n*36; reopening of, 212–13; residential use of, 171; restoration of, 157–58, 169–70, 172–79, *174*, 187–88, *190*; size of, 102. *See also* Durgin Park (restaurant)

North Market Street, narrowing of, 78–79, 80

O'Connor, Thomas, 145–47

Old City Hall, 153, 182, 183, 234, 256*n*9

Old Feather Store, 69, 248*n*19

Old Grampy Joe's Place, 229

Old South Meeting House, 29–30, 148–49

Old State House, 42, 119, 149, 256*n*9

Oliver Noyes and Associates, 9

O'Neil, Thomas P. ("Tip"), 164

Otis, Harrison Gray, 33, 119

Otis, James, 22, 23

Pantheon (Rome), 89

Paris, Treaty of, 28

Park, Eldridge, 118–19

Parkman, Samuel, 65

Parris, Alexander, 54, *70*; architectural significance of, 231–32; architectural style of, 71, 105; career of, 69–71; and colonnade, 91–93; and dominance of market house, 96;

double dome designed by, 93–95, 209, 253*n*47; and Fanueil Hall Market, 71–72, 73–75; and Fanueil Hall Market preservation, 173, 195; fee paid to, 112; granite columns used by, 89; Hammond-Faxon building(s), *139*; lost plans of, *ii, iv*, 121, *124*, 236, 255*n*28; and market house budget, 249*n*2; and Mill Creek rerouting, 85; navy affiliations of, 253*n*52; and North/South Market Street facades, 99–100; and pavilion, 119; and rebuilding on resold properties, 86; written descriptions of market, 170, 255*n*28

Parthenon (Athens), 89

Patten's Restaurant, 136–37, 138

Paul Revere Copper, 224

Pemberton, Samuel, 24

Pendleton, John and William, *113*

Penn, James, 6

Philadelphia, 10, 32, 125

Philadelphia Wharf, 120

Phillips, John, 35, 39, 53, 245*n*24

Phillips, William, 29, 83

Pie Powder Court, 6, 18

Pierpont, W., *19*

Police Court, 48

Pollard, Benjamin, 47

Porter, Edward G., *135*

Portsmouth (N.H.), 99, 232, 253*n*52

President (ship), 32

Preston, Thomas, 24

Providence (R.I.), 122

Provident Institution for Savings, 105

Prudential Center, 206

Puritans, 1–4, 6, 7, 240*n*19

pushcart vendors: English heritage of, 8; at Fanueil Hall Market, 117, *137*, 208; and handmade crafts, 264*n*52; at market house reopening, 203; and Market Square assymetry, 125; and Market Square expansion, 50, 51, 53; restricted at Market Square, 39, 49

Quartering Act, 23

Quincy (Mass.), 75

Quincy, Abigail (sister), 40

Quincy, Abigail Phillips (mother), 40, 47

Quincy & Company, 264-65*n*60

Quincy, Edmund (justice, great-grandfather), 40, 243*n*3

Quincy, Edmund (justice, great-uncle), 24

Quincy, Edmund (Puritan ancestor), 4, 40–41

Quincy, Edmund (son), 64, 246*n*37

Quincy, Eliza Susan (daughter), *iv*, 236

Quincy, Eliza Susan (wife), 48

Quincy, John, Sr., xv, 229, 246*n*37, 264-65*n*60

Quincy, Josiah, *ii, iv, 231*; becomes mayor, 39, 43–44; belief in spirits, xvi; birth of, 40; career of, 41–43; centralization of municipal authority, 44–45, 47–48; defeated as mayor, 119; detractors of, 244-45*n*15; family background of, xv, 40–41; final market expansion report, 113–15; as Harvard president, 119, 254-55*n*25; and "Iron Hat," 135–36; and land acquisitions, 54–59, 60–66, 80, 246*n*28; lays market house cornerstone, 84; leadership of, xv, xvii–xviii, 106–7, 233–34; lost records of, xvi, 236; on lot auctions, 73; and Market Square expansion plans, 49–54; moral character of, 47–49, 79, 229–31; and naming of Fanueil Hall Market, 109–11, 112; portrait of, 236; and press coverage, 88; purchases City Wharf, 123, 127; redeveloped market house dedicated to, 204; reelected as mayor, 63–64; and repositioning of market

house, 76–80; sanitation improvements made by, 45–47, 244*n*12, 244*n*14; statue of, 234; supervision of construction, 89–90, 97–99, 187, 232, 253*n*52

Quincy, Josiah (grandfather), 24–25, 40–41

Quincy, Josiah, Jr. (father), 22, 24–25, 40, 42, 242*n*11

Quincy Market, 220. *See also* Fanueil Hall Market; Fanueil Hall Marketplace™

Quincy Market Cold Storage, 130

Quincy Market House Hotel, 118

Quincy, Old Grampy Joe's Place (family name for market house), 229

Quincy, Samuel, 25

rats, 144

Redman, John, *74*, 75, 90, 112

Revenue Acts, 25–26

Revere, Paul, 22, 27, 224

Rhodes, Daniel, 121

Rice, Alexander H., 128

Robbins, Robert, 86

Rodgers, Bill, 266*n*16

Roe Buck Passage, *52*, 72, 212; congestion in, 38–39; widening of, 59, 84

Roe Buck Tavern, 39, 68–69

Rouse, James W./Rouse Company, 170–72, 181, 182–83, *184*; disputes over maintenance fees, 219, 221–23; and Fanueil Hall Market preservation, 232–33; hired as phase II developer, 184, 185, 260*n*5; as mall developer, 170, 260*n*6; and market house reopening, *202, 203*, 264*n*56; and marketplace management, 201–3, 213–15, 217, 220–23, 259*n*43, 265*n*8; and 99-year sublease, 185–87; and redevelopment costs, 199; and redevelopment financing, 188–93, 261*n*22; remerchandizing of marketplace, 226–27

Rowson, William S., *124*, 170
Roxbury (Mass.), 145
Royal Exchange (London), 16
Ruggles, Samuel, 15, 17

Salem (Mass.), 122
Sargent Wharf, 138
school desegregation, 189
Seider, Christopher, 24
Shambles, 30, *31*, 38, *50*, *52*; defi-
  nition of, 243*n*24; and Mar-
  ket Square expansion, 51
Shaw, Robert Gould, 83
Shawmut Peninsula, 1, *3*
Sherley, William, 28
Shults, A. B., *131*
slave trade, 10
Smibert, John, 14–15
Snow, Caleb, 97, 235
Society for Promoting Theatri-
  cal Amusements, 27
Society for the Preservation of
  New England Antiquities,
  155
Sons of Liberty, 23, 24, 26–27
South Boston: relocation of
  fishing trade to, 133–34; relocation of merchants to, 145
South Boston Savings Bank,
  262–63*n*36
South Cove, 33
South End, 32
South Market, 11–12
South Market building: architectural significance of, 105;
  architectural style of, 99–103,
  103; changes to appearance of,
  120, 123; city acquisition of,
  166–67; climate control in,
  198; completion of, *110*; congestion in, *133*; construction
  of, 84–86, *98*; demolished
  stores in, 260*n*50; deterioration of, 138, 141–43, 144–45,
  152, 158, *163*, *168*; goods sold
  in, 117–18, 129; granite for,
  82–83; lot auctions for, 71–73,
  83–84, *104*; and market house
  dominance, 96–97; and master ground lease, 260*n*1;
  opening and occupancy of,
  97, 102, 108–9; Parris as archi-

tect of, *70*; real estate taxes on,
  264*n*46; redevelopment costs
  of, 262–63*n*36; reopening of,
  211–12; residential use of, 171;
  restoration of, 157–58,
  169–70, 172–79, *173*, *174–76*,
  178, 187–88, *190*; size of, 102
South Market Street: extension
  of, 127; peddlers in, 125;
  widening of, 77–80
Spear, Nathan, 76–77, *140*. *See
  also* Nathan Spear's Wharf
Speleotis, Charles J.: and BRA,
  169, 179; and legal ownership
  of streets, 258*n*35; on marketplace success, 233; on 99-year
  sublease, 187; on redevelopment costs, 199; on redevelopment financing, 192
Stahl Associates, 153, *156*
Stahl, Frederick ("Tad"), 167,
  172, 177–79; and Fanueil Hall
  Market preservation, 232–33;
  and market house reopening,
  203, 205; on marketplace success, 216; restoration feasibility study by, 153–59, *156*, *157*
Stahl-Bennett Architects, 164,
  169, 177
State House, 32, 240–41*n*28
State Street Bank and Trust
  Company, 153, 189,
  262–63*n*36
steamships, 125, 130
Steele, John, 11
Stobart, John, *107*
streets: improvements to,
  115–16; legal ownership of,
  255*n*37, 258*n*35; made into
  pedestrian mall, 213; widen-
  ing of, 52–53, 84–85
Stuart, Gilbert, *ii*, *iv*, 236
Stuart Highland Regimental
  Group, 203
Sudbury High School, 204
Suffolk Insurance Company,
  105
Suffolk Municipal Court, 42
Sullivan, Leo, 205
Sumner Tunnel, 138
supermarkets, effect of, 145
Symonds, Henry, 248*n*19

Teachers Insurance and Annuity
  Association of America, 188,
  261*n*22
Thompson, Benjamin/Ben-
  jamin Thompson and Associates, *184*, *204*; architectural
  modifications made by,
  193–99, *194*, *198*, 263*n*43; on
  benefits of marketplace redevelopment, 190–91; and Design Research, 257*n*23; on
  effects of tourism, 220; and
  Fanueil Hall Market preservation, 232–33; hired as redevelopment architect, 167, 185;
  and hiring of phase II developer, 181, 183; illustrations by,
  94, *154*, *185*, *190*; on market
  house atmosphere, 209, 214;
  and market house reopening,
  202, 203, 205, 206; on marketplace success, 216, 217; redevelopment proposal of, 155;
  restaurants owned by, 210,
  212; Rouse and, 170–72
Thompson, Jane, *204*; on market
  house atmosphere, 209; and
  market house reopening, 203;
  on night landscaping of marketplace, 263*n*41; redevelopment proposal of, 155; restaurants owned by, 210, 212;
  on Rouse proposal, 259*n*43
Thorndike, Israel, 83
Tilden, Thomas, 85
Tokyo, 216
Torrey, Charles, 83
tourism, 130–33, 220–21
Town Court, 7
Town Cove, 2–3, *3*, 36; reclamation of, 66–67
Town Dock, *54–55*; congestion
  at, 36, *36–37*; and expansion
  of Dock Square, 30; Fanueil
  Hall at, *15*; and Market
  Square expansion, 54–56, 68;
  marketplace at, 5; reconstruction of, 54; replacement of,
  115
Town House, 6–7, 10, 23–24,
  240*n*19, 240–41*n*28. *See also*
  Old State House

town meetings, 7, 8, 15–16, 17–18; at Fanueil Hall, 19; on Market Square expansion, 57–59

Tracey, Charles, 85

Tramountain/Trimountain, 1–2, 4–5, 9, 33. *See also* Beacon Hill

Triangular Warehouse, 62, *63*, 69, 72

Tuck and Reed Company, 83

Tudor, William, 41

Union Warren Savings Bank, 193

United Freight Railroad Company, 137

United States (ship), 32

United States Bank, 105

U.S. Department of Agriculture (USDA), 141

U.S. Department of Housing and Urban Development (HUD), 150, 152–53, 188; Historical Preservation Grants, 159, 162–64, 166, 172–73

U.S. House of Representatives, 42

urban renewal, 150–51, 256*n*4, 257*n*13

urban revitalization, Fanueil Hall Marketplace as model of, 216

Uring, Nathaniel, 8–9

Van Arkle and Moss, 167–69, 181, 260–61*n*10

Vietnam War, protests against, 166, 189

wagon vendors. *See* pushcart vendors

Wagstaff, G. E., *114*

Walsh Brothers Construction Company, 224

War of 1812, 241*n*43

Warner Brothers, 220, 226

Warren, Joseph, 22, 28

Washington (schooner), 75

Washington, George, 28–29

waterfront, *107*; congestion and pollution in, *36–37*, 36–38; deterioration of, 138–40; and highways, 141; India Wharf as example of renewal at, 51; market access to, 52–53, *135*; restoration of, 151, 256*n*4

Waterstone's Booksellers, 220, 226

Watson, James, 11

Webb, Roger S., 170, 183; and Fanueil Hall Market preservation, 232–33, 257–58*n*23; redevelopment proposal of, 181–82; restoration feasibility study by, 153–59, *156*, *157*

Webster, Daniel, 48, 60

West End, 32, 256*n*4

Westford quarry, 82, 89, 90, 97, 250*n*8

wharves, *54–55*; deterioration of, 137–39; and Market Square expansion, 54–56; restoration of, 171. *See also specific wharf*

White, Kevin H., *184*; on delays in market reconstruction, 165–66; and Fanueil Hall Market preservation, 232–33; and hiring of phase II developer, 182–83, 184–85, 259*n*43; and market house reopening, *202*, *203*, 206; on marketplace success, 217; and redevelopment financing, 189, 191–92, 193; and urban renewal, 162

Whitehill, Walter Muir, *146*; and Fanueil Hall Market preservation, 147, 150, 152–53, 155–57, 158, 172, 232–33; and federal landmark status, 193, 259*n*48; and marketplace oversight, 220–21

Whitney, Ann, 129

Wild, Paul, 111, 205

Willard, Solomon, 84

Williams, Eliphalet, 62

Willoughby, Francis, 11

Winthrop, John, 2, 6, 33, 240*n*19, 255*n*37

Works Progress Administration (WPA), 138

World War II, 139–40

Yorktown (Va.), 28